ART AND FASHION

Dr. Alice Mackrell

Batsford

First published 2005

© Alice Mackrell 2005

Volume © B T Batsford 2005

The right of Alice Mackrell to be identified as Author of this work has been asserted by her in accordance with the Copyright, Designs and Patents Act 1988.

0 7134 8873 5

A CIP record for this book is available from the British Library.

Design by Lee-May Lim

Printed in Malaysia
for the publishers

B T Batsford
The Chrysalis Building
Bramley Road
London W10 6SP

An imprint of **Chrysalis** Books Group plc

✳ Contents

To the Memory of

Mrs Stella Mary Newton OBE

Acknowledgements

For their help and advice I would like to thank: Hélène Alexander (The Fan Museum), Conrad Atkinson and Ronald Feldman Fine Arts (New York), Matthew Bailey (National Portrait Gallery, London), Susie Bell (National Galleries of Scotland, Edinburgh), Michelle Bennett (Kimbell Museum of Art, Fort Worth), Nicola Birtwisle (B T Batsford), Sue Daly (Sotheby's, London), Lizabeth Dion (Museum of Fine Arts, Boston), Martin Durrant (V&A Images, London), Marcia Erickson (North Carolina Museum of Art), Scott Hisey (Cincinnati Museum of Art), Antony Hudek (Courtauld Institute of Art, London), Gill Huggins (Museum of Costume, Bath) Roger Huggins (BT Batsford), David L Kencik (San Diego Museum of Art), Joan R Kropf (Salvador Dalí Museum, St Petersburg), Kate Lau (Walters Art Museum, Baltimore), William Mackrell (Chelsea College of Art and Design, London), the late Richard Martin (Metropolitan Museum of Art, New York), Ursula Oldenburg (Bridgeman Art Library, London), Nancy Osborn, Tina Persaud (B T Batsford), Irving Solero (the Museum at the Fashion Institute of Technology, New York), Polly Sartori and Talia Katz (Sotheby's, New York), Louise Sorensen (Courtauld Institute of Art, London), Grace Thompson and Jon Whiteley (Ashmolean Museum, Oxford).

Dr Alice Mackrell
Hampstead, London

1 Introduction

The links between art and fashion go back at least to the Renaissance.[1] Artists of the stature of Jacopo Bellini, Antonio del Pollaiuolo and above all Antonio Pisanello, were not only depicting fashions in their paintings, but also creating costume models and designing textile patterns and embroidery.[2] Life and fashion at the Renaissance court was a major theme of the exhibition *Pisanello: Painter to the Renaissance Court*, held at the National Gallery, London, from October 2001 to January 2002. Pisanello, one of the most celebrated artists of the Renaissance, worked for several influential courts in Italy: the Visconti in Milan, the Este in Ferrara and the Gonzaga in Mantua. The section of the exhibition entitled 'Chivalry and Court Culture' described the cultural and sartorial life of the Italian Renaissance courts. Italian rulers of the 15th century were keen to show their engagement in warfare as more than just politically and economically inspired. Important to them were the codes of honour and gallantry gleaned from the story of Saint George and the dragon, and from the much-read French literature on chivalry. Pisanello's accuracy in the depiction of dress and armour were of immense importance to ruling princes in reflecting court chivalry. The up-to-date appearance of the armour (paintings of which appeared in the exhibition alongside surviving examples) denoted modern fighting skills, while the lavish, fashionable costumes were a vestimentary hallmark of the distinctive social standing of the ruling families. The exhibition featured many of Pisanello's studies of costume and embroidery, showing the spirit of individualistic creation in the 15th century, and attesting to his involvement in the design process.

The exhibition also provided the background to an understanding of the dress and subject matter of Pisanello's great painting, *The Vision of Saint Eustace*, to which an entire room was devoted in the exhibition. The picture tells the story of Saint Eustace's conversion to Christianity. While out hunting, Placidus, a soldier of the 2nd-century Emperor Trajan, had a vision of a stag who spoke to him with Christ's voice. Placidus became a Christian and changed his name to Eustace. Although ostensibly a religious painting, Pisanello responded to the passion for hunting, one of the chief courtly pleasures of his day, by painting Saint Eustace as a 15th-century prince engaged in this aristocratic privilege. Hunting was also widely associated with virtue, and seen as a training ground for military action, being the setting for a large group of chivalric legends. Saint Eustace, as well as being an historical figure, is thus presented at the same time as a contemporary role model of the ideal Christian knight. These values help to interpret Pisanello's painting of the saint in the height of court fashion, wearing a close-fitting golden tunic edged with fur and a blue *cappuccio*, (a hood, or in French, *chaperon*), with fur that matched that of the tunic. Pisanello's authenticity in dress extended even

Antonio Pisanello, The Vision of St Eustace *(mid-15th century), tempera on panel (National Gallery, London/www.bridgeman.co.uk). Pisanello painted the saint in the height of court fashion.*

to the saint's gilded Italian rowel-spurs, a sign of knightly status and easily identifiable with surviving examples of the period.[3] The painting thus afforded the patron the opportunity to identify with Saint Eustace both as a royal huntsman and as a Christian knight.

The painters of the Renaissance were very much aware of the artists of classical antiquity, and studied their surviving works, especially of sculpture, for the representation of appearance and clothing. The Italian Humanist writers praised Pisanello's ability to depict nature in all its forms in the way Greek and Roman artists had once done. To achieve this, Pisanello drew from life, and also made studies of ancient sculpture and coins, which he incorporated into his works. Coins were especially valued for study during the Renaissance, for they were tangible manifestations of the ancient world and, with the depiction of individual ancient rulers, much information could be gleaned from them.

Introduction

The new spirit of Humanism, emphasizing the individualistic and the particular, was highlighted in the exhibition *Virtue and Beauty: Leonardo's Ginevra de'Benci and Renaissance Portraits of Women*, held at the National Gallery of Art, Washington, in 2001. The emergence of Humanism in the early Renaissance (c.1420–1500) 'encouraged the kind of personal interaction represented by the frontal gaze of the new format', first adopted in the 1470s by Leonardo for his portrait of Ginevra, and by Sandro Botticelli in *Woman at a Window (Smeralda Brandini?)* of about 1470–1475.[4]

> 'Though she was the daughter of a wealthy banker, [Ginevra] is depicted wearing a plain brown dress against a peaceful landscape. An accomplished poet, Ginevra was the sister of one of Leonardo's lifelong friends and belonged to an elite literary circle ... the work reflects the painter's own leanings.'[5]

The Renaissance rediscovery of the classical articulation of cloth and the shape of the body beneath it, and the development by artists of their own way of representing the clothed appearance of their day, was taken up by Giorgio Vasari in his book *The Lives of the Painters, Sculptors and Architects (Le Vite dei più eccellenti pittori, scultori ed architettori Italiani*, first published in 1550; a second, enlarged edition appeared in 1568), the key source-book on Italian Renaissance art. Vasari believed that art was primarily an imitation of nature and that perfecting the means of its representation was the way for painting to progress. He supported the belief of the Italian Humanists that this process had been taken to the zenith of perfection in classical antiquity but had declined in the Middle Ages. Vasari charted the innovations and improvements in the delineation and appearance of the human figure in painting by Italian artists from the 14th century to his own time, using the word *rinascita*, 'rebirth', to describe this process that we refer to today by the equivalent French term, 'renaissance'.

Cimabue and his follower Giotto had begun this movement towards greater realism in the late 13th and early 14th centuries by introducing 'graceful heads and delicate colouring', attractively posed figures, the show of emotions and more realistic drapery. Giotto's monumental achievement of endowing his figures with a new solidity and naturalism was noted by his contemporaries, Giovanni Boccaccio and Dante Alighieri. In *The Decameron*, Boccaccio remarked that it was Giotto who had 'brought back to light an art that had been buried for centuries'. Boccaccio noted Giotto's verisimilitude in following nature, making things look actual. Giotto's great advance in naturalism was also noted by Dante in *The Divine Comedy*, where he said that Giotto had surpassed Cimabue. The beginnings of the Italian love of sumptuous textiles can also be seen in Giotto's fresco cycle in the Arena Chapel in Padua. Here he shows a very early interest in textiles as objects of fashionable appeal, and an indication of the commercial world of textiles in the 14th century.

Of the great masters of the High Renaissance (c.1500–1527, the terminal date being marked by the sack of Rome by the forces of the Holy Roman Emperor Charles V), Leonardo, Michelangelo and Raphael, it was the latter 'in whose works the ideals' of the period find 'their most complete expression'.[6] At the early age of 25, Raphael was already in the front rank of artists at the papal court in Rome. His early death at the age of 37 in 1520 'plunged into grief the entire papal court', according to Vasari. His enormous influence was widely extended throughout Europe by the engravings of his works made by Marcantonio Raimondi. Until the later 19th century, his reputation among critics as the greatest painter who ever lived influenced artists from Reynolds to Ingres. In the words of Vasari:

> 'But the most graceful of all was Raphael of Urbino, who studied what had been achieved by both the ancient and modern masters, selected the best qualities from all their works, and by this means so enhanced the art of painting that it equalled the faultless perfection of the figures painted in the ancient world by Apelles and Zeuxis, and might even be said to surpass them were it possible to compare his works with theirs. His colours were finer than those found in nature, and his invention was original and unforced, as anyone can realize by looking at his scenes, which have the narrative flow of a written story ... His figures expressed perfectly the character of those they represented ... and his draperies ... appear wholly realistic.'[7]

Raphael created many portraits that show great inventiveness in the subtlety of characterization of his sitters and in the depiction of their fashions. They also provide a remarkable document of the Roman intellectual and cultural classes in which he moved, for example in his portrait of Baldassare Castiglione, dated about 1515, in the collection of the Musée du Louvre. Castiglione wrote a treatise entitled *Il Libro de Cortegiano*, a book of manners, deportment and dress. Castiglione considered that black, more than any other colour, gave grace to a garment. The fashion for black dominated male fashion, and this is brought out in a dazzling way in Raphael's portrait. The portrait shows how deeply interested Raphael was in the character of Castiglione, translating his intellectual and moral character into pictorial terms by means of dress, the beautiful black velvet of his hat and cloak framing the whiteness of his linen shirt. The structure and solidity of the body is emphasized by the width and depth of the clothes, even down to the detail of the brim of the wide hat with its dark outline, which adds to the stability of the face.

That Vasari recognized the 16th-century artistic expansion of endeavour in the realm of fashion is attested by the high praise he gave to Francesco Salviati, who studied under Andrea del Sarto, and worked mainly in Rome and Florence for the papal court and wealthy Tuscan families. Of Salviati, who also made designs for tapestries, Vasari wrote: 'He gave lovely grace to his heads of every style ... he also continually clothed his figures with new fashions in dress, and he was fanciful and varied in his depiction of headdresses, footwear and every other sort of adornment.[8]

Titian (Tiziano Vecellio), the greatest of the Venetian painters of the Renaissance, was arguably the most significant international artist of the 16th century, as the groundbreaking exhibition devoted to him at the National Gallery, London and the Museo Nacional del Prado, Madrid during 2003 showed. His remarkable skills as a portraitist were recognized by Vasari, who knew many of his portraits at first hand. A large section of the exhibition was devoted to Titian's wide range of portraiture – the imperial Habsburgs, the papal Farnese, the ruling Venetian élite and members of the various Renaissance courts – confirming how his reputation as a master portraitist was established in his own lifetime. It was not just the quantity but the quality of his portraits that impressed contemporaries like Vasari, who noted how 'alive' they appeared, and his pupil, Palma Giovane, who wrote of his technique of 'laying in his pictures with a mass of colour which served as a groundwork for what he wanted to express'. Titian revolutionized the technique of oil painting with his expressive brushwork – 'bold, sweeping strokes' that astonished Vasari. Titian's supreme mastery of oil technique enabled him to bring out in his portraits great insight into character as well as the structure, behaviour and texture of clothing. The opulence of Titian's style showed the unlimited potential of oil to represent the sensuous and tactile powers of textiles. His capability in this respect perhaps owed much to Venice's position in Italy as the centre of the pigment trade and of the manufacture of textiles, two industries that interacted:

> 'There are many documented cases of painters sending to Venice for colours (including Titian himself when he was working away from home), and such was the importance of painting and associated crafts in the city that by Titian's time it had become possible to buy painting materials from specialist colour suppliers instead of the general apothecaries operating elsewhere in Italy. In Venice he could procure the finest and most costly grades of ultramarine ... Pigments were also manufactured from imported raw materials, and Venice was well known for the quality of its vermilion, lead-tin yellow (one type of which was associated with glassmaking) and especially its lead white. The existence of an extensive dyeing industry meant that painters were able to obtain the best and most intensely coloured red lakes, pigments prepared from dyestuffs used in the production of luxury textiles. In oil these lakes formed sumptuous glazes, which could be built up to achieve a translucent depth of colour like that of stained glass. These red lakes with other translucent pigments, including green glazes based on verdigris, were essential to Titian's technique.'[9]

Titian's portrait of Ranuccio Farnese, dated 1542, is one of his most revolutionary in the genre, in which he uses paint as an expressive substance, acutely observing his sitter and scrutinizing every detail of his dress. A member of a powerful and aristocratic family, yet only twelve years old in the portrait, Titian conveys how responsibility far beyond his tender years came to him through the cloak of office he wears. Sent to Venice by his grandfather, Pope Paul III, to become prior of an important property belonging to the Knights of Malta, the cloak is far too large and heavy, sliding off his youthful shoulders yet poignantly characterizing the role of a boy as a man. Limiting his palette to black, white and red, Titian brilliantly renders the black velvet of the cloak, which offsets the fashionable red doublet adorned with golden stripes and embroidery. The way Titian has lit the portrait draws attention to both Ranuccio Farnese's alert, intelligent face and to the garments he wears, animating them by bringing out details such as the gleam flowing over the sleeves of the cloak and the busy pattern shining across the doublet. Titian threw down the gauntlet to future artists.

Studio of Bronzino, Eleonora di Toledo *(c. 1550), oil on panel (Reproduced by permission of the Trustees of the Wallace Collection, London). The wife of Cosimo de Medici is sumptuously dressed, her gown dripping with pearls. Several artists in Northern Europe – including Albrecht Dürer and Hans Holbein the Younger – designed jewellery.*

'Rubens's equestrian *Philip IV* was hung alongside Titian's equestrian image of his great-grandfather in Velázquez's re-hanging of the Hall of Mirrors in the Madrid Alcázar. Van Dyck's passion for Titian emerges from his British Museum *Sketchbook*, which shows him hunting down Titian's works in Italy ... In England Van Dyck worked for Charles I and the Whitehall group, which favoured the Venetian style, and he formed his own collection of Titian's works, among them some twenty portraits, including *The Vendramin Family* and *A Man with a Quilted Sleeve*.'[10]

Another theme that preoccupied Vasari in his *Lives of the Painters* was the art of the gem-engraver. The Italian city-states were wealthy and their princely ruling families were great patrons of the arts, Vasari singling out the Medici family of Florence. The goldsmith was regarded as highly as the painter and the sculptor. His work was closely allied to theirs, jewellery mirroring in miniature the exacting standards of precision and purity found particularly in sculpture. Many artists of the Renaissance were involved in jewellery design. Ghiberti, Filippo Brunelleschi, Donatello, Domenico Ghirlandaio, Antonio del Pollaiuolo and Sandro Botticelli (who was also a designer of embroidery) are some of the great artists of the Renaissance who began their artistic careers as apprentices to goldsmiths, learning the techniques of jewellery, described in detail by Benvenuto Cellini in *Due trattati uno intorno alle otto principali arti dell'oreficeria* (Florence, 1568). The *Virtue and Beauty* exhibition showed how the study of jewellery in Renaissance portraits is important for the period's new emphasis on personality and appearance in painting.

'The sitter in Domenico Ghirlandaio's *Giovanna degli Albizzi Tornabuoni* (1488/1490) ... her jewellery — most strikingly, a ruby-encrusted, pearl-laden pendant — distinguishes her as Lorenzo de'Medici's first wife, who died in childbirth.'[11]

Another Medici portrait, of Eleonora di Toledo, wife of Cosimo de'Medici, from the studio of Bronzino (shown opposite), shows the sitter in magnificent state dress. Wearing a sumptuous dress of Italian silk velvet, she is dripping with pearls — on her headdress, around her neck, on the parlet on both sides of her square neckline and draped across her bodice, amply demonstrating her status as the wife of the Grand Duke of Tuscany.

In Northern Europe, several artists designed jewellery that accessorized the elaborate, fashionable dress of that region. Albrecht Dürer, from Nuremberg, whose father was a goldsmith, designed jewellery. Hans Holbein the Younger, originally from Augsburg, came to London and became court painter to King Henry VIII. He is credited with over two hundred jewellery designs.

'... his jewellery designs created a new court fashion, as seen in portraits of Tudor society. Few Holbeinesque jewels survive, for their material value was usually less dependent on the cost of precious stones than on the delicacy of the figural scenes; because of changes in court fashions, many pieces were remodelled or destroyed.'[12]

In his drawings and paintings Holbein not only meticulously delineated the jewellery worn by his sitters, but also recorded how these objects provided valuable information about the details of dress and contemporary posture. In the front view of his drawing of *An Unknown English Lady* of about 1535, one hand is at waist level showing her touching the undersleeve, while the other hand is just below waist level and is clasping a rope of beads, thus allowing the viewer to study both the complex cuts of the oversleeve and undersleeve as well as appreciating the correct position of standing (shown right).

> 'England towards the end of the 16th century saw the fashion for a new type of jewel "to celebrate the reign of Elizabeth I: oval pendants containing miniature portraits. Nicholas Hilliard, the court painter and jeweller, not only suggested but also probably executed the first ones himself".

The two most celebrated are the Armada Jewel and the Drake Jewel, enamelled gold pendants set with diamonds and rubies and enclosing miniature portraits of the Queen.

> "On the Continent, the closest comparison were *Gnadenpfennige* (enamelled portrait medals) usually with armorials on the reverse. They were set within enamelled scrollwork and worn on gold chains." [13]

The 16th century was the great age of travel and exploration, with a quest for knowledge that included the costume and customs of other nations. This had tremendous results for fashion, as the first printed costume books appeared in the second half of the century, heralding a new visual source.[14] With the invention of movable type around 1450, associated with Johannes Gutenberg of Mainz, books could be printed cheaply, and many costume books were published in several editions and translations. The most famous of the genre – indeed the costume book that best epitomizes Renaissance man's search for an encyclopedic knowledge of dress – is Cesare Vecellio's *De gli habiti antichi et moderni di diverse parti del mondo*, published in Venice in 1590. Vecellio, a cousin and assistant to Titian, divided his book into two parts: Book I consists of 361 woodcuts of costumes in Europe and Book II contains 59 woodcuts of Asian and African clothing. A second, enlarged edition, entitled *Habiti antichi et moderni di tutto il Mondo*, was published in Venice in 1598; it contained 507 woodcuts, including a survey of the dress of the New World, with descriptions in both Latin and Italian. The great merits of Vecellio's book as a record of fashion are twofold: first, he emphasized the dress of his own region, and second, he recorded textiles that were made by Venetian drapers, who would have been *au fait* with current fashionable tastes, which they sold to the Italian courts. As J L Nevinson has pointed out: 'when we find an indoor dress of 1590 illustrated and described in detail and are also informed of the Venetian shop where its fabric could be had,

Hans Holbein the Younger, An Unknown English Lady *(c. 1535), drawing (Courtesy of the Trustees of the British Museum, London). In his drawings Holbein provided valuable information about the details of dress and contemporary posture.*

surely we are not very far from the idea of a fashion plate.'[15] When Vecellio's book was reprinted in Venice in 1664, the great Titian was believed to have done some of the artwork, and for the next two centuries it was considered to be Titian's book, a tribute to Vecellio's contribution to art and fashion.

Marcus Gheeraerts II, who was brought by his artist father from Bruges to England in 1568, was the subject of the exhibition *Marcus Gheeraerts II: Elizabethan Artist* at Tate Britain, London in 2003. The exhibition showed how this important late-Elizabethan and Jacobean artist was one of the earliest identifiable painters in England to use oil on canvas rather than on a wooden panel. This enabled him to produce full-length portraits, introducing a new style of naturalism and humanity into English portraiture, with repercussions for fashion. Since the Middle Ages England had excelled in ornament with needlework, and during the Elizabethan period embroidery flourished. Flowers and plants were distinctive English motifs on embroidery and their sources were the woodblock images published in contemporary herbals. Gheeraerts produced a number of so-called 'pregnancy portraits', showing women wearing loose-fitting linen robes or jackets embroidered with a whirling design of flowers and fruits rendered naturalistically against a background of meandering stems. A linen jacket was featured in the exhibition alongside the portraits that would have been worn as informal dress: dated 1600–1625, it was embroidered (in silk, silver and silver-gilt thread) with oak leaves, acorns, peapods, honeysuckle and pansies against a background of scrolling stems.[16]

The interaction of art and fashion continued apace in the 17th century. In France, the artists most closely associated with fashion engraving during the reign of King Louis XIII (1610–43) were Jacques Callot, Jean de Saint-Igny and Abraham Bosse. Callot's most illuminating illustrations of fashion were his twelve etchings in the series *La Noblesse de Lorraine* (1624) in which he observed most perceptively the fashionable dress of the *dames* and *seigneurs* of his native region. It is during the reign of Louis XIII that the term *la mode* is used to apply to clothing. The caption to the frontispiece in a collection of fashion engravings published in 1624 read:

'Les mignonnes du temps qui court
n'ont d'autre soin qu'estre à la mode.'[17]

In 1630 Jean de Saint-Igny entitled his series of engravings *Diversitez d'habillements à la mode*, and about 1634 Abraham Bosse produced the engravings for his *Pièces concernant la mode et les édits*.[18]

Abraham Bosse was an engraver at the court of Louis XIII. A teacher at the Académie Royale de Peinture et de Sculpture in Paris from its foundation in 1648 until 1661, he wrote a treatise on the art of engraving. The son of a master tailor, Bosse's *oeuvre* was prodigious – some 1,500 prints – making him a rich and authoritative source for art and fashion in 17th-century France. His engraving of

Cesare Vecellio, A Venetian Noblewoman *(From* Vecellio's Renaissance Costume Book, *Dover Publications, New York, 1977, Plate 99). Vecellio was a cousin and assistant to Titian.*

La Galerie du Palais, of about 1640, illustrates the fashionable shopping venue in Paris in which a great choice of accessories, all lavishly displayed, could be purchased, including gloves, fans, ribbons, lace collars and cuffs (shown above).

Elsewhere in Europe, artists clearly found inspiration in dress. Rubens, the great Flemish Baroque artist, designed tapestries and pageant decorations, and also produced costume studies for his subject paintings and portraits, compiling a large collection of drawings known as the *Costume Book*. Anthony Van Dyck, Rubens's principal assistant in his workshop, was himself the son of a cloth and silk merchant and 'known for his sumptuous costume. Van Dyck must have been acutely aware of the power of dress'.[19] In 1632 Van Dyck moved to London, where he was appointed by King Charles I as 'Principal Painter in Ordinary to their Majesties'. He remained at the Caroline court until his death in 1641, apart from a few brief visits to the Continent. During this period he was primarily occupied with portraits, and such was the power of his portraiture that it is through his work that our knowledge of the fashions worn at the court of Charles I is mainly gleaned.

Abraham Bosse, La Galerie du Palais *(c. 1640), engraving (The Metropolitan Museum of Art, New York, Rogers Fund). A range of accessories – gloves, fans, ribbons, lace collars and cuffs – could be bought at La Galerie du Palais, a fashionable shopping venue.*

Introduction ☐

The exhibition entitled *The Swagger Portrait*, held at the Tate Gallery, London in 1992, had as its subtitle *Grand Manner Portraiture in Britain from Van Dyck to Augustus John 1630–1930*, and demonstrated how Van Dyck invented a new conception of portraiture while he was court painter in the 1630s. The swagger portrait, the portrait as a public statement, began with Van Dyck.

'His swagger portraits were showy displays of how glamour can be given expression in brushstrokes and were insightful social documents of monarchy and aristocracy. Fashions at the court depended on the monarch and his circle. Newness and diversity were ways they could set the tone and underline their superiority. This was ever more important during the reign of Charles I when the middle classes were slavishly keen to ape the fashions at court. An avid collector of paintings and a lover of masques, Charles's love of finery and application of an artistic temperament to clothes is affirmed by his wardrobe accounts. The portraits of Van Dyck depict the new, relaxed sartorial atmosphere. It is the textiles, silk, satin, taffeta and lace that Van Dyck captures with such brio and finesse.'[20]

English fashion was given a fillip by the marriage in 1625 of Charles to Henrietta Maria, sister of King Louis XIII of France, and Van Dyck painted many portraits of the new queen. The first portrait in *The Swagger Portrait* exhibition was Van Dyck's *Portrait of Queen Henrietta Maria with Sir Jeffrey Hudson* of 1633. While the queen is shown in hunting costume, which mirrors the masculine style of dress in her bodice, deep lace collar and wide-brimmed plumed hat, Van Dyck also depicts the French style of ease and elegance.

'One detail that has not appeared before in English or any other portraits of 1632 is the wide and short sleeve worn alone without a gown or half oversleeve, but it certainly was not a fiction. It is unlikely that Van Dyck would reproduce the lace gorget, the ribbon decoration, or pattern of the fabric in such a detailed and coherent manner only to invent the shape of the sleeve, which is constructed in a way that reveals a convincing anatomy of the arm beneath. The joint of the sleeve to the bodice under the gold shawl, the fall of the fabric and the puckering around the elbows reveal that Van Dyck made a close study of the garment. This is evidenced by a detailed preparatory sketch of the dress, which still exists. Not only are the general lines of the bodice and skirt copied precisely from the drawing onto the painting, but small details are also the same: the pattern of the lace gorget, the placement of the ribbons and the line of the braiding on the skirt. The sleeves are identical in both sketch and painting – even the folds, creases and shadows made by the bend of the elbow correspond.'[21]

An unequalled responsiveness to the tactile qualities of fabrics and their relationship to dress can be found in the Dutch 'little masters' of the 17th century, such as Gabriel Metsu, Gerard ter Borch and Gerrit Dou. Their meticulously wrought small scenes of everyday life – with an almost enamelled appearance to

Gerard ter Borch, Portrait of a Young Man,
(c. 1663–1664), oil on canvas (National Gallery, London).

Anthony Van Dyck, Portrait of Queen Henrietta Maria with Sir Jeffrey
Hudson *(1633)*, *oil on canvas (National Gallery of Art, Washington,
Samuel H. Kress Collection). The Queen is portrayed in hunting costume.*

Wenceslaus Hollar, An English Noblewoman,
*engraving from Theatrum Mulierum (1643) (Chrysalis
Image Library).*

Diego Velázquez, King Philip IV of Spain in Brown and Silver, (c. 1631–1632), oil on canvas (National Gallery, London)

their surface — the diligent yet delicate characterization of their sitters, and the splendour of the materials of their costumes, made them very fashionable painters to collect in 18th-century France. They so influenced the *troubadour* painters of early-19th-century France that they were christened the Dutch *petits-maîtres*. Dou was a pupil of Rembrandt, Metsu was a pupil of Dou, and ter Borch had first-hand knowledge of Rembrandt in Amsterdam and Haarlem. Rembrandt's name conjures up a whole period, Holland's 'Golden Age', and this great era was the subject of an exhibition in Paris in 1970–71 under the title *Le Siècle de Rembrandt*. His multi-faceted talent included fashionable portraiture and self-portraiture. Indeed, the long series of self-portraits in various costumes, dating from 1629 to 1669, reflects so many aspects of society.

The Bohemian artist Wenceslaus Hollar worked in England as an etcher, engraver and illustrator from 1632 until his death in 1677. He excelled in costume studies, specializing in women's fashions. His first English series was entitled *Ornatus Muliebris Anglicanus*, which was published in 1640. Consisting of 26 engravings, the range of the work is conveyed in the sub-title: the *Several Habits of English Women from Nobilite to the Country Woman as they are in these times*. His next series, *Theatrum Mulierum*, first published in 1643 with 36 prints, was reprinted in 1646 in a new edition enlarged to 100 prints under a new title, *Aula Veneris*. It was an original study based largely on Hollar's own sketches of women's dress, made during his travels around Europe. His best-known series of women's costumes is *The Four Seasons*, which exists in two formats: a set of three-quarter-length figures published in 1641, and a set of full-length figures published in 1643–44. Hollar was also celebrated for his accomplished studies of the capacious furs of the 1640s, especially that most salient of accessories, the muff.

At this same period in Spain, Francisco de Zurbarán and Diego de Silva Velázquez were painting portraits noted for their fundamentally realistic basis. Although Zurbarán worked for King Philip IV in Madrid in 1634–35, he is known largely for his portraits of saints executed in the 1630s. These portraits show a union of the mystical and the realistic, for he is attentive to the definition of the details of Spanish dress, most notably the distinctive bags and shoes. Velázquez was appointed painter to Philip IV in 1623 and also held a succession of other court appointments, including the Gentleman of the Wardrobe in 1636, which would have made him very cognizant of contemporary fashion. He would have benefited from seeing the Titians in the Spanish royal collection and also from the visit to court in 1628 of Rubens, his first contact with a celebrated painter, and with whom he became friendly. With scrupulous accuracy Velázquez delineated the formality of the stiff Spanish Baroque silhouette in his portraits right up to his death in 1660, the year he supervised the marriage ceremonials, which included dress, of the Infanta Maria Teresa with King Louis XIV of France.

The last quarter of the 17th century saw the flowering of French fashion engraving. It was this period that Auguste Garnerary, the renowned *troubadour* artist who created fashions for the Empress Joséphine, would later find so attractive, compiling in about 1820 a costume book of lithographs entitled *Costumes du siècle de Louis XIV*. During the reign of King Louis XIV (1643–1715) everything concerned with art and fashion was precisely organized. The word *mode* became established in literature as denoting sartorial style. In his *Essai d'un Dictionnaire Universel* of 1685, Antoine Furetière gave this definition: '*Mode ... se dit plus particulièrement des manières de s'habiller reçues à la Cour.*'[22]

The exhibition *A Fanfare for the Sun King*, held at the Fan Museum, Greenwich, London, in 2003, showed how Louis XIV 'took a personal interest in everything that went on in his kingdom'.[23]

> 'We know that Louis XIV, the Sun King, was meticulously interested in everything that concerned him or his image. All his commissions were accompanied by written instructions, often in his own hand ... Everything that touched on his 'Gloire', France's fame or reputation, was part of a well thought out 'propaganda' ... By studying French fan leaves of the 17th century ... we discover the world described in the journal *Mercure Galant* in every detail. For example, in one of the fans belonging to The Fan Museum, we see the royal family of France gathered together on the occasion of the Twentieth Birthday of the Grand Dauphin in 1681. The King and Queen are seated while other members of this large family stand around them in full Court dress. Madame's dress matches a description in one of his own letters! (Madame was the King's sister in law).'[24]

One new way in which French fashion was disseminated abroad was through fashion journalism. In 1672 Jean Donneau de Visé founded *Le Mercure Galant*, a popular magazine that was aimed directly at fashionable women. This was an expanding readership due to feminist agitation, for periodicals heretofore had been a male preserve. *Le Mercure Galant* published literary and scientific works as well as news of the social world of the court and articles on fashion. In 1677 *Le Mercure Galant* obtained a *Privilège du Roy* and was reorganized under a new title, *Le Nouveau Mercure Galant*. From 1678 to 1685 the *extraordinaire* or supplementary numbers were published, in which the fashion articles were accompanied by engravings, *gravures de mode*. Jean Le Pautre's engraving entitled *Intérieur d'une boutique parisienne de mode* appeared in the *Le Nouveau Mercure Galant* supplement of January 1678 and featured an array of bolts of mainly floral fabrics, which were popular for fashionable women in the 1660s and 1670s, as well as various female items including slippers, gloves, ruchings, ribbons, caps, bows and scarves. Another innovatory way that French fashion was methodically and stylishly publicized and promoted by the government was the granting of permission, through the Petite Académie (an erudite institution akin to a fine arts commission), for the publication of large quantities of *gravures de mode* of men's and women's dress, which were avidly collected, most importantly abroad. The Crown authenticated each print with its own seal of approval, *avec*

Privilège du Roy. These *gravures de mode* were exquisitely drawn and hand-coloured by artists of the calibre of J D de Saint-Jean, who was made an *agréé* of the Académie Royale de Peinture et de Sculpture in 1687, Sébastien Le Clerc, who engraved Charles Lebrun's tapestry series *L'Histoire du Roi*, Jean Paul Le Pautre, who engraved for *Le Nouveau Mercure Galant*, and Antoine Trouvain, whose series of fashion engravings entitled *Appartements royaux* offered a unique insight into the court at Versailles. Trouvain's *gravures de mode* depicted women at court, and in particular the King's mistress Madame de Montespan and his second wife, Madame de Maintenon (shown on page 20), dressed in the height of French Baroque fashion, wearing the heavy *manteau* and the complicated *fontange* headdress, and absorbed in intellectual pursuits, especially reading, embodying the concept of the *femme savante* (educated woman). A rich flourishing and interaction of art and fashion was to ensue, for Madame de Pompadour, King Louis XV's mistress and the 'godmother and queen of Rococo', later found inspiration in these *gravures de mode.*[25]

'Pompadour's images were the apogee of an already solidly established and influential visual and iconographic tradition. In life, Pompadour reinvented herself in the image of Montespan and Maintenon. In art, she and her portraitists created her persona out of the pictorial conventions of the *femme savante*.'[26]

Madame de Maintenon

Antoine Trouvain, Madame de Maintenon, *(1695), engraving (Cabinet des Estampes, Bibliothèque Nationale de France, Paris)*

1   Rococo and Neo-Classicism

Descending the long staircase in the Sainsbury Wing of the National Gallery, London, into the lower galleries that housed the exhibition *Madame de Pompadour: Images of a Mistress* (October 2002 to January 2003), the doorway-entrance that riveted one's attention showed straight ahead her ravishing portrait painted by François-Hubert Drouais in 1763–64 (shown on page 22). Madame de Pompadour, seated in her boudoir at her tambour frame, engaged in embroidery work yet surrounded by her books and a portfolio of engravings reminding the viewer of her intellectual and artistic achievements, wears a sumptuous *robe à la française* of painted silk with a meandering pattern of naturalistic light-green leaves and salmon-pink flowers, trimmed at the elbows with three rows of large *engageántes* (cuffs with two or three ruffles) made of fine French needle lace. With four striking bows of matching striped silk at her elbows, throat and bosom, and a broad border of fine lace stitched into the hem of her dress, this garment epitomizes the Rococo taste – serpentine curves, three-dimensional ornamentation and clear, delicate colours.

The Rococo style has been the subject of debate for centuries:

> 'The term Rococo seems to have been first used in the closing years of the 18th century, although it was not acknowledged by the Académie Française until the 1842 supplement to its dictionary, which defines it as the type of ornament that characterized the reign of Louis XV and Louis XVI. The term was originally derogatory, probably derived from the term *Rocaille*, on the model of the Italian barocco. *Rocaille*, which had originally referred to the shell-work employed in garden grottoes, began from 1736 to be used to designate a specific mode of decoration.'[1]

The preoccupation with the natural world, especially the collecting, identifying and cataloguing of new plants and flowers, would have a tremendous influence on the movement away from the heavy fabrics of the Baroque to the light and fluid fabrics of the Rococo, as depicted so beautifully in Drouais's portrait of Madame de Pompadour.

The Goncourt brothers, in their 12-volume *L'Art du XVIIIe. siècle* (1859–75), undertook much valuable research on the sources and aesthetics of the Rococo style. In the 20th century, writers such as Fiske Kimball, in the catalogue of the exhibition *The Creation of the Rococo*, held at the Philadelphia Museum of Art in 1943, argued against the theory that the Rococo was the final phase of the Italian Baroque and wrote eloquently on its development in France, especially in relationship to the decorative arts, critically analysing its salient characteristics of asymmetry, naturalism, graceful play on three-dimensional surface decoration and

François-Hubert Drouais, Madame de Pompadour *(1763–1764), oil on canvas (National Gallery, London/www.bridgeman.co.uk). The serpentine curves, three-dimensional ornamentation and clear, delicate colours on her dress epitomize the Rococo taste.*

light colours. Kimball also pointed out that the word 'Rococo' was first used in the *atelier* of the great Neo-classical artist Jacques-Louis David in the 1790s by the artist Maurice Quaï, leader of the group called *les primitifs*, who wanted to return to classical sources as a creative stimulus for art and dress, which meant at that time, according to the supplement to the dictionary of the Académie Française, 'all that was old and out of fashion in the arts, literature and costume', while in the *Enciclopedia universale dell'arte* (1966), Hans Sedlmayr and Hermann Bauer showed convincingly that the term Rococo embraced all the arts and architecture, and demonstrated the fundamental unity of the style. This was most imaginatively brought out in the exhibition *The Art of Love: Madame de Pompadour and the Wallace Collection,* held at the Wallace Collection, London, from October 2002 to January 2003. The gallery walls were covered in white silk woven with silver, which evoked the wall coverings in Madame de Pompadour's private apartments. This magnificently set off the strong, clear greens, pinks and blues of the Sèvres porcelain on display. The fabric woven with silver scrolls, which covered the walls of the second room in the exhibition, echoed the gold embroidery on the white satin dress Madame de Pompadour wore in the pastel of 1755 painted by Maurice Quentin de La Tour, which was reproduced in the exhibition (the original portrait is in the Musée du Louvre). The exhibition conveyed her all-embracing taste for the Rococo, for, on her death in 1764, it took more than a year to compile an inventory of her possessions: porcelain, marquetry furniture, marble garden statues, tapestries, silk fabrics, jewellery, gold snuff boxes, drawings, prints and paintings by François Boucher.

Madame de Pompadour, who in 1745 became *maîtresse en titre,* the mistress of King Louis XV, and was ennobled as the marquise de Pompadour, became both the inspiration for, and the arbiter of taste of, the Rococo style, until her death. As a powerful patron of the Rococo arts, she had the wherewithal to employ some of the most accomplished masters of the decorative arts and some of the most renowned French painters and sculptors of the era: Jean-Marc Nattier, François-Hubert Drouais, Carle van Loo, Joseph-Marie Vien, Étienne-Maurice Falconet, Edmé Bouchardon, Jean-Baptiste Pigalle, Jean-Baptiste Greuze and, above all, François Boucher.

In both art and fashion, Boucher is the artist forever associated with the Rococo style. For the Goncourt brothers, Boucher was 'one of the men who indicated the taste of a century'.[2] The son of a painter who was probably his first teacher, Boucher mastered many branches of the arts including fan painting, tapestry designing, stage designing and book illustration, while several of his pastoral paintings were used as a basis for a series of porcelain figure groups for Vincennes and Sèvres. He was inspired by the subjects and delicate manner of Jean-Antoine Watteau, one of the key artists of the Rococo, and especially by his paintings of *fêtes galantes,* social gatherings of elegantly dressed people in park settings. These paintings, and his series of etchings entitled *Figures de mode,* depicting female and male figures wearing fashionable clothes in landscape settings, show Watteau as a foremost exponent of the interaction of art and fashion. Boucher, an outstanding draughtsman, made etchings after Watteau's drawings, under the title *Figures des différentes caractères.* He also made twelve etchings of the set of 30 *Diverses figures chinoises peintes par Watteau ... au*

Jean-Antoine Watteau, Gilles and His Family *(c. 1716–1718), oil on panel (Reproduced by permission of the Trustees of the Wallace Collection, London). Watteau, a key artist of the Rococo, was known for his paintings of elegantly dressed people in park settings.*

château de La Muette (published in 1731), which explored the asymmetrical element in Chinese art, *chinoiserie* being a prominent motif in the Rococo style. His prints captured Watteau's refined sensibilities, the lightness and elegance of, for example, the *sacque* with the distinctive *plis Watteau*, so-called because of his exquisite handling of the flowing falls of unbroken columns of pleats. Engraving these images for publication, Boucher became influential in spreading the Rococo style across Europe.

Boucher's prodigious talents did not escape the attention of the King's new mistress, and between 1747 and her death in 1764 he flourished under the patronage of Madame de Pompadour. She embellished her châteaux with textiles, tapestries, porcelain and modern French paintings, achieving a symbiosis between the decorative and fine arts. She commissioned from Boucher tapestry designs for her private theatrical productions at her château de Bellevue, and designs for sculptures for her château de Crécy, that were used as models for porcelain at Vincennes and Sèvres. The paintings she commissioned from Boucher include masterpieces such as *Arts and Sciences,* now in the Frick Collection, New York, and *The Rising of the Sun* and *The Setting of the Sun,* both in the Wallace Collection, London. Madame de Pompadour also commissioned Boucher to portray her several times, where he perfectly met her requirements to be seen as a woman of culture and education, a *femme savante,* surrounded by her books, prints, maps and musical instruments.[3] Although women in 18th-century France had no legal rights, they occupied a powerful position in society, as both Louis-Sébastien Mercier in the 18th century and the Goncourt brothers in the 19th century pointed out. In *Le Tableau de Paris,* Mercier maintained that fashion was the one area in which they could express their creativity and exert their authority: 'Dress, adornment. This is what constitutes their joy and their glory.' For the Goncourt brothers, in their book *La Femme au XVIIIe. siècle,* women were: ' ... the commanding voice ... the century was filled with female marvels, female excitements ...'[4]

These views were mirrored in the person of Madame de Pompadour. She was an enlightened patron, not only of artists, but also of poets and *philosophes.* She herself was a woman of great cultural accomplishments: a musician, an actress and an engraver, studying drawing with Jacques Guay — the gem engraver whose jewellery she often wore — and with Boucher. She published a number of her prints in a limited edition that she gave to friends and members of the royal family.

Madame de Pompadour also wanted to be seen as a woman of great taste and fashion, a *belle savante.* As Madeleine Delpierre wrote in her book *Dress in France in the Eighteenth Century,* Madame de Pompadour 'promoted a taste in dress that reflected the visual arts of the period'.[5] She popularized the *robe à la française,* a gown made of beautiful silk, which became one of the most enduring fashions of 18th-century France. Evolving from the *sacque,* the voluminous nature of that dress gave way to a defined waistline. The *robe à la française* had pleats at the

François Boucher, Madame de Pompadour (1759), oil on canvas (Reproduced by permission of the Trustees of the Wallace Collection, London). In both art and fashion, Boucher is the artist forever associated with the Rococo style.

back organized into crisp folds, and close-fitting sleeves that terminated at the elbow where the pleated wing cuffs of the *sacque* were replaced by overlapping tiers of ruffles that echoed the lace sleeve ruffles immediately underneath, called *engagéantes*. The gown was worn with *paniers* (the hoops under the skirt that held it in shape) that were elliptical in form (with the short axis from front to back), instead of the round ones worn with the *sacque*. Other features of the *robe à la française* were a ladder of ribbons called *échelles* on the stomacher (the long, triangular panel forming the front of the bodice), trimmings of lace, ruching and *passementerie* at the neckline, at the sleeve ruffles, down the front opening of the dress, and across the front opening of the *jupe* or petticoat. The awesome construction and cut of the gown, with the huge skirt pushed out with the *paniers*, formed a silhouette that made possible the Rococo influence of the fabric design and the profuse use of trimmings. The exquisite painted silk in Drouais's portrait of Madame de Pompadour, for example, with its pattern of convoluted flora and leaves and the trimmings of lace and ribbons embellishing the *robe à la française,* softened and brought out the symmetry of the dress. All the elements harmonized and, and as worn by Madame de Pompadour, conveyed the sophisticated and delicate nature of the Rococo.

It was Boucher, in his many portraits of Madame de Pompadour, who defined her *chic* and who made her an icon of stylishness. In the most celebrated, dated 1759, located in the Wallace Collection (shown on page 25), Boucher modelled the composition on his earlier portrait of Madame Bergeret, dated 1746 (shown opposite). Madame Bergeret is situated in a garden wearing a resplendent silk gown with a tight bodice and puffed sleeves, which are highlighted with ribbons. An important motif, which would become identified with Madame de Pompadour, is the profusion of roses in the portrait of Madame Bergeret: they are emerging from a bronze vase, decorating her sleeves and hair, and arranged on the garden bench and in the foreground plane. In Boucher's portrait of Madame de Pompadour in 1759 in a garden setting at the château de Bellevue, which was noted for its abundance of roses, she wears a *gris-rosé* taffeta dress and a rose in her corsage, the distinctive colour associated with her. Boucher shows how her *robe à la française* is an integral part of the whole, harmonizing with the flowers, foliage, garden furniture and sculpture, a statement par excellence of the Rococo style.

The English artist William Hogarth, writing in *The Analysis of Beauty* in 1753, declared the basis of beauty to be the waving line. As Richard John points out in his article 'Rococo', in *The Dictionary of Art*:

> 'Although Hogarth did not specifically intend his *Analysis of Beauty* to be a manifesto for the Rococo, his conviction that beauty and grace could only be found in the serpentine line was the closest anyone came in Europe to offering a theoretical justification for the style ... Hogarth asserted: "Such shell-like winding forms, mixt with foliage twisting about them are made use of in all ornaments; a kind of composition calculated merely to please the eye. Divest these of their serpentine twinings and they immediately lose all grace."[6]

In his book, Hogarth referred to dress to underline his theory. The English textile industry was influenced by the Rococo style. The most celebrated English silk designer, Anna Maria Garthwaite (1690–1763), was noted for her naturalistic, asymmetrical

François Boucher, Madame Bergeret *(1746), oil on canvas (National Gallery of Art, Washington/ www.bridgeman.co.uk). Boucher used this painting as a composition model for his later painting of* Madame de Pompadour *(page 25).*

floral designs, which she began producing in 1742. In the following year she started 'using C-scrolls reversed on each other. Late in life, she recommended that the silk-designer "ought to follow the principles Mr Hogarth gives in his *Analysis*, observing the Line of Beauty", demonstrating that even the minor arts had acquired a new self-importance through the influence of the Rococo.'[7]

The English artist whose work most conjures up fashionable ladies in their silks and gauzes – indeed, whose portraiture not only captured a living likeness, but also epitomized the English elegance of Rococo fashion, is Thomas Gainsborough. Trained in London by Hubert-François Gravelot (the son of a Parisian tailor and a former pupil of François Boucher), Gainsborough was very much aware of Rococo art and fashion. Gravelot's important series of fashion drawings of the mid-1740s clearly inspired Gainsborough, especially the angular figures of his early period. Gravelot was well acquainted not only with the works of Boucher but also of Watteau, whose imagery Gainsborough readily adopted. This is already evident in Gainsborough's portrait of *Miss Lloyd* (shown far right), traditionally identified as a member of the Lloyd family of Ipswich. Gainsborough painted her about 1750, soon after his return from London to his native Sudbury, in Suffolk. A small-scale painting of a figure in a parkland setting with ornamental classical objects, it shows the influence of his mentor and the Rococo charm of Gravelot's friend, Francis Hayman, with whom Gainsborough studied in the early 1740s, as well as the example of Watteau. The graceful ease and informality of Miss Lloyd, together with the attention to detail of the dress and its rich textures, already demonstrates Gainsborough's extraordinary skill in the rendering of appearance and fabrics. The fluidity of the paint animates the surface of the silk and gauze fabrics and the fashionable straw hat in Miss Lloyd's lap.

Gravelot was associated with the St Martin's Lane Academy, founded by Hogarth in 1735. Gainsborough mixed in this circle of artists and would have been stimulated by Hogarth (who visited Paris in 1743 and 1748) and the master's lively debates on the asymmetrical curve. 'Ultimately rooted in Hogarth's theories about the serpentine "Line of Beauty"', Gainsborough was also well served in being so attuned to contemporary fashions by the fact that his family were in the textile trade. His father was a clothier and crêpe-maker and his sister was a milliner. He would have been well aware of the trends in fashionable dress after his training, and 'would have trained his eye on noticing the materiality of stuffs'.[8] This was brought out in the 'Portraiture and Fashion' section of the exhibition on Gainsborough held at Tate Britain, London, the National Gallery of Art, Washington and the Museum of Fine Arts, Boston during 2002–03, where comparisons with fashion dolls and fashion plates showed Gainsborough to be *au fait* with current fashions. This room of the exhibition showed how Gainsborough used fashion dolls as models, with several examples of them on display. The dress worn by Mrs Henry William Berkeley Portman in his portrait of her dated c.1764–65 was compared to the equally exquisite one worn by the British doll, dated c.1755–60, known as the 'The Queen of Denmark', made for one of the

Above left and right: Hubert-François Gravelot, An English Lady and Gentleman, drawings engraved by L. Truchy, 1744–1755 (Chrysalis Image Library). Gravelot's fashion drawings were an inspiration for Gainsborough.

Right: Thomas Gainsborough, Miss Lloyd (c. 1750),
oil on canvas (Kimbell Art Museum, Fort Worth).
Gainsborough was well acquainted with
contemporary fashions as his family was in the
textile trade.

British royal princesses. Both wear costume that is magnificently harmonized, consisting of a sack dress and petticoat, stays, chemise and stiffened hoops. This was underlined in William Hoare's portrait of Christopher Anstey with his daughter, dated c.1776–78 (shown on page 30), where the toy doll she is showing to her father evoked the elaborate dress and hairstyles of the 1770s, seen in the portraits of the fashionable women painted by Gainsborough, and exhibited in this section of the exhibition.

In the absence of fashion magazines with fashion plates at the beginning of the 18th century, fashions were transmitted via dolls, or *poupées*. Dressed in the latest fashions, *poupées* were sent out from Paris to the European capitals to be displayed in the windows of fashionable shops for all to see. Louis-Sébastien Mercier described how the *poupées* were a delight to behold in the shops of the *modistes* in the rue Saint-Honoré, the fashionable shopping street in Paris.[9] The English also sent out dolls dressed in the latest fashions, while the milliners, like the *modistes*, advertised their dolls in their windows.

The use of dolls as models for artists was well established:

'A number of artists associated with St Martin's Lane, including Gravelot and Hayman, are known to have painted from poseable dolls. Gainsborough, in turn, took up the practice, perhaps using dolls for his costume studies of the 1760s and quite definitely using figurines as models for *The Mall* and the 'Richmond Water-walk.'[10]

William Hoare, Christopher Anstey with his Daughter, Mary *(c. 1776–1778), oil on canvas (National Portrait Gallery, London). The child is keen to show off her doll. The earliest dolls, dressed in the latest fashion, were sent out from Paris to be displayed in the fashionable shop windows in European capitals.*

Dolls and female identity were themes taken up by Jean-Jacques Rousseau in his novel *Émile* (1762), in which girls are exhorted to play with dolls, since in time they would become dolls themselves. This is charmingly visualized in William Hoare's painting. Best known for his satirical poems about life in Bath, a city of fashion and entertainment, Anstey is depicted deep in thought composing a poem while his daughter tries to distract him with her very fashionable doll, whose attire and feathered coiffure can also be seen in the fashion plates of the 1770s.

As a painter of fashionable life, Gainsborough also made use of fashion plates. These were images made specifically to illustrate to people the types of clothes they should wear to keep up to date with fashions, and also gave guidance on whether the clothing shown would suit the taste and style of the individual wearer. Fashion plates evolved in the 18th century, with their origin in the 16th-century costume books. *The Lady's Magazine*, published in London and edited by Oliver Goldsmith from 1759–63, boasted the earliest fashion plate. The number for December 1759 issued a full-page black-and-white engraving entitled 'Habit of a Lady in 1759' with the accompanying editorial text:

> '... I have engaged the ingenious Mr. Walker to execute a design of a Lady in a perfectly genteel undress; and for the assistance of those in the country, who, as they have not opportunities of seeing the originals, may dress by that figure, I shall endeavour to accommodate to it certain plain instructions.'[11]

Many of the English fashion plates of the last quarter of the 17th century show figures in landscape settings, walking and conversing in parks. Gainsborough brought these elements of fashion plates to the fore in his visually engaging drawings of the 1780s, such as *Study of a Lady,* which have a 'specifically modern way of looking'. 'A Hogarthian aesthetic of serpentine beauty is still evident, in that the drawings do not simply document or describe fashionable ideals, but in the very gracefulness of their technique embody those ideals.'[12]

The archaeological discoveries of the Roman cities of Herculaneum (from 1738 onwards) and Pompeii (from 1748), buried by an eruption of Mount Vesuvius in AD 79, provided exciting visual evidence of ancient art, the discoveries of which were disseminated to a wide public through the publication, with plates, of *Le Antichità di Ercolano esposte* (The Antiquities of Herculaneum Revealed, 10 vols, 1755–92). The French painter Joseph-Marie Vien, for example, who was studying in Rome along with many other avant-garde artists and designers at the time of the excavations at Herculaneum and Pompeii, drew inspiration from this work in the 1763 painting *La Marchande d'amours (The Cupid Seller)* (shown on page 34), which he closely based on a Roman painting discovered at Gragnano, near Naples, in 1759, and which had been engraved in volume 3 of the *Antichità* by Giovanni Battista Nolli. New theories arose, fuelled not only by a reaction against the Rococo style, which was seen as frivolous and capricious, but also by a genuine desire to re-create the art and fashions of the ancient world, a continuation of the flowering of classicism that went back to the Renaissance. However now, with a new, more scientific and more historically based interest in the past, stimulated by these great archaeological discoveries, there was a movement towards developing a contemporary style that was informed by this new information. Johann Heinrich Wilhelm Tischbein, who twice visited Rome, described that city as the 'the true centre of the arts'. His compatriot, the archaeologist and art historian Johann Joachim Winckelmann, who became a key figure in the Neo-classical movement, wrote *Gedanken über die Nachahmung der griechischen Werke* in 1755, the year he settled in Rome. Translated into English in 1765 by the artist and writer Henry Fuseli, under the title *Reflections on the Painting and Sculpture of the Greeks*, it contained the key phrase, 'noble simplicity and calm grandeur'. Winckelmann's assertion that 'there is only one way for the Moderns to become great, and perhaps, unequalled: by imitating the Ancients', was a clarion call for artists consciously to imitate antique art in style and subject matter. In 1764, Winckelmann wrote another erudite tome, *Geschichte der Kunst des Altertums*, in which for the first time the term 'history of art' was used in the title of a book. A very influential publication, it was soon translated into English *(History of Ancient Art)* and also into French *(Histoire de l'art chez les anciens)*. In England, the artist Sir Joshua Reynolds, who had studied in Italy from 1750 to 1752, became the first President of the Royal Academy in London in 1768. He compiled his *Discourses on Art,* which he addressed to the students and members of the Royal Academy between 1769 and 1792. Published separately and in collected editions, and translated into Italian, French and German, Reynolds advocated mastery of the 'Grand Style' and a 'timeless dress'.

In France, the comte de Caylus – scholar, collector and Europe's most renowned antiquary – published a detailed description of the wall paintings of Herculaneum in 1751, and followed this with *Recueil d'antiquités, egyptiennes, étrusques, grecques, romaines et gauloises* (1752–67). Along with other like-minded scholars and collectors such as J-P Mariette and the abbé Jean-Jacques Barthélémy, Caylus felt the Rococo had had its day. In the annual *salons* in Paris, the *philosophe* Denis Diderot led the attack on the Rococo style, in particular the paintings of Boucher. In his article entitled 'Style' in *The Dictionary of Art*, James Elkins writes that '"Rococo" ... was coined by Jacques-Louis David's pupils "for the meretricious taste of the age of Pompadour"'.[13] The fashionable dress of Madame de Pompadour in particular came in for censure. Boucher's portrait of her painted in 1756 (in the Alte Pinakothek, Munich), in which she wears a *robe à la française* of sea-green taffeta trimmed with lace and pink roses, and with the bodice decorated with rows of pink and silver striped silk, elicited this response of ridicule from the critic, baron Grimm, in the *Correspondance littéraire*, when the painting was exhibited at the *salon* of 1757: '... it is so laden with ornaments, pompoms, and all sorts of frills, that it must surely hurt the eyes of everyone of taste.'[14]

Two Ladies in the Newest Dress, *from drawings taken at Ranelagh, May 1775, engraved for the Lady's Magazine, June 1775 (Chrysalis Image Library).*

Thomas Gainsborough, Study of a Lady *(c. 1783–1785), chalk drawing (Courtesy of the Trustees of the British Museum, London).*

Yet Madame de Pompadour, even nearing the end of her life, showed herself to be a true patron of the arts by embracing the new trends. She supported the visit to Italy of her brother the marquis de Marigny, who was the *directeur des Bâtiments du Roi*, which did much to encourage the study of the antique. She commissioned paintings from Vien and owned furniture *à la grecque*. The work table at which she sits in the portrait by Drouais discussed at the beginning of the chapter, with its swags and goats' heads, is boldly in the new style and likely to have been made for her by the *ébéniste du Roi* (cabinet-maker of the King) and *maître-ébéniste* (master cabinet-maker), Jean-François Oeben, in the early 1760s. Richard John notes in his article 'Goût grec' (literally, 'Greek taste') in *The Dictionary of Art* that this was a stylistic term for the first phase of French Neo-classicism.

> 'The style was effectively inaugurated by a set of furniture, comprising a combined writing-table and cabinet and a clock made for the Parisian financier Ange-Laurent de La Live de Jully from designs (1756–1758) by the painter and amateur architect Louis-Joseph Le Lorrain. The monumental and unfrivolous style of these pieces, executed in ebony-veneered oak with heavy gilt-bronze mounts, was quite different from the current Rococo idiom.'[15]

Among the objects uncovered at the Temple of Isis in Pompeii were bronze tripods. In The *Virtuous Athenian*, Vien's engraving of 1763 (he also painted a version of the scene), he included a tripod that spawned a very popular piece of furniture, called the *athénienne*. The furniture, together with the dress worn by the Athenian girl — a long tunic over a chiton that is split at either side exposing her legs to mid-thigh — presented an image of the classical past that did much to infuse a spirit of excitement for the antique.

Contemporaries looked to Vien to inspire women to abandon their Rococo capriciousness for classical simplicity, singling out his engravings and paintings, especially *La Marchande d'amours* (shown on page 34), as being 'dans le goût et le costume antique', with Diderot especially praising the dress when this painting was exhibited at the *salon* of 1763. Vien prophetically gauged the new taste, launching the fashion for antiquity with the dress of his statuesque, concupiscent ladies in *La Marchande d'amours*. Their dress was practically identical with the Neo-classical chemise that would later be worn by the *élégantes* of the *Directoire* (1795–99), with its high waistline, low *décolletage*, bare arms and unfussy sandals, complemented by simple hairstyles or modest turbans. Enthusiastic for the classicist ideas expressed in Winckelmann's publications of 1755 and 1764, and underlined by his association with the antiquarian comte de Caylus (who addressed the study of costume as a corollary to art in his *Tableaux tirés de l'Iliade et de l'Odyssées d'Homère et de l'Enéide de Virgile: avec des observations générales sur le costume,* 1757), Vien's work followed this new direction when he returned to Paris. He immediately started to dress his female sitters in the new antique style, a notable example being his portrait of the marquise de Migieu of

1764. In a setting of antique furniture and a sculpture bust of her father, Vien portrayed the marquise in a fashionable blue dress with its square neckline and elbow-length sleeves, but adding artistically invented details such as a sash emphasizing a higher waistline and the arrangement of the material as drapery. In 1771, Vien painted King Louis XV's mistress, Madame du Barry. Like her predecessor, Madame de Pompadour, she was in the forefront of art and fashion and played a key role in the creation and dissemination of the new classical taste. She commissioned furniture, porcelain and architecture. The Pavillon de Louveciennes (1769–71), which the King presented to her, was a proclamation of the new style in architecture, in which antiquity triumphed. The daughter of a dressmaker, Madame du Barry was very fond of clothes, and in 1760 she herself became an assistant in the shop in Paris of the celebrated dressmaker, Labille,

Joseph-Marie Vien, The Cupid Seller (1763), oil on canvas (château de Fontainebleau/ www.bridgeman.co.uk). Vien inspired women to abandon their Rococo tastes in clothes, endorsing instead classical simplicity.

which many artists frequented to procure trimmings for fashions depicted in their portraits, most notably Drouais. Vien represented her as a Muse in a *chemise à l'antique*. The catalogue of *The Age of Neo-classicism* exhibition, held in London in 1972, confirms the seminal role of Vien in art and fashion: '... Vien, whom legend was to transform into the father of Neo-classicism, did mark a turning-point in the history of taste, as much or more by the fresh simplicity of his style as by his antiquarian subject matter.'[16]

The 1770s in France were notable for the re-emergence of costume books that conveyed a specialist antiquarian knowledge of dress. Michel-François Dandré-Bardon spent the years 1726–31 studying in Rome. Received into the Académie Royale de Peinture et de Sculpture in 1735, he pursued an academic career, becoming a Professor at the Académie in 1752. As a vivid draughtsman and theoretician, he wrote and illustrated a number of books, including his *magnum opus, Costumes des anciens peuples*. Published in six volumes in 1772–74, he dedicated it to the marquis de Marigny in recognition of his encouragement of *le goût grec*. André Lens's book, *Le Costume des peuples de l'antiquité*, appeared in 1776. He believed artists should imbue their work with 'la simplicité et la noblesse des formes grecques ou romains' ('the simplicity and nobility of Greek and Roman forms'). That the great artist Jacques-Louis David was *au fait* with this costume book can be seen in his portrait, painted in 1799, of the *Directoire élégante,* Madame de Verninac, whose pose and arrangement of the folds of her *chemise* and shawl are clearly based on Lens's engraving (plate 121) of a Roman matron. In her dress and pose, David presents Madame de Verninac as both fashionable and erudite, a sitter with a knowledge of the classical world. David's influence on other artists in portraying sitters in classicized dress – conveying their subjects as both fashionable and with an awareness of the antique – can be seen in an anonymous artist's portrait, painted after 1800, of Madame de Servan, the wife of the minister of war, which is almost a direct copy of David's portrait of Madame de Verninac.

Neo-classicism became the dominant movement in the fine and decorative arts, architecture and fashion in Europe from the late 18th century, as knowledge grew ever more widespread about the archaeological discoveries extending from southern Italy to Egypt and the Near East. The term 'Neo-classical', however, was not coined until the 1880s. It was defined very lucidly in the opening pages of the catalogue of the comprehensive *The Age of Neo-classicism* exhibition:

> 'The word "Neo-classical" was first applied to works of art of the late eighteenth and early nineteenth centuries at a time when they were generally out of favour and when the very notion of a classical revival was suspect – in the 1880s. The more obviously opprobrious "pseudo-classical" was also used, especially for the paintings of David and his contemporaries. Such terms were never used by the artists and critics of the late eighteenth century. It is important to remember what we now call Neo-classical was described by them as quite simply the "true" or "correct" style.'[17]

In late-18th-century France, Vien had many followers and disciples who created the fashions of the time, as well as visually recorded them. A report in the *Mémoires secrets* for 3 June 1781 commented on fashion being more than ever 'the object of the inventive genius of our artists'. One of the major painters at the epicentre of art and fashion was Elisabeth-Louise Vigée Le Brun.

> 'Perhaps more than any single individual in the last quarter of the eighteenth century, Vigée Le Brun influenced the development of women's costume. She helped to popularise a more natural look by introducing into her portraiture light-weight gowns, as opposed to the corseted and bulky "robes à la française" which had long been in vogue. She also spurned the great masses of ornately dressed and powdered hair women were forced to endure for the sake of being fashionable.'[18]

Vigée Le Brun was the daughter of the pastellist Louis Vigée, under whom she studied. Vien, as a pioneer of the Neo-classical style of dress, won her admiration. She described him as the artist 'who first gave us the exactitude and style of the ancient Greek and Roman costumes'.[19] By 1770 she was a practising portrait painter in her own right. In 1776 she married the picture dealer, J-B-P Le Brun and their *hôtel* in Paris became a *salon* attended by fashionable society. Beautiful, and with an unerring sense of style, she was sought out as a portraitist by ladies of fashion. Her *Mémoires*, which were published in three volumes from 1835 to 1837 and translated into English, chronicle her times and works and vividly demonstrate her natural flair for costume and her influence on fashion:

> 'As I had a horror of the current fashion, I did my best to make my models a little more picturesque. I was delighted when, having gained their trust, they allowed me to dress them after my fancy. No-one wore shawls then, but I liked to drape my models with large scarves, interlacing them around the body and through the arms, which was an attempt to imitate the beautiful styles of draperies of Raphael and Domenichino ... above all I detested the powdering of hair and succeeded in persuading the beautiful Duchesse de Gramont-Caderousse not to wear it when she sat for me. Her hair was black as ebony, and I parted it on the forehead, arranging it in irregular curls. After the sitting, which ended around dinner time, I did not alter her hair at all and she left directly for the theatre; being such a pretty woman she was quite influential and her hairstyle insinuated itself into fashionable society and eventually became universal.'[20]

In her *Mémoires*, Vigée Le Brun noted that she favoured wearing gowns of simple white muslin and her hair unpowdered and styled by herself. This is evident in her many self-portraits. One that dates from about 1781, in the collection of the Kimbell Art Museum, Fort Worth, shows her wearing a loose-fitting muslin gown, adorned only with a coral bow and caught high up under the waist with a coral sash and a black, lace-trimmed shawl. Called *la robe en gaulle,* this is the same style of dress

Elisabeth-Louise Vigée Le Brun, Self-Portrait *(c. 1781), oil on canvas (Kimbell Art Museum, Fort Worth). The high-waisted silhouette favoured by the portraitist Vigée Le Brun moved fashion towards a new contemporary style.*

worn by Queen Marie-Antoinette in Vigée Le Brun's portrait of her from 1783. Summoned to Versailles in 1778 to paint the Queen wearing a white satin *robe à paniers*, court dress, Marie-Antoinette became her friend and patron and helped to ensure that Vigée Le Brun was received into the Académie Royale de Peinture et de Sculpture in 1783. This proved to be a turbulent year, for the commissioned portrait – showing the Queen in muslin *déshabille* rather than in court dress – caused a scandal when shown at the *salon* of 1783, and signalled a break with tradition and convention. The *robe en gaulle* would have a profound impact on future sartorial

Attributed to Elisabeth-Louise Vigée Le Brun, Queen Marie-Antoinette *(c. 1783), oil on canvas (National Gallery of Art, Washington, Timken Collection). The portrait of the Queen in a loose-fitting muslin gown, as opposed to court dress, caused a scandal when first shown and had to be withdrawn from the salon of 1783.*

Toiles de Jouy, Manufacture Oberkampf de Jouy-en-Josas (Bibliothèque Forney, Paris)

developments in the Neo-classical period. With regard to its construction and material, it moved fashion ahead towards a new contemporary style, its simplicity in stark contrast to the Rococo *robe à la française*, and emerging as the transitional form of the high-waisted silhouette of the *Directoire chemise*, as well as 'prefiguring that which will eventually become generalised under the term 'empire'.[21]

With Queen Marie Antoinette's immediate influence on muslin, which became the fashionable fabric in the 1780s and thence throughout the Neo-classical period, her dress also had political and international implications, for 'she was also infuriating the Lyons silk manufacturers, jettisoning their extravagant outer layer and choosing to aggrandise cottons imported from India'.[22]

The *robe en gaulle* was derived from *la robe à la Créole*, worn by ladies on the plantations of the French West Indies and brought to France in the 1770s. Vigée Le Brun recalled in her *Mémoires* how she had seen Queen Marie Antoinette wearing this style of dress at Marly in the mid-1770s. The *Correspondance secrète* related in September 1779 the Queen's love for the pastoral life.[23] She and her ladies-in-waiting required a simpler attire when affecting the role of milkmaids at the hamlet at Versailles and at the dairy at Rambouillet. The *robe en gaulle* was a comfortable dress, quite simply a tube of muslin put on over the head. Very different from the established, structured form of silk dress, which was stepped into and had, as we have seen, a number of component parts, *la robe en gaulle,* with its sleeves of elbow or wrist length tied with ribbons, was gathered on a drawstring round a low neckline with falling collars, its fullness drawn in at the waist by a sash. Vigée Le Brun's painting had to be withdrawn from the *salon* of 1783, which only helped to popularize the dress it depicted. The very next year, the dress was illustrated as the *chemise à la reine* in *La Gallerie des modes et costumes français d'après nature gravés par les plus Célèbres Artistes en ce genre* (1778–87) (*The gallery of French fashions and costumes, drawn from life, engraved by the most celebrated artists in this medium*), which contained the first set of French fashion plates, keeping women abreast of current taste. The widespread use of muslin and naturalistic-style floral-printed cottons as the favoured female dress materials can be seen, not only in the extant specimens of dress, but also in the fashion plates of *Le Cabinet des modes*. This began to be published in Paris in 1785 with hand-coloured plates drawn mainly by Sébastien-Jacques Le Clerc (who drew the *chemise à la reine* in *La Gallerie des modes*) and Claude-Louis Desrais (who also drew for *La Gallerie des modes*), and was the first magazine devoted to news about French fashion to be published with regular frequency.[24] Another source in which the new styles began to be widely seen was the pattern books containing the exquisite French printed cottons known as *toiles de Jouy*.

The abbé Jean-Jacques Barthélémy's *Voyage du jeune Anacharsis en Grèce (Voyage of the young Anarcharsis to Greece),* published in Paris in 1788 (and reprinted and translated many times), was an account of Greek antiquity in fictional form, which did much to encourage interest in ancient Greek life and also travel to Greece, for Anacharsis was a Scythian prince of the sixth century

BC, noted for his wide travels and extraordinary wisdom. Inspired by the abbé's book, Vigée Le Brun held in the year of its publication her celebrated *souper grec*, or Greek supper party, considered one of the exceptional social events of the reign of King Louis XVI. Through it, Vigée Le Brun stamped her vestimentary authority on the fashion ethos of the *ancien régime* by wearing a white tunic, and clothing her female guests in draperies from her studio. Thus she continued to influence fashion right up to the final years of the *ancien regime*.[25]

An artist fundamental to the links between art and fashion in late-18th-century France is Jacques-Louis David, who has already been mentioned. He first trained under Boucher, who was a distant relative. Recognizing that their artistic temperaments were different, Boucher recommended him to study under Vien. David won the *Prix de Rome* in 1774, and went to Rome the following year with Vien, who had been appointed Director of the French Academy. David quickly forsook the Rococo for the new Neo-classical style. In 1784, he painted *The Oath of the Horatii*, which was commissioned by the comte d'Angiviller, *directeur des Batîments du Roi*. When the painting was exhibited at the Salon of 1785,

> 'David's fame was established throughout Europe and the influence of the painting, which was regarded by all as the manifesto of the Neo-classical School, was considerable ... No other artist had achieved greater purity in his forms and in his emphasis on outline. One can almost sense an uncontrollable desire to rival sculpture bas-relief.'[26]

Like his *Oath of the Horatii*, David's painting *Brutus and the Bodies of his Sons* (1789) was also rapturously received at the *salon*, and both were reproduced upon the stage as *tableaux vivants* during the French Revolution. As 'pageant-master of the Republic', he designed uniforms for the new revolutionary government, and his direction of the revolutionary festivals made thousands of participants and tens of thousands of onlookers familiar with his version of classical dress. He clothed the women who took part in simple, antique-style white gowns that helped to make the white *chemise* the most important gown of the 1790s.[27] David's study of the antique in Italy for five years (1775–80) had instilled in him a profound knowledge of classical costume, and the dress he portrayed in his history paintings, like the *Horatii and Brutus*, were the subject of much interest and debate in the *salons*. That the costume of the women in his history painting of 1799, *The Intervention of the Sabine Women*, was acknowledged to be close to *Directoire* fashion, showed how *au courant* he was with the current taste. Again he strove for the purity of sculpture bas-relief, arranging his figures in a wide frieze. He defined the tall, slender, statuesque women in the *Intervention of the Sabine Women* with sleek, clean contours. His superb use of draperies suggested the shape of the human form underneath. The duchesse d'Abrantès, a contemporary chronicler of the time, wrote in her *Mémoires* that 'it was then the fashion for ladies' dresses to fall like the draperies of the antique statues'.[28] Even if David's imprisonment as a supporter of Robespierre lessened his influence among

Attributed to the circle of Jacques-Louis David, Portrait of a Lady *(c.1794–1795), oil on canvas (San Diego Museum of Art, Gift of Anne R. and Amy Putnam). The painting captures the sculptural quality of white muslin.*

Engraved fashion plate from Le Journal des Dames et des Modes, October 1797, Plate 8 (Private Collection). This was the leading fashion magazine of the time. Many of the social elite were used as models for the plates.

Engraved fashion plate from Le Journal des Modes et Nouveautés, July 1797, Plate 4 [renamed Le Journal des Dames et des Modes from September 1797] (Bibliothèque Doucet, Paris)

the leaders of the Thermidorean Reaction of July 1794, he was still the period's principal portraitist. John Carr, an Englishman who visited Paris during the Peace of Amiens (1802–03), noted in his book *The Stranger in France* how he had seen in a restaurant 'admirably painted after the taste of Herculaneum' in the fashionable Tuileries Gardens where the cream of society gathered, 'some beautiful women present, dressed after the antique, a fashion successfully introduced by David'.[29] He painted some of the leading *élégantes* of *Directoire* society, such as Madame Récamier and Madame de Verninac, discussed above, while *A Portrait of a Lady,* which may be of Madame Tallien, is attributed to the circle of David. All of them capture the pronounced sculptural quality of the white muslin *Directoire* chemise. David represented in his portraits the simplification held out as the ideal to the creators of fashion. That this ideal was accepted in its essentials can be seen in the hand-coloured fashion plates of the leading fashion magazine of the time, *Le Journal des dames et des modes*, which were drawn from life, recording immediate fashion by some of the period's minor masters, including E-C Voysard, P-L Baquoy, J-F Bosio, M Deny, Claude-Louis Desrais, Philibert-Louis Debucourt and Carle and Horace Vernet. Many of the models in the fashion plates were *élégantes* (an élite social group numbering between 60 and 80) easily recognized by those who moved in *Directoire* society, whether promenading down the Champs-Elysées or walking by the elegant waterways in the gardens of Tivoli or Frascati, or eating and dancing there in the decorative temples.[30] David's portraits go far towards endorsing the essential accuracy of the fashion plates in *Le Journal des dames et des modes*. The last great *chef d'atelier* before Jean-Auguste-Dominique Ingres, David counted among his pupils François Gérard, Anne-Louis Girodet de Roussy-Trioson, Antoine-Jean Gros and Ingres himself, all of whom were fashionable portrait painters.

When studying the Neo-classical period, most people think immediately of France. By the 18th century, France was recognized as the worldwide leader of fashion for women. However, there were reverberations elsewhere, particularly in England. By the 1770s, fashionable ladies clad in classically inspired white dresses were a feature of the portraiture of Thomas Gainsborough, George Romney and Sir Joshua Reynolds. Romney's significance as a Neo-classicist rests largely on his drawings and paintings of Lady Hamilton, made during the 1780s. Wearing plain white dresses with classical overtones, she performed her celebrated 'attitudes' at social gatherings. These were dramatic *tableaux vivants* in which she exhibited every possible variety of classical pose and expression, based on representations in paintings and sculpture. She so bewitched Romney that he persuaded her to sit for him again and again.

In his portraiture, Reynolds alluded to the Old Masters, especially Raphael and Michelangelo, and to classical sculpture, which he had studied extensively in Italy, to enhance the dignity of his sitters. He advocated the use of draped cloth which, with its noble folds, would impart a 'timeless' quality to the dress, and therefore a dignifying effect. In the seventh of his *Discourses on Art,* he addressed fashion and his theory of 'timelessness'.

> 'He therefore who in his practice of portrait-painting wishes to dignify his subject, which we will suppose to be a lady, will not paint her in the modern dress, the familiarity of which alone is sufficient to destroy all dignity. He takes that his work shall correspond to those ideas and that imagination which he knows will regulate the judgement of others; and therefore dresses his figure something with the general air of the antique for the sake of dignity, and preserves something of the modern for the sake of likeness. By this conduct his works correspond with those prejudices which we have in favour of what we continually see; and the relish of antique simplicity corresponds with what we may call the more learned and scientific prejudice.'[31]

Reynolds' portrait of Lady Frances Warren (shown far right) is one of his earliest full-length portraits of fashionable ladies, executed in the grand manner to which

Joshua Reynolds, Mrs Elizabeth Carnac *(c. 1775),
oil on canvas (Reproduced by permission of the
Trustees of the Wallace Collection, London). The
height of the hairstyle and headdress was the
current fashion in 1775.*

Joshua Reynolds, Lady Frances Warren *(1759),
oil on canvas (Kimbell Art Museum, Fort Worth)*

he was devoted. She is recorded in the artist's sitter books in January 1758 and
May 1759, nearly a decade after Reynolds wrote his *Discourses on Art*. His portrait
of Mrs Elizabeth Carnac is dated about 1775, the height of her hairstyle and her
extravagant headdress being in accordance with current fashion. Both Lady Warren
and Mrs Carnac evince a faultless balance of classically draped clothing and a

modern hairstyle. Such elegance and ideal beauty, with its 'veneration of antiquity', made Reynolds the arbiter of the Neo-classical style in England.

Finally, some of the outstanding caricaturists in France and England must be mentioned, for these artists reconciled the demands of caricature with an accurate portrayal of dress.

The late 18th century was noted not only for its trenchant political debate but also for its fierce shopping. Urban dwellers saw fashionable shops springing up, and the streets of their cities paved and better lit. The French caricaturists at the century's end, such as Philibert-Louis Debucourt, Jean-Baptiste Isabey, Louis-Léopold Boilly and especially Carle Vernet, with their candid depictions of modern life, were artistically perceptive enough to fasten onto the essentials of fashion, often down to the smallest details. During the *Directoire*, Carle Vernet drew the *incroyables* and *merveilleuses*. Rather than precise sartorial labels, these terms were coined to express the public's sheer astonishment at the new male and female fashion. His *incroyables* and *merveilleuses* were published as a series of aquatints in 1797. They may seem a preposterous distortion of fashion, but a clear indication of Vernet's accuracy was the indignation of the *incroyables* at his caricatures of them.[32] In fact, a close look at Vernet's caricatures of the *incroyables*, and their female counterparts the *merveilleuses*, serves more to dispel their sartorial grotesqueness: it is far less the costumes than the wearers who are distorted. The strongest proof that Carle Vernet's caricatures gave an authentic rendering of their subjects is the appearance as a fashion plate in *Le Journal des dames et des modes* (in spite of its title, men's fashions were included) of his *homme dégagé*, and the endorsement by Pierre de La Mésangère, the editor, that the fashions were actually worn. They can be observed being worn by the very top of society in Philibert-Louis Debucourt's engraving of Frascati, which was one of the most modish places in Paris where those of *bon ton* flocked. Carle Vernet's *homme dégagé* enjoyed the status of a model for aspiring men of fashion — so caricature suffered the indignity of being turned inside out to become a new reality. The *habit dégagé*, with its dark-woollen, double-breasted coat, tight-fitting across the chest and down the sleeves, and cutaway at the skirts, *pantalon à la hussarde* (close-fitting pantaloons in the style of the French Hussars, light cavalrymen and the most glamorous of army units) and boots that hugged the legs, created a quasi-antique look.

The golden age of caricature in England was the theme of *Followers of Fashion: Graphic Satires during the Georgian Period*, a touring exhibition in the United Kingdom during 2002–03, featuring the caricatures of, among others, William Hogarth, James Gillray, Thomas Rowlandson and George Cruikshank. Delineating the 'atmosphere of clothes', the people who wore them, their foibles and affectations and their society with great inventiveness and wit, their protean variety was conveyed in the very subheadings of the essay in the exhibition catalogue: 'fashion and nature', 'fashion and society', 'contemporary impressions of fashion' and the 'caricaturists' vision'.

Habit dégagé *(based on Carle Vernet's* Homme dégagé*), engraved fashion plate from* Le Journal des Dames et des Modes, *4 April 1799, Plate 99 (Bibliothèque Doucet, Paris). Vernet was one of the outstanding caricaturists of fashion in the late 18th century.*

2 Romanticism

Romanticism began as a literary movement. The term 'Romantic' was first used by the German critic Friedrich Schlegel in 1798 to define modern poetry. It was drawn from the French word, *romance*, referring back to a medieval literary form. 'He chose as his badge a word derived from "Romance", admittedly once a description of the old French language but, more significantly, of medieval stories of courtly love or mysterious phenomena which appealed directly to the imagination.'[1]

Historical revivalism, especially an admiration for the Middle Ages, had been growing in France since the mid-18th century. It was Jean-Baptiste de La Curne de Sainte-Palaye who brought the Middle Ages to life through his publications, *Mémoires sur l'ancienne chevalerie (Memoirs on the old chivalry)* (2 vols, 1759) and *Histoire littéraire des troubadours (Literary history of the troubadours)* (3 vols, 1774). La Curne de Sainte-Palaye invited his readers to share his dreams by the mesmeric repetition of a phrase that he made particularly his own. Again and again he invoked *le bon vieux temps* – the good old days.[2]

He had a central role in the revival of interest in the Middle Ages through his evocation of a whole set of values that he equated with life in *le bon vieux temps:* high aspirations, chivalric deeds and the devotion of a knight for his lady. Medieval dress, lovingly and minutely described, was central to La Curne de Sainte-Palaye's presentation of the Middle Ages. It was the *romans de chevalerie* (novels of chivalry), republished by the comte de Tressan, which proved the principal means for the diffusion of La Curne de Sainte-Palaye's vision of the Middle Ages among a wider public. The comte de Tressan's interest in medieval romances went back to 1732, when he found a collection of them in manuscript form in the Vatican Library. In 1775 he launched the *Bibliothèque universelle des romans* (universal library of novels), a publication that appeared regularly until 1789. The popularity of the comte's *romans de chevalerie* were much enhanced by numerous illustrations closely integrated with the text. Indeed, the *Bibliothèque universelle* proved so popular, that after a hiatus during the turmoil of the French Revolution, publication was resumed in 1798. At the turn of the century, the atmosphere had changed decisively: writings defending tradition were published, such as *Le Génie du christianisme ou beautés de la religion chrétienne (The Genius of Christianity or Beauties of the Christian Religion)* (1802) by François-René, vicomte de Chateaubriand; Napoléon signed the Concordat with Pope Pius VII in 1802, which made Catholicism again the official religion of France; and Napoléon took the title of Emperor in 1804. In these changed circumstances, the cult of the Middle Ages, which in France came to be known as *le style troubadour,* was set to become a central theme of Romanticism.

Another key tendency of Romanticism was the cult of personality. The celebration of individual character and social status took on a fresh aspect in the form of a new kind of fashionable society portraiture. In England, this sophisticated, urbane style was mastered by Sir Thomas Lawrence, who greatly influenced Eugène Delacroix. As a self-proclaimed movement, Romanticism emphasized an intense, personal and subjective response and the seeking of inspiration in the creative imagination. The French poet and critic Charles Baudelaire later posed the question, in his review of the *salon* of 1846, 'what is Romanticism?', and went on to answer that it was 'a manner of feeling'. The expression of emotion and the power of intuition led to an examination of the role of the artist in society. Self-revelation and a new attitude to creativity on the part of the artist underpinned Romanticism. Cultural *salons* called *cénacles* were formed and prestigious art magazines that explored artistic freedom, such as *L'Artiste*, were founded. The Romantic sense of mission had a powerful influence on artists in exploring the self, for example, as *dandy*, *Jeunes-France* or *artiste-flâneur*, where the rendering of costume played an important part in the understanding of the creative personality as a force or voice within society.

Nor did Romanticism totally break with Neo-classicism. 'Romantics frequently sought to make classicism a living experience rather than a dead ideal, and aspects of Neo-classicism ... have been seen as a hybrid version of Romantic classicism.'[3] Although Romanticism started as a literary movement, it came by association to embrace the other arts, including the visual arts. It was Baudelaire who gave a definition of Romanticism that expressed the idea of a modern world whose means could include a heightened historical awareness, when he wrote that 'Romanticism and modern art are one and the same thing, in other words: intimacy, spirituality, colour, yearning for the infinite, expressed by all the means the arts possess'.[4]

While the themes of Romanticism were a constant presence not only in France but across much of Europe, this chapter concentrates almost exclusively on France. French artists produced some of the greatest masterpieces and influenced the course of fashion. Painting and fashion were closely related and the iconography created by the artists changed fashion, inspiring new fashion trends, such as a sense of national identity, a quest for a new expression of beauty and an unbridled freedom of the imagination.

In the last chapter, we saw how the spirit of Neo-classicism affected fashionable French masculine attire during the *Directoire* period. Men's plain dark clothing was cut and tailored in a figure-hugging manner, emphasizing shape as a way of suggesting classical form. But, as Anne Hollander notes in her book to accompany the exhibition *Fabric of Vision: Dress and Drapery in Painting*, held at the National Gallery, London, in 2002:

> 'Except in classicised portrait sculpture, men in 1800 could never appear in true
> classical garb – draped togas, long gowns or tunics that bared sizeable expanses of

leg, arm and chest – because, during centuries of European custom, those features of dress had become feminine. Women's clothing in all classes had permitted exposure of the neck and chest since the fourteenth century, of shoulders and the lower arms since the early seventeenth, and of ankles in the mid eighteenth. Women had always worn versions of tunic, gown and mantle, and their clothing had never divided their legs. At the beginning of the nineteenth century ... women could re-make themselves in Neo-classical earnest simply by re-designing their hair, re-modelling their underwear and making their gowns and mantles of thin fabric with no surface ornament ... In the closing decades of the eighteenth century men urgently needed a shift in elegance, a way to re-clothe their bodies without effeminately denuding and draping them, something to fit them visually into the new political and social climate and the Neo-classical aesthetic scheme. This scheme demanded a candid and simple aspect, indicating respect for enlightened political views as well as for natural virtue and feeling and not the outward magnificence that once denoted superiority of rank.[5]

Le Monument du Costume, a series of engraved plates after designs by Jean-Michel Moreau (known as Moreau le Jeune) with a text by Rétif de la Bretonne, was published in 1789, and is the most complete example of the life and dress of the privileged on the eve of the French Revolution. In his book *The Culture of Clothing* Daniel Roche writes of the 'Rococo air' of the aristocratic fops at court. The death throes of the *ancien régime* saw them wearing the *habit à la française* made of silk, the coat richly decorated with embroidery that emphasized its surface rather than its shape. A splendid visual example from *Le Monument du Costume* is 'La Petite Toilette', drawn by Moreau le Jeune and engraved by P-A Martini, in which the young marquis is shown by his tailors a new coat, amply cut and decorated with floral embroidery, laid out on the chair beside him (shown on page 48).

Around 1730, a Frenchman called Césare de Saussure visited England and noted that fashionable men 'dress simply'. 'They are rarely seen in gold braiding, they wear a small coat called a frock that is without pleat or adornment, with a collar on top. They have a little round wig, a plain hat and a stick in hand, but their cloth and linen is of the finest and most handsome.'[6]

By the 18th century France was recognized as the centre of women's fashionable dress. The reputation of 'Parisian Mode' was consolidated in the 19th century. But due to an advanced woollen industry and exceptional tailoring techniques developed in London during the 18th century, fashionable men's dress became associated with the label 'London Tailoring'. While fashionable women's dress was in a constant state of flux, that of men retained a basic form, the English suit. The English suit, in fact, has been the focal point of fashionable men's dress for over two hundred years.

In Gainsborough's portrait of *Mr and Mrs William Hallett* (*The Morning Walk*), dated about 1785 (shown on page 49), it is noticeable how Mr Hallett's simple figure-hugging black woollen suit is bereft of adornment. It was Neo-classicism in tandem with Romanticism that made the new, simpler modes both very attractive and desirable for fashionable men.

Jean-Michel Moreau (Moreau le Jeune), La Petite Toilette (being groomed), *drawing engraved by P-A Martini,* Le Monument du Costume, *1789 (published originally in 1777 in the* Seconde Suite d'Estampes pour servir à la histoire des Moeurs et du Costume des Français dans le dix-huitième siècle*), (Chrysalis Image Library).*

'These were already being romanticised in real life by the famous Beau Brummell, who as dandy-in-chief of London society at the turn of the century, was renowned for his perfect clothes and figure, but also known for his utterances – for example, 'to be well dressed is to be unnoticeable'. More significantly, anecdotes circulated about his numerous rituals for preserving the perfect cleanliness of his body and its linen, and others about how many artisans and craftsmen were needed to achieve the perfect fit and condition of his simple garments, gloves and boots. There is in the tone of Brummell's celebrity a Romantic and erotic intensification of the Neo-classical theme, with its emphasis on the purity of the linen folds and the clarity of their arrangement,

Thomas Gainsborough, Mr and Mrs William Hallett ('The Morning Walk') *(1785), oil on canvas (National Gallery London).*

the beauty of the body, the preservation of the smooth line of the figure and its extremities. It suggests the creation of classical nude sculpture out of the clothed male form, to be accomplished by tailoring and groooming.'[7]

It is something that was taken up with great aplomb by the French Romantics. As the late, great Sir Hardy Amies said in one of his waspishly witty remarks: 'The English suit is the universal grammar of the cultivated gentleman or him who aspires to be one. It remains the sole reason Frenchmen might envy us.'[8]

Above: John Cook, Beau Brummell *(c. 1798), engraving (Courtesy of the Trustees of the British Museum, London).*

Left: Ferdinand-Victor-Eugène Delacroix, Louis-Auguste Schwiter *(1826–1830) oil on canvas (National Gallery, London). Schwiter was an absolute Anglophile and Delacroix has painted him as the ascetic black-suited dandy in the distinctive English manner.*

Carrick à collets rond, engraved fashion plate from Le Journal des dames et des modes, 15 February 1812, Plate 1206 (Private Collection).

No French Romantic painter better summarized what was the English masculine style of fashion than Eugène Delacroix in his portrait of Louis-Auguste Schwiter, dated about 1826 (shown far left). For Baudelaire, Delacroix was the supreme, indeed, the epitome of the Romantic artist. Baudelaire considered Delacroix not only as the kindred spirit of Raphael, Michelangelo, Rembrandt and Rubens, but also as the first modern painter. His artistic education was obtained by studying the Old Masters in the Louvre. Defining Romanticism as 'a call for artistic freedom', Delacroix's prodigious talent included designing historical costumes for a Romantic drama, drawing many series of carefully detailed studies of medieval dress and armour compiled from books of hours, a series of paintings during the 1820s on subjects in *le style troubadour,* magnificent portraits and the writing of a voluminous journal, all of which contribute to an understanding of Romanticism in fashion. He dominates the critical writings of Baudelaire, who eulogized him in the poem 'Les Phares' (from *Les Fleurs du mal,* 1857). Delacroix and succeeding generations identified the dandy, held to be a particularly English character, with Beau Brummell and Lord Byron. According to Baudelaire, Delacroix 'in his youth had thrown himself into material vanities of dandyism, and ... how with the collaboration of Bonington [the English artist with whom he travelled to London in 1825 and shared a studio in Paris in 1826] he had laboured to introduce a taste for the English cut in clothes and shoes among the youths of fashion.'[9]

His portrait of Louis-Auguste (later baron) Schwiter, who was also a painter and a staunch Anglophile, is considered an icon of Romanticism. A highlight of the exhibition *Constable to Delacroix: British Art and the French Romantics,* held at Tate Britain, London, and the Metropolitan Museum of Art, New York, during 2003–04, the portrait is the consummate image of the ascetic black-suited dandy in the distinctive English manner. Baron Schwiter's demeanour, like that of so many of the Romantic artists, is of a dandy aspiring to perfection through the impeccable simplicity of his clothes.

'The early Romantic and still Neo-classic proposition for male dress, requiring that artless country garments be recut to fit Apollo, was then further homogenised to create a High Romantic version in the form of a full-length suit. Eugène Delacroix's 1826 standing portrait of twenty-one year old Louis-Auguste Schwiter offers a beautiful example of the male classical figure unified by clothes instead of nudity. This young man's ideal body is carved by the painter out of soft black suiting, his shoulders shown delicately augmented by padding, his neck strengthened by a standing collar, his mid-section flattered by the curves of a smoothly fitted coat and waistcoat, his legs lengthened by the continuous black modelling of his trousers ... He [Delacroix] shows how painters' imaginative perceptions of male tailoring were expanding to allow for broader emotional suggestions. This is a Romantic Parisian dandy, not a romanticised country squire ... He is outdoors, but not engaging with Nature; he stands on a stone terrace strewn with leaves and flowers, facing, we must think, a sumptuous interior

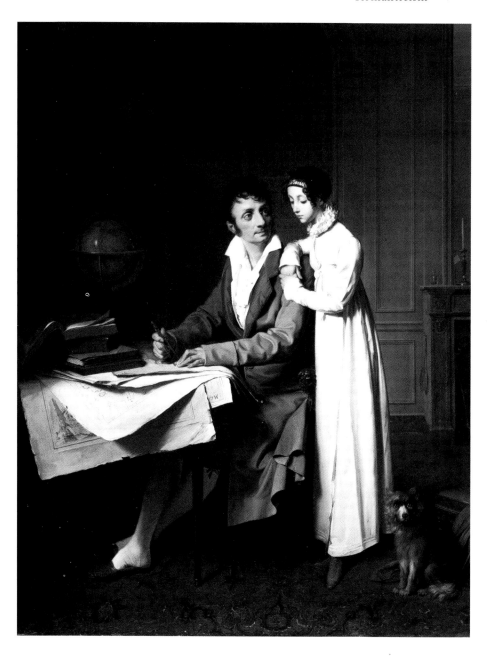

Louis-Léopold Boilly, The Geography Lesson *(1812), oil on canvas (Kimbell Art Museum, Fort Worth).*

through high windows behind us — who is he waiting for? He is in evening dress; and while his soft hair is lifted by natural breeze, his feet are shod for the ballroom. Behind him are steps leading down to a park — there are even distant mountains against the light-streaked sky. This is a Balzacian image, made of sharp social observation infused with mystery and sexuality. The complete blackness of the baron's evening suit was a recent innovation including the long black trousers, a Brummell invention. Knee-breeches had been required with dress coats throughout the second decade of the nineteenth century, and many dress suits were then still in colours. Delacroix shows the baron's evening black striking a new and resonant note, initiating the Romantic allure of black clothing that has affected all fashions for both sexes with an enduring tenacity ever since. Its celebration here by Delacroix foreshadows his various versions of Hamlet and Horatio in the *Graveyard*, especially the one in the Louvre from 1839, where the black-clad Dane, even resembles the baron.[10]

Delacroix's portrait of baron Schwiter was painted under the spell of Sir Thomas Lawrence. The leading London portraitist, Lawrence transformed French portrait painting, after exhibiting at the *salons* of 1824 and 1827. The comte de Forbin, director of the French Royal museums, considered Lawrence the leader of the British School and secured his appointment as a chevalier of the *Légion d'honneur*. To Gustave Planche, writing in his *Études sur l'école française, 1831–1852* (2 vols, 1855) the drab frock coat and top hat posed obstacles to painterly invention, and it was Lawrence who overcame them, investing as much interest in modern costume as he did to the face in his portraits. Delacroix, in his portrait of the baron, was paying *hommage* to Lawrence, for he had visited him in London in 1825, the year before he started to paint Schwiter. Lawrence was also the subject of an essay written by Delacroix in 1829. It is significant that Delacroix's portrait of baron Schwiter was later owned by Edgar Degas, who painted a swagger portrait of his friend, the artist James Jacques-Joseph Tissot, about 1867–68, as an exemplar of the *artiste-flâneur*.

During the Paris Opéra's winter season of 1799–1800, at a formal performance given in the presence of the First Consul, Napoléon Bonaparte, Madame Tallien and two of her friends attended dressed as nymph-huntresses, in short tunics that hardly reached the knees, with their bare feet decorated with rings wrapped in sandals with purple straps. Joséphine, the future Empress, persuaded Napoléon to inform them that 'the time of fable was over and the reign of History had begun'.[11] The Romantics had a passion for history and were obsessed by a sense of the past. Overthrowing the *Directoire* by a military coup in 1799, Napoléon established himself as First Consul, and from 1804 to 1814, as Emperor.

> 'No single person exemplifies the Romantic hero-genius better than Napoléon. And if he did not create these types, his reputation both depended on them and brought them to full flowering. He was the ultimate self-made man, the absolute image of wish-fulfilment – the individual who came from nowhere to realise an extraordinary destiny … All this is reflected in the arts of the period. To Napoléon's years of glory belong the heroic images of the man himself conjoined with the heroes of history…'[12]

Appointed *premier peintre de l'Empereur* (first painter of the emperor), Jacques-Louis David recorded in his *Sacre* (shown on page 58) the ceremony that was held on 2 December 1804 in the splendid Gothic interior of the cathedral of Notre-

Edgar Degas, James-Jacques-Joseph Tissot (c. 1867–1868), oil on canvas (Metropolitan Museum of Art, New York, Rogers Fund). Degas painted a 'swagger portrait' of his best friend Tissot.

Dame, Paris, decorated with red and blue fabric and gold fringes by the *architectes de l'Empereur*, Charles Percier and Pierre-François Fontaine. Making a model of the nave of the cathedral and filling it with dolls specially dressed by his pupil, Madame Mongez, David put aside his classicist preferences and chose as his schema Rubens's striking *Le Couronnement de Marie de'Médicis (the Coronation of Marie de'Médicis)* with its kneeling figure of the Queen, a painting that was and still is in the collection of the Musée du Louvre.[13]

Queen Marie de'Médicis was the second wife of King Henri IV, one of the most popular kings in French history, who reigned from 1589 to 1610. The Romantic devotion to historical revival was made manifest in the dress at the coronation, brought out by David in a vivid, painterly style. Regulated by imperial decree, the *grand habillement* was designed by the artist Jean-Baptiste Isabey, who in 1804 was appointed *dessinateur du Cabinet de l'Empereur*. Isabey was aided by Jean-Baptiste Regnault, one of the outstanding history painters of the period, who also painted portraits of the fashionable. *Le Livre du Sacre de S M l'Empereur Napoléon* contains the engravings by Isabey of the dress and also those of Percier and Fontaine, of the decorations of Notre-Dame.[14] The Emperor's *grand habillement* consisted of a white satin tunic embroidered in gold and fringed at the ankles with a matching belt, a ruff of Alençon lace and a matching lace cravat, the Imperial mantle of velvet (*pourpre*) lined with Russian ermine ornamented with tufts of black astrakhan, white shoes with gold embroidery based on a strap design imitating laces, a collar of the *Légion d'Honneur* and a circlet of gold laurel leaves. The imperial jeweller, Biennais, supplied the circlet as well as the regalia, which consisted of a sceptre based on that of the 14th-century King Charles V, and the Hand of Justice and sword that were supposed to have been Charlemagne's.

According to David's biographer, E-J Delécluze, Napoléon paid a visit to David's studio and, on seeing the painting of the *Sacre*, approvingly told the artist that he had made him a *chevalier français*. The evocation of the motifs of historical dress from France's medieval past served to underline his concept of monarchy. In her book *La France*, Lady Morgan, noting this identification, wrote that 'the court of the new Charlemagne ... assumed a character of Gothic grandeur, wholly destructive to that tone of republican simplicity which Brutus Bonaparte had once contributed to establish'.[15] The costume of the dignitaries of the First Empire and of the royal household was based on the Emperor's *petit habillement*, which he wore for the journey to Notre-Dame and for the festivities surrounding the coronation. He was clearly inspired by the new costume of the *Ordre du Saint Esprit* (Order of the Holy Spirit) (founded in 1578) which had been approved by King Louis XVI in 1788, and which also consciously imitated the dress of the monarchy of King Henri IV. These chivalric links with the past appealed to the Emperor and artists-cum-designers of costume such as Isabey. The outfit consisted of the *habit à la française*, white velvet breeches embroidered with gold at the seams and with diamond buttons and garter-buckles; a vest of white velvet,

Jean-Baptiste Isabey, Self-Portrait (c. 1805), ivory miniature (Reproduced by permission of the Trustees of the Wallace Collection, London). In 1804 Isabey became the Emperor's designer.

embroidered with gold and decorated with diamond buttons; a coat of crimson velvet faced with white velvet and decorated with a mass of gold embroidery; a short cloak of crimson velvet, lined with white satin and fastened with a clasp of diamonds; white velvet shoes laced and embroidered with gold; gold-embroidered silk stockings with a design of the Imperial crown worked in the corner, and a hat of black velvet with white feathers, in the style of Henri IV. All the courtiers in David's painting wear a costume similar to the Emperor's *petit habillement*.

The Empress Joséphine's costume, also designed by Isabey, was made by her principal *couturier*, Louis-Hippolite Leroy. The dress of white silk brocaded in silver retained the high waist of the Neo-classical style of dress. The heavy mantle, with straps over the shoulders to hold it up, was made of velvet, embroidered and lined with ermine like the Emperor's. It drew attention to some of the graceful historical details on the dress such as the fine gold embroidery and jewelled bands on the short, puffy sleeves that imitated the Renaissance fashion for slashing, in vogue from the 15th to the 17th century, whereby, as a form of decoration, the top fabric was slit to reveal another underneath. There was also exquisite gold embroidery in vertical bands down the front of the dress in the style called *à la Reine Mathilde*. Yvonne Deslandres, in her article entitled 'Joséphine and *La Mode*', pointed out the reference to some of the embroidered garments that appeared in *La Tapisserie de la Reine Mathilde*, known in English as the Bayeux Tapestry, which was exhibited in Paris in 1803 while the invasion of England was being prepared.[16] (There had been a long French tradition that Queen Matilda, the wife of William the Conqueror, had embroidered the tapestry.) According to Madame Rémusat, a *dame du palais* who was charged with carrying the offerings at the *Sacre*, the highlight of the Empress Joséphine's gown was the raised collar of silk lace embroidered with gold, called the *collerette à la Médicis* or *chérusque* (the names were interchangeable during the First Empire).[17] It had been brought to France originally by Catherine de'Médicis when she married King Henri II. The collar is a prominent feature of the dress of Queen Marie de'Médicis, the wife of King Henri IV, in Rubens' painting of her coronation, and in practically all of the portraits painted of her.

France is a nation in which women have always been an important force in the realms of art and fashion. Chapter 1 focused on this aspect of French civilization, with the prominent roles of Madame de Pompadour and Queen Marie-Antoinette in collecting and commissioning art and in initiating the choice of fashions.

'The gigantic painting of the imperial coronation by David is called the *Sacre de Joséphine* since it records the moment when the Emperor, immediately after crowning himself in the presence of the Pope, is preparing to crown his wife. By his gesture and by David's brush, Joséphine's dress sense was given monumental authority.'[18]

As Emperor, Napoléon saw dress as a means of propaganda. A luxurious new court signalled power and glory. The Empress's magnificent court costumes of

Lyons silk and Alençon lace that promoted French fabrics, together with her fabulous jewellery, would give special brilliance to court ceremonies and would serve as a model for that adopted by the ladies of the court for all official functions, and indeed, by those throughout the First Empire. The Empress Joséphine was noted for the extreme elegance of her deportment when she wore the Neo-classical style of contemporary fashion. It showed her off to the greatest advantage and also kept the link with classical antiquity. The details of her coronation dress, however, show a scintillating and astute derivation from France's historic past, all beautifully rendered by David in his painting (page 58).

To the Emperor, who described her as incomparable, the Empress also represented the eternal qualities of the feminine. His valet, Constant, described her as having an 'exquisite figure'. The First Empire's alluring, sensuous, exotic side stems from her. In the annals of fashion history, the Empress Joséphine is forever remembered as the arbiter of official court dress of the First Empire. Little known, however, is her patronage of the *troubadour* painters and of her translation of many of the costumes and accessories depicted in their paintings into fashionable dress. This represented her own personal taste, which she raised to exquisite heights during the First Empire, manifested in her portraits and echoed in the portraits of an array of fashionable women and in the many fashion plates of *Le Journal des dames et des modes* that were inspired by her. She was admirably suited in character and taste to be a great patron of the arts, especially of *le style troubadour*. The subject matter in these paintings had a common thread of being centred around an admiration for women, and the choice of so many subjects where women played a primary role as paradigms of gentility and refined behaviour reflecting the ideals of a distant age of chivalry would have been very attractive to her. Mademoiselle Avrillion, *première femme de chambre de l'Impératrice*, wrote in her *Mémoires* of her mistress's love of the arts and of her many pleasurable conversations with baron Dominique-Vivant Denon, whom Napoléon in 1802 had appointed *directeur des musées*. The Empress was a most knowledgeable and assiduous collector who regularly visited the *salons* and she had a genuine interest in the history of France. She was a member of the Académie Celtique, which was founded in 1804 for the encouragement of research into 'Celtic, Gallic and French antiquities'.[19]

In his biography of Jacques-Louis David, Delécluze recounts, in his chapter entitled 'Les Elèves à leur atelier' ('The pupils in their studio'), that some of his pupils were already, from the earliest years of the 19th century, abandoning the study of antique art in the Louvre (home of the Musée Central des Arts, which had been established in 1793 by decree of the Revolutionary government, and renamed the Musée Napoléon in 1803) for a new rallying point, the Musée des Monuments Français, under its *conservateur*, Alexandre Lenoir.[20] Soon after the Catholic Church had been nationalized in November 1789, the religious houses were closed and their treasures confiscated. In 1790 the Commission des Arts selected the couvent des Petits-Augustins to house the artefacts, which included paintings, sculpture, tombs and stained glass. The artist, writer and archaeologist Alexandre Lenoir set about restoring the treasures, and in 1793 a list of objects was published. The results of Lenoir's labours were seen when, on 25 October 1795 the Commission des Arts appointed him *conservateur* and on 1 September 1796 the Petits-Augustins officially became the Musée des Monuments Français, and was opened to the public. Delécluze singled out Fleury François Richard, Pierre Révoil, comte Auguste de Forbin, François-Marius Granet and Jean-Baptiste Vermay, who went there in search of French subjects for their paintings, and to consult Lenoir's vast descriptive catalogue, *Musée des monuments français* (5 vols, 1800–1806), which stressed the Musée as a source of information about dress.[21] Lenoir prefaced the entries for each century with a dissertation on the costume of the period. The Musée des Monuments Français had many ups and downs throughout the curatorship of Lenoir, whom the Empress appointed *conservateur des objets d'art de la Malmaison*, which further strengthened the ties between the *troubadour* painters and herself. In 1802, Napoléon signed the Concordat with Pope Pius VII that re-established Catholicism as the official religion and opened up Catholic churches as places of worship again. The Emperor was under a great deal of pressure to return the treasures to their rightful places. In Lenoir's own words, 'it was the protection of the Empress Joséphine which allowed the Musée to survive'[22] She enjoyed visiting the museum, and in 1812 acquired a painting of the room housing its 13th-century collection by Charles-Marie Bouton. The museum flourished until 1816, and throughout this period Lenoir's five-volume catalogue had a great influence on the *troubadour* artists, a testament in itself to its historical accuracy. The works of this new generation of artists had the unequivocal support of the Empress, and she was their pivotal and outstanding patron. She liked and admired their paintings, small cabinet-size pictures in the manner of the 'little Dutch masters' of the 17th century such as Gabriel Metsu, Gerard ter Borch and Gerrit Dou, whose works could be studied in the Louvre. These paintings, which celebrated the history of the French nation rather than of classical antiquity, reflected a sentimentality and an etiquette and code of conduct derived from the system of *chevalerie,* central themes found in the writings of La Curne de Sainte-Palaye, which were also essential to these artists. The chief ingredients of these paintings were a small domestic interior filled with illustrious French historical personages from the Middle Ages and the Renaissance, making them far more accessible by rendering them foremost as human beings; a minute description of their dress, accessories and furnishings, a diffused light, brilliant, jewel-like colours reminiscent of illuminated manuscripts and a smooth, porcelain-like finish. These paintings were well suited both in scale and in spirit to the delicate interiors of the Empress's private home, the château de Malmaison, especially the music room and the picture gallery, with their Gothic décor. Between 1804 and 1812 she purchased or commissioned some 24 of these paintings for Malmaison. She made her collection 'relatively accessible to visitors of distinction ... so there is no doubt about Joséphine's predilection for the genre

Jacques-Louis David, The Consecration of the Emperor Napoléon and the Coronation of the Empress Joséphine *(detail) (1806–1807), oil on canvas (Musée du Louvre, Paris/www.bridgeman.co.uk). The Romantic devotion to historical revival was made manifest in the dress at the coronation, brought out by David in a vivid, painterly style.*

having contributed greatly to its success and diffusion'.[23] Her collection included works by the comte Auguste de Forbin, Jean-Antoine Laurent, Jean-Baptiste Vermay, Marie-Philippe Coupin de la Couperie and above all, Fleury François Richard, whom she appointed *peintre de l'Impératrice* (painter of the Empress) in 1808. She owned nine of his paintings, including *Valentine de Milan pleurant la mort de son époux (Valentine of Milan mourning the death of her husband)*, the new genre's manifesto painting. Richard wrote of her formidable knowledge about art when she invited him to Malmaison after the *salon* of 1808. Contemporaries described these paintings as *le genre chevaleresque* or *le genre anecdotique*, as Delécluze related in his biography of David.[24] *Le style troubadour*, as a term, was unknown to contemporaries – it is found for the first time in Émile Littré's great *Dictionnaire de la langue française* (2 vols, 1863–72), where it is defined as the prevailing taste of the First Empire. *Le style troubadour* is a useful term for bringing out the interrelationship of different elements associated with the cult of the Middle Ages, such as *le bon vieux temps, les moeurs chevaleresque*, the idealization of women and the mystery of the Gothic. The Middle Ages, for the early Romantics, embraced everything that was thought to lie between the 12th and the 16th centuries.[25]

The salient achievement of the Empress Joséphine was to draw inspiration from the costumes and accessories found in the *troubadour* paintings and to select and combine them into a most attractive effect in fashion. Indeed, *Le Journal des dames et des modes* acknowledged early on that it was a fashion in itself to go to the exhibitions at the *salons*.[26] The costumes of the time of King Henri IV, especially the *collerette à la Médicis*, pervaded court and fashionable dress. Of all the 16th-century French kings, he was the most popular, a *roi chevalier*, noted for his *galanterie* and patronage of the arts. One of the Empress Joséphine's favourite paintings in her collection was *Henri IV chez Gabrielle d'Estrées* by Fleury François Richard. She was inspired by the example of Queen Marie-Antoinette, whom she saw as a kindred spirit (she surrounded herself at Malmaison with gothic-style furnishings that had belonged to the Queen), and shared her delight in the world of the *romance*. King Henri IV, the first of the Bourbon line to become King of France, had been an enduring hero in the 18th century, with many novels and plays written about his life, the most notable being Voltaire's *Henriade* of 1723. La Curne de Sainte-Palaye used the enormous influence of King Henri IV's memory with the public to raise his reputation to an even higher level when, in 1781, in the new edition of *Mémoires sur la ancienne chevalerie*, he included a third companion volume, *Mémoires sur la chasse*, a kind of updating of the chivalric code to apply to Henri. Many hoped that King Louis XVI, when he succeeded to the throne in 1774, would inaugurate *le bon vieux temps*. The comte d'Angiviller enhanced the iconic stature of King Henri IV by commissioning paintings in which his heroic deeds were depicted. In an historical revival that was so fashionable, dress played an important part. As King Louis XVI lacked the necessary flair to translate the theme of Henri IV into dress, it was

Queen Marie-Antoinette, an avid reader of the *romans de chevalerie*, as well as an enthusiastic theatre-goer to plays about King Henri IV, who supported the revival of dress *à la Henri IV* and influenced the nascent *style troubadour*. Court balls, masquerades and fêtes formed the crucible in which Queen Marie-Antoinette forged a fashion for dress *à la Henri IV*, which were drawn as fashion plates by Claude-Louis Desrais and Pierre-Thomas Le Clère (or Le Clerc) for *La Gallerie des modes*.[27]

Three portraits of the Empress Joséphine in the Wallace Collection, London, show her fondness for the *collerette à la Médicis* and how she put her own distinctive style of shape and material onto it. An ivory miniature by Louis-François Aubry, of about 1805–1810 (shown right), shows her in a rich, blue velvet gown, decorated with pearls, onto which is mounted a large, high-standing embroidered white lace *Médicis* collar; an unfinished painting of about the same date by Pierre-Paul Prud'hon (shown far right) sees her sketched in a black dress with a low-cut neckline and a high, sharply-pointed *Médicis* collar made of muslin or *blonde* lace; and another ivory miniature, by the Italian painter Ferdinand Quaglia and dated 1814, depicts her wearing an elaborate white and gold dress, decorated with pearls and with the *Médicis* collar made of delicately scallop-shaped lace that sits gracefully on the puffed sleeves, drawing attention to the fine gold embroidery while echoing the lace cuffs. The portraits by Aubry and Quaglia attest to how the Empress harmonized her dress with her jewellery. Her favourite jewel, to judge from these portraits (and also the enormous quantity listed in the inventory of her collection at the château de Malmaison), was the pearl. Pearls were favoured and used more extensively than any other jewel during the Renaissance, as the exhibition *Virtue and Beauty: Leonardo's Ginevra de'Benci and Renaissance Portraits of Women* revealed, and, as the portraits of Queen Marie de'Médicis, Eleonora di Toledo and the Venetian Noblewoman from Vecellio's costume book, illustrated in the Introduction, bear witness. The *Mercure de France*, the journal read by high society, reported in March 1806 that pearls were preferred to diamonds and were especially popular for ornamenting the hair.[28] The portraits of Aubry and Quaglia also show how, in keeping with the spirit of the Renaissance, the Empress Joséphine wore her pearls, whether they be simple strands of pearls or a glittering pearl tiara, low across the brow in the manner of a *ferronnière*. Many troubadour artists, such as Anne-Louis Girodet de Roussy-Trioson and Jean-Auguste-Dominique Ingres, copied Leonardo da Vinci's *La Belle Ferronnière*, which was in the Louvre, thus spreading the influence of this fashion.

There are many beautiful portraits of fashionable ladies who copy the Empress Joséphine's fashion for pearls. One of her *dames du palais*, Madame la maréchale Ney, was painted by François Gérard wearing a dark velvet Renaissance-style dress with a square-cut bodice edged with gold, which provides a glorious backdrop for a double strand of pearls and a pearl pendant on the centre of her bodice. Her hair is adorned with pearls and her forehead with a pearl *ferronnière*.

Louis-François Aubry, The Empress Joséphine *(c. 1805–1810), ivory miniature (Reproduced by permission of the Trustees of the Wallace Collection, London). The miniature shows the Empress wearing an embroidered lace* Médicis *collar.*

François Gérard, Mary Nisbett, Countess of Elgin *(c. 1804), oil on canvas (National Gallery of Scotland, Edinburgh).*

Pierre-Paul Prud'hon, The Empress Joséphine (c. 1805–1810), oil on canvas (Reproduced by permission of the Trustees of the Wallace Collection, London). Here the Medici collar is made of muslin or blonde lace.

Another stunning example is the portrait of the comtesse de Périgord, princesse de Courlande, painted by Robert Lefèvre in 1812. He excelled in painting the tactile qualities of the rich fabrics and jewellery of the First Empire, so much so that contemporaries gave him the soubriquet 'the French Van Dyck'.[29] The comtesse is depicted wearing the same style of dress and pearls as Madame la maréchale de Ney. Further interesting *troubadour* details include the way the pearls are used with gold bands to hold in the puffs at the top of her sleeves, and the repeat of the motif across the bodice of her dress. Foreign ladies were also painted by these leading French artists, and their portraits (together with their recorded comments about them) confirm that they compare favourably with their

Ferdinand Quaglia, The Empress
Joséphine *(1814),*
*ivory miniature (Reproduced by
permission of the Trustees of the
Wallace Collection, London).*

French counterparts. Mary Nisbett, Countess of Elgin, was painted by Gérard wearing a black velvet dress embroidered in gold around the bodice, the puffed sleeves and in bands down the front, in the style designed by Isabey for the Empress Joséphine (shown on page 60). Around her neck she wears gold chains, another Renaissance revival of the Empress's, suited to the picturesque garments of Romanticism. Suspended from the Countess's gold chains are cameos and a jewelled pendant. Her hair is adorned with a tiara or comb edged with pearls, which harmonizes with her pendant pearl earrings. Writing to her mother, the Countess said that her portrait 'was done by the best painter here and he took unconscious pains about it'. In an article in *Le Journal des dames et des modes*, the editor singled out Jean-Baptiste Isabey, François Gérard and Robert Lefèvre as the artists most sought after by the *élégantes* for showing off their fashionable dress.[30] And in a further article, the editor wrote that to be of *bon ton*, an *élégante* absolutely had to have her portrait painted by one of these artists.[31] They were the leading portrait painters associated with the Napoleonic era: Isabey and Gérard received the appointment *premier peintre de l'Impératrice* in 1805 and 1806 respectively, while Lefèvre was the Emperor Napoléon's official court painter.

Another 16th-century French monarch, King François I, was also very popular during the First Empire. *Roi chevalier,* celebrated for his *galanterie* and renowned for his patronage of the arts, the first nucleus of the collection of the Musée du Louvre can be traced back to him. He introduced Italian Renaissance culture to France by inviting such masters as Leonardo da Vinci to the country, and by adding to his collection works by Titian and Raphael. In 1547, the last year of his life, the construction of the Louvre began. He was also the fashion-conscious king who epitomized the taste of the Renaissance. The Empress Joséphine was fond of the simple, little black velvet *toques* with an ostrich plume that were in the style of those worn by François I. The *troubadour* artist Auguste Garneray, who studied under Isabey, made a series of drawings of these Renaissance *toques* in the Musée du Louvre, and his inventive genius was interpreted most skilfully by Monsieur Leroy, who designed them for her. She wore one of these fetching *toques* in an ivory portrait miniature painted by Jean-Baptiste Isabey, dated about 1806 (shown left). Isabey was the Empress's favourite portraitist. In 1785 he went to Paris where he began his career by painting snuffboxes. He received patronage from Queen Marie-Antoinette, designing clothes and painting portrait miniatures of her. But his real ascent to fame came through his pupil, Hortense de Beauharnais, the Empress Joséphine's daughter, who introduced him to the Emperor and Empress. He painted several portrait miniatures of them that became so celebrated that reproductions of them decorated the snuffboxes of the fashionable. As both a portrait painter and a designer of costumes, Isabey is perhaps more than any other artist associated with the fluency and luminous quality of art and fashion in *le style troubadour,* so highly prized by the Empress Joséphine. He imbued the Empress's *toque* with a theatrical air, framing her Romantic hairstyle of 'dishevelled' curls. Such fresh and graceful attention to detail derived from his

Jean-Baptiste Isabey, *The Empress Joséphine,* c. 1806 *Ivory miniature (Private Collection). Isabey, a painter and designer of costumes, was the Empress's favourite portraitist.*

role as principal decorator and costume designer for the imperial theatres. An unmistakable offshoot of *troubadour* paintings, the same *toque* can be seen in Jean-Antoine Laurent's *Jouer de hautbois*, exhibited at the *salon* of 1806, which was in the Empress's collection. The *Mercure de France* in 1806 paid tribute to this particular *toque*, made so fashionable by the Empress.[32] It was seen again in Pierre Révoil's *L'Anneau de l'Empereur Charles-Quint (The Ring of Emperor Charles V)*, where both King François I and the Emperor Charles V wear it. Shown at the *salon* of 1810, where it was snapped up on behalf of the Emperor's household (perhaps under the influence of Denon's commendation of *troubadour* paintings as being 'peculiarly French'), this painting was so popular that it was re-exhibited in 1814.[33] The *toque* in Isabey's portrait of the Empress Joséphine harmonized well with the high-standing embroidered white lace *Médicis* collar and one of her favourite garments, a dark velvet *pelisse*. The *pelisse*, a velvet coat often edged with wide bands of fur, originated from those worn during the 12th to the 15th centuries, and it can be seen in many *troubadour* paintings. Eleanor d'Este wears one in Louis Ducis's *Le Tasse lisant à la princesse Eléonore d'Este (Tasso reading to Princess Eléonore d'Este)*. The Empress's *pelisse* is close-fitting with the sleeves puffed at the top in an elaborate cutwork design in the Renaissance manner. The inventory of her collection at Malmaison lists five *pelisses*. Fashion plates in *Le Journal des dames et des modes* from 1807 to 1814 show how quickly the Empress Joséphine's sartorial flair passed into *la mode*, and how it was in vogue throughout the First Empire.[34]

Jean-Baptiste Isabey, The Empress Joséphine, *ivory miniature (Reproduced by permission of the Trustees of the Wallace Collection, London)*

The Empress always had a liking for headwear and she devised many inventive ways to wear the long, gossamer veils, made of lace, muslin or silk net, that are so often seen in *troubadour* paintings, such as *Le Départ du chevalier (The Departure of the Knight)*, a watercolour painted by her daughter, Hortense de Beauharnais, who became a successful *troubadour* artist in her own right. In the painting by baron Antoine-Jean Gros, *The Empress Joséphine Accompanying the Emperor at the Salon of 1808*, she wears such a veil flowing down her back, setting off her dark red velvet *pelisse* with its slashed and puffed sleeves and its trimming of ermine. This rich fur had been worn by royalty and the aristocracy since the Middle Ages, and is also seen, for example, on the *surcôte* worn by Valentine de Milan in Fleury François Richard's painting of her. It also featured on the Empress's coronation costume, and on the many garments in the fashion plates of *Le Journal des dames et des modes*. Isabey painted delightful portrait miniatures of the Empress in which the veils are draped around her face. In one particular example in the Wallace Collection, London, the Empress's veil covers her head, falling to one side and echoing but not intruding on her scalloped collar framed with gold chains – themselves one of the Empress's favourite revivals of Renaissance jewellery – without disturbing the arrangement of the curls in her hair, which are ornamented with flowers (shown above right). In the inventory of her possessions, 26 veils in different materials and laces are listed in her collection. Again, the *Mercure de France* commented on the veils made so fashionable by the

Empress, the favourite materials, and the manner of wearing them.[35] In Ingres's portrait of Madame Rivière, shown at the *salon* of 1806, she wears a translucent veil of white silk net that swirls around her hair, which is styled in a manner very similar to the Empress's. The Romantic feeling of the portrait is heightened by the way Madame Rivière wears the veil with a cashmere shawl. French Romantic artists and writers had a fascination for the exoticism of the East, from the paintings of seraglios by Delacroix to the *odalisques* of Ingres, and from the writings of the vicomte de Chateaubriand to those of Victor Hugo and Théophile Gautier, who all explored oriental themes. This enchantment would find itself translated into French fashion. Arriving in the wake of Napoleon's Egyptian campaign in 1798, the cashmere shawl was the indispensable accessory throughout the first half of the 19th century and up to about 1870, even as French copies were made. In his portrait of Madame Rivière, and again in his portrait of Madame de Senonnes (shown on page 67), Ingres captures all the Romantic traits of the cashmere shawl, its sensuous texture, its luxurious curves and its circuitous lines.

Winning the *Prix de Rome* at the École des Beaux-Arts in 1801, a dearth of state funds delayed Ingres's departure for Italy. He had a studio and lived in the couvent des Capucines, a convent secularized during the French Revolution and given over to artists, whose numbers included Pierre Révoil and Fleury François Richard. Ingres's sensibilities and technique alike were revealed in his mastery of the porcelain-like portrait with opulent costume, wielded to create a painting of rich, deep characterization, and his early fame presaged a long succession of portraits over six decades that gave a window on the cutting edge of fashion.

In studying the objects in the Musée des Monuments Français, Lenoir pointed out that the costume was what most interested the artists studying there.[36] He encouraged them to do their own collecting and preserving of medieval and Renaissance works. Fleury François Richard possessed specimens of dress from both the Middle Ages and the Renaissance, while Delécluze referred to Pierre Révoil as a 'peintre, antiquaire'. Révoil himself wrote of his 'joli cabinet des gothicités' and amassed a cornucopia of medieval and Renaissance objects that included furniture, tapestries, paintings, manuscripts, armour and jewellery, which provided him with 'un repertoire des costumes' ('a repertoire of costumes'). His collection of some 839 articles was sold in 1828 to the Musée du Louvre and formed the foundation for the museum's Département des Objets d'Art.[37]

From her collection of devotional jewellery, it is evident that Empress Joséphine was very aware of the religious side of *troubadour* painting and of the religious spirit of her time. Napoléon's policy of reconciliation with the Catholic Church culminated in the Concordat in 1802, making Catholicism again the official religion in France, and in the same year Chateaubriand wrote *Le Génie du Christianisme*, evoking a nostalgia for Catholicism and the beauties of Roman Catholic ritual. Lenoir's Musée des Monuments français 'fostered historical and Catholic yearnings' and 'its relics helped inspire the self-styled "aristocrats" among Jacques-Louis David's pupils'.[38]

Above: Engraved fashion plate from Le Journal des dames et des modes, *1813, Plate 1292 (Bibliothèque Doucet, Paris)*

Left: Engraved fashion plate from Le Journal des dames et des modes, *1811, Plate 1113 (Bibliothèque Doucet, Paris)*

Troubadour paintings, by reflecting on the tender passion inspired by courtly *romance* and on the virtues of a chivalrous code of conduct, had a religious quality about them, foreshadowing the new religious art that was soon to develop. In Louis Ducis's painting, *Le Tasse lisant à la princesse Eléonore*, the Princess wears on the bodice of her dress a ruby pendant in the shape of a cross attached to her pearls, a fashion of the Renaissance. The wearing of reliquary crosses (crosses containing a compartment for relics) was also popular during the Renaissance, for fabulous jewels were displayed not only as a symbol of wealth and status but also as a protective power. In the inventory of the Empress's collection at Malmaison, three crosses are listed: one made of rubies, one of opals and another of various precious jewels. Jewelled crosses inspired by the *troubadour* painters and the Empress Joséphine endured throughout the First Empire. *Le Journal des dames et des modes* noted their popularity among the *élégantes*.[39] Madame de Senonnes, perhaps the most iconic *élégante* of the First Empire, in her portrait painted by Ingres, wears a magnificent cross (shown right). Indeed, this portrait is a supreme example of art and fashion in *le style troubadour*. A student of David, Ingres was widely championed as a bastion of Neo-classicism, a counterpart to Delacroix and the Romantics. However, before his departure for the Villa Medici in Rome in October 1806, his studies at the Louvre, where Napoléon had assembled masterworks of the Italian Renaissance, offered alternatives to Davidian classicism. With his assiduous research there and his years in Rome, where he immersed himself in studies of the Renaissance painters, Raphael above all (he devised some 14 possible subjects for paintings based on the life of Raphael), together with his family background (his grandfather having been a master tailor and his wife a *modiste*), Ingres was well suited to render Romantic fashions conceived in the spirit of historicism, especially those imbued with Renaissance styles. Madame de Senonnes's red velvet dress, imitating the split and slashed sleeves of the Renaissance by the application of white satin puffs to the surface of the sleeves, her hair, styled *à la Madonna*, and her jewellery, which so beautifully complements the dress, all show his admiration for Raphael. The catalogue of the exhibition, *Portraits by Ingres: Images of an Epoch*, held at the National Gallery, London, the Metropolitan Museum, New York and the National Gallery of Art, Washington, during 1999–2000, pointed out:

> 'Her luxurious gown, high-waisted and full at the back, was made from a generous length of red velvet, whose slashed-sleeves and pocket-slit, revealing silver-satin, appear to be a tribute to Raphael's *La Fornarina* ... No less than Ingres's homage to Raphael, Madame de Senonnes's costume demonstrates a revival of interest in the Renaissance. Her hairstyle 'à la Madonna' is pulled into a chignon with a jewelled comb, which is matched by her earrings. Madame de Senonnes is all baubles, bangles and beads, wearing a rich array of rings and chains with pendants and a cross, bejewelled with diamonds, rubies, peridots and aquamarines.'

Jean-Auguste-Dominique Ingres, Madame de Senonnes *(1814), oil on canvas (Giraudon/ www.bridgeman.co.uk). French Romantic artists had a fascination for the East. Its translation into French fashion can be seen in the popularity of the cashmere shawl (brought back from Egypt by Napoleon), shown here to the side of Madame de Senonnes.*

The same style of dress is worn by the niece of Cardinal Bernardo Dovizi il Bibbiena in another of Ingres's paintings venerating Raphael, *The Betrothal of Raphael and the Niece of Cardinal Bibbiena* (shown overleaf), which is frequently cited as one of the painter's major contributions to le style *troubadour.*

Baudelaire detected in Ingres's work 'an ideal that is a provocative adulterous liaison between the calm solidity of Raphael and the affectations of the fashion plate'.[40] Ingres's device of a mirror, often used in nineteenth-century fashion plates (although, as the *Ingres* exhibition catalogue points out, it derives from Boucher's

Jean-Auguste-Dominique Ingres, The Betrothal of Raphael and the Niece of Cardinal Bibbiena *(1813), oil on paper mounted on canvas (The Walters Art Museum, Baltimore). Baudelaire on Ingres's work: 'An adulterous liaison between the solidity of Raphael and the affectations of the fashion plate.'*

portrait of Madame de Pompadour in the Alte Pinakothek, Munich), not only serves to convey the meticulously painted detail of costume, but also brings 'an air of mystery' to the portrait, a salient *troubadour* quality. It is significant for art and fashion that James Tissot copied Ingres's portrait of Madame de Senonnes, and in the catalogue entry of the sale of Tissot's copy at Christie's, London (10 June 2003), the seminal influence of Ingres's painting on Tissot as a future *peintre de mode* is noted.

A great achievement of Lenoir was to awaken in artists the need to compile their own costume books, he himself having set the tone with his vast five-volume publication, *Musée des Monuments français*.[41] He also continually referred *troubadour* artists studying in the museum to one crucial work, Dom Bernard de Montfaucon's *Les Monumens de la Monarchie françoise* (5 vols, 1729–33), which was an indispensable source for Richard, Révoil and Ingres, among others. Assisted by La Curne de Sainte-Palaye and by artists such as Antoine Benoist, Montfaucon's *magnum opus* described and illustrated the visual remains of the monarchy from the Middle Ages. It is one of the classic works on the history of French dress, and essential to the development of *le style troubadour*.

One of the first artists who studied in Lenoir's museum to compile a costume book was Nicolas-Xavier Willemin, who exhibited at the *salons* from 1800 to 1824. The culmination of his research was entitled *Monumens français pour inédits pour servir l'histoire des arts, des costumes civiles et militaires* (1806–25), devoted to the dress of medieval and Renaissance France. Willemin included a large number of plates of the statues of *chevaliers* in Lenoir's museum, his attention invariably riveted by some detail. One of the most interesting was his engraving of 'Ceintures des XIVe. et XVe. Siècles', for it shows the interaction of art and fashion. The Empress Joséphine liked wearing the cashmere shawl tied tightly around her waist and flung over her left shoulder in the manner of a *chevalier's* military belt, exemplified in baron Gros's portrait of her painted in 1809. Resting her hand on a fine leather-bound book, which seems to comprise those illuminated manuscripts that she and the *troubadour* painters admired so much, her personal preference for fashion in *le style troubadour* is clearly demonstrated in the way she wears her shawl and gauze veil edged with gold and gold-tasselled cords, offsetting the two gowns she wears of cashmere and of muslin or silk gauze, one over the other.

Another celebrated costume book, *Recueil des costumes français ... depuis Clovis jusqu'à Napoléon Ier* was the joint production of the *troubadour* artists Firmin-Hippolyte Beaunier and Louis-François Rathier; their two-volume work was published in 1810. Dedicated to the Empress Joséphine, this was in effect an acknowledgement of her great contribution to Lenoir's museum, her remarkable patronage of the *troubadour* artists, and her exquisite blending of the dress and accessories found in their paintings and costume books with fashion. She played a significant part in the triumph of the Romantic movement in painting and fashion. The great scholar of the Napoleonic period, Frédéric Masson, proclaimed the Empress as 'one of the mothers of Romanticism'.[42]

Le style troubadour had been immensely popular and successful under the First Empire. Under the Restoration of the Bourbon monarchy, following the abdication of Napoléon in 1814, it continued to flourish, the Bourbons being intent on stressing their Royal and Catholic origins. Just as Denon during the First Empire had collected works for the French public collections, the comte de Forbin, the new director of museums under the Bourbon Restoration, continued the policy of buying or commissioning. The venue for *troubadour* paintings was the Louvre, where the Musée Charles X was founded in 1826 and inaugurated in 1827. The comte de Forbin also undertook a major commission for the Galerie de Diane in the château de Fontainebleau for a set of 24 paintings on the theme of France from its origins under Clovis to King Henri IV, laying emphasis on the latter as the founder of the Bourbon dynasty. These were painted during the years 1817–18.

The number of paintings on French national-history themes increased at a staggering rate, continuing France's obsession with its medieval and Renaissance past. Much of the subject matter was repetitive, and it is the paintings and literature of this period, from the Restoration in 1814 to the July Monarchy, that attracted such devastating comment from Romantic writers and critics such as the Goncourt brothers and Théophile Gautier. The Goncourts described the art of the *troubadour* painters as 'emasculated', 'childlike' and 'troubadouresque', with a 'mawkish and insipid sentimentality'. Gautier, in his *Histoire de l'art dramatique depuis vingt-cinq ans* (6 vols, 1858), and in his *Histoire du romantisme*, which was published posthumously in 1874, looked back on the period from about 1824 to 1840 and disparagingly called certain literary and theatrical characters, as well as drawings and watercolours, 'troubadour'.[43]

Paintings on subjects relating to King Henri IV, not surprisingly, were numerous, with their particular relevance and appeal for the restored dynasty. They received tremendous critical approbation at the *salon* of 1817, the first one to take place after the Restoration under King Louis XVIII.

In 1817 François Gérard triumphed with his *Entry of Henri IV into Paris*, a royal commission celebrating the origins of the ruling dynasty and the recent return of Louis XVIII ... Révoil's celebrated, and much imitated, *Henri IV Playing with his Children* (1817), appeared in the same exhibition, together with a dozen other illustrations from this monarch's life.'[44]

Another devotee of King Henri IV, and indeed, one of the staunchest painters in *le style troubadour,* was Ingres. His originality as a *troubadour* painter was manifested early on, at the *salon* of 1806, where the critics dubbed his *Napoléon on the Imperial Throne*, his self-portrait, his portrait of Madame Rivière and two other portraits of the Rivière family, as 'Gothic'.[45] Ingres was an avid reader of history and a scrupulous documentarian who made copious *cahiers* or notebooks in which he included 15 themes on King Henri IV alone for consideration as paintings. On his return to Paris in 1824, he breathed new life into *troubadour* painting, as the catalogue of the exhibition, *Constable to Delacroix* pointed out: 'Conscious of the burgeoning popularity of *troubadour* painting following the Restoration, he exhibited a series of easel pictures in the genre, of which *Henri IV and the Spanish Ambassador* enjoyed international recognition and several imitators.'[46] The full title of the painting, in fact, is *Henri IV jouant avec ses enfants, au moment où l'ambassade d'Espagne est admis en sa présence* ('Henri IV playing with his children at the moment when the Spanish ambassador is admitted to his presence'), and it is one of Ingres's finest paintings in *le style troubadour*. The exquisite domestic interior and the subject matter, imbued with the charm and humour of the King playing with his son as the Ambassador of

Spain visits, inspired sympathetic feelings for the newly restored monarchy, while the scrupulously accurate costume, the porcelain-like finish in the manner of the 'little Dutch masters' of the 17th century, and the small cabinet size reflected the taste for miniaturist precision and splendour of collectors during the Restoration period.

Both art historians and costume historians have examined the subject of cultural exchanges between Britain and France in the aftermath of the Battle of Waterloo in 1815 and Napoléon's final exile. 'Hardly had Allied troops dispersed from Paris after their victory in 1815, than new invasions took place.' During the period of High Romanticism in France (1820–40), the country was swept by an enthusiasm for British literature, from Shakespeare to Byron, and especially for Sir Walter Scott. 'Between 1822 and 1837 nearly 230 paintings illustrating passages from Scott adorned the major exhibition halls in France.'[47] At the forefront of British authors, 'the popularity of Sir Walter Scott is not only to be measured by the number of translations of his works, but also by the amount of tartan worn'.[48] Yet the Scottish influence in the realm of literature, art and fashion can be dated long before its supposed inception following the occupation of Paris by the British army. Napoléon's devotion to Ossian dated back to his years as First Consul. One of his favourite books in his library at the château de Malmaison was an edition of the supposed poems of Ossian that had been published by James Macpherson between 1760 and 1763 and then quickly translated on the Continent (they are now believed to have been original compositions by Macpherson). He commissioned paintings on the theme of Ossian from Anne-Louis Girodet de Roussy-Trioson and François Gérard in 1800 for the *Salon Doré* at Malmaison. Less well known is the Empress Joséphine's passion for things Scottish during the First Empire.[49] Her collection of paintings included one by the comte de Forbin entitled *Ossian chantant ses poésies et s'accompagnant sur une harpe* ('Ossian singing his poems, accompanying himself on a harp'). The most sought-after painting at the salon of 1808 was Jean-Baptiste Vermay's *Marie Stuart, Reine d'Ecosse, recevant la sentence de mort que vient de ratifier le parlement* ('Mary Stuart, Queen of Scots, receiving the death sentence ratified by parliament'). It was sold at the beginning of the exhibition, and the Empress, who admired the painting so much 'that she would have liked a second version', was obliged to order a copy. She linked her love of Scottish themes in paintings to fashion and it was her interest that contributed to the early influence of Scottish fashion motifs in *le style troubadour*. Her inventory includes costumes with Scottish trimmings and ornamentation and the fashion plates and commentaries in *Le Journal des dames et des modes* demonstrate how quickly her taste was embraced by the fashion industry. As early as the summer of 1806, *Le Journal des dames et des modes* carried two fashion plates showing *élégantes* wearing Scottish scarves. In the Spring of 1807, the *Journal* reported that Scottish ribbons were much in use on hats. And exactly a year later, the fashion editor of the *Journal* wrote that the use of Scottish ribbons was more in vogue than ever.[50] Some of the most charming evocations of the Scottish theme in fashion can be enjoyed in Horace Vernet's series, *Incroyables et Merveilleuses*, commissioned between 1810 and 1818 by Pierre de La Mésangère, the editor of *Le Journal des dames et des modes*, in which the *merveilleuses* wear scarves and *brodequins écossais*. Vernet was the grandson of Jean-Michel Moreau (Moreau le Jeune), one of the great visual chroniclers of the fashions of late-18th-century France, and the son of Carle Vernet, the source of the original *Incroyables et Merveilleuses* from the Directory period, discussed in Chapter 1. Horace Vernet's set of thirty-four plates shows the continued close connection between the Parisian art world and fashion illustration.

When Emperor Napoléon divorced the Empress Joséphine and married Princess Marie-Louise of Austria in 1810, the new Empress made no difference to dress in *le style troubadour*, and so the graceful and delightful fashions of Joséphine were preserved. According to the duchesse d'Abrantès, another indefatigable chronicler of *la mode*, Marie-Louise, even though she had the same financial resources, lacked the elegance and flair of her predecessor. The Empress Joséphine's successor as arbiter of taste in art and fashion at court during the Restoration was Marie-Caroline, the duchesse de Berry. She too wholeheartedly embraced *le style troubadour*. *Troubadour* themes, as we have seen, had begun to affect the decorative arts during the First Empire, and the Empress employed *troubadour* artists, most notably Auguste Garneray, to undertake commissions in the *style à la cathédrale* at the château de Malmaison where she had a Gothic gallery built in 1805. During the Restoration period the *style à la cathédrale* flourished with a passion due largely to the patronage of the duchesse. She also supported the revival of such historic ceremonies as the *prix de Jeux Floraux*, a poetry prize first established in 1324. The daughter of King Francis I of the Two Sicilies, she married in 1816, at the age of 18, the duc de Berry, the younger son of the future King Charles X. The unfortunate duc was assassinated at the Paris Opéra in 1820. The duchesse moved into the Pavillon de Massan in the Palais des Tuileries in Paris, which became the centre of court life under King Louis XVIII and then under King Charles X from 1824 to 1830. Such an exalted setting was the perfect venue for her to become the leader of art and fashion in *le style troubadour*. She was an avid collector of *troubadour* paintings, especially of artists who had been favoured by the Empress Joséphine, and like her, made them accessible to art *aficionados*, thus fostering and influencing contemporary taste in art and fashion. Among her favourite paintings were two by Révoil, *Henri IV jouant avec ses enfants* (the subject also treated by Ingres) and *Marie Stuart séparé des ses fidèles serviteurs (Mary Stuart separated from her faithful servants)*. She was painted by all the leading portraitists. Sir Thomas Lawrence painted her in 1824, producing a portrait that shows her adherence to the style of dress of the Empress Joséphine, with her Renaissance-style square-cut *décolletage* adorned with a centrally placed Renaissance-style jewel and pearl pendant, and the small raised lace trimmings framing her short, puffy sleeves, while her *toque* made of tartan recalls the

Empress's fondness for Scottish things. In her portrait by Robert Lefèvre, painted about 1825 (shown above), she emulates Joséphine in her long veil, the perfect accessory to frame her display of Renaissance-style jewels, the centrally placed pendant on the bodice of her Renaissance-style dress and the jewelled *ferronnière* worn low on her brow. Achille Devéria's portrait of Madame Victor Hugo wearing a Renaissance-style dress, cross and *ferronnière* shows how fashionable women of the Restoration period followed the duchesse de Berry in reflecting this brilliant period of *le style troubadour*.

The duchesse also continued the tradition of court balls in historic dress. Although more associated with Queen Marie-Antoinette, the duchesse d'Abrantès also gives vivid accounts in her memoirs of the Empress Joséphine's court balls. The duchesse de Berry's most celebrated ball in a similar vein took place at the Palais des Tuileries in 1829. All the guests wore dress based on the court of King François II. She came dressed as his wife, Queen Mary Stuart. Her choice of artists to design the costumes showed her to be in the artistic milieu of *le style troubadour:* Jean-Baptiste Isabey, Auguste Garnerary and Alexandre-Evariste Fragonard. Fragonard was the son and pupil of the 18th-century artist, Jean-Honoré Fragonard, whose paintings of gallant subjects are amongst the most complete expression of the Rococo, and whose *portraits de fantasie* are another facet of *le style troubadour*. Alexandre-Evariste was a *troubadour* artist with a prodigious talent across a range of design, from decorative objects in the *style à la cathédrale* to fancy dress and theatrical costumes noted for their historical verisimilitude. Eugène Lami, an astute chronicler of elegant society, compiled a series of hand-coloured lithographs entitled *La Quadrille de Marie Stuart*, to document the occasion. Accounts were given in the leading fashion journals and in the duchesse's biography written by the vicomte de Reiset.[51]

While the Empress Joséphine and the duchesse de Berry transformed the costumes in *troubadour* paintings, where women figure so prominently, into fashionable dress, intimations of the *style troubadour* were already evident in men's fashionable dress during the First Empire. Perhaps this was a reflection of the definition of Romanticism given by the French writer Stendhal: an art form that takes for its subjects the men and mores of the times. Horace Vernet's series of *Incroyables et Merveilleuses* were like those that his father Carle Vernet had produced during the *Directoire* period in that they were not so much caricatures as fashion plates, exact in the details of costume. Horace Vernet's *incroyable* of 1810 shows his devotion to the fashions of *le style troubadour*. With his refined gestures and impeccable deportment, so essential to a stylish appearance, his hair is carefully cut *à la François Ier* and he wears a beautifully tailored coat that has full set-in sleeves, imitating the shape of 16th-century doublets seen in *troubadour* paintings. Horace Vernet was an exceptional designer of fashion plates and contributed to *Le Journal des dames et des modes*. During the 1820s the *Journal* featured fashion plates in which men are attired in dress that echoes the tailoring of 16th-century costume and that are

Capote de Perkale écrue. Fichu et Brodequins écossais. Ombrette de Perkale.

Engraving from Vernet's series, Incroyables et Merveilleuses, *published by Pierre de la Mésangère, Paris, 1810–1818 (Chrysalis Image Library).* Incroyables *and* Merveilleuses *were words coined during the Directoire period to express the public's sheer astonishment at the new fashion, rather than precise sartorial labels.*

accompanied by captions that use precise vocabulary. For example, one *costume parisien* in 1823 featured a very fashionable *gilet-cuirasse*, a waistcoat-breastplate, which reflected the close parallels in design between the doublet and armour in the 16th century.

The floundering Bourbons were unable to sustain their rule in the face of a rapidly expanding economy and a rising bourgeois society, ranging from a wealthy upper-middle class to a petty bourgeoisie of small shopkeepers and traders. The social tensions of this situation led to the July Revolution in 1830, the abdication of King Charles X, and the accession of Louis-Philippe, duc d'Orléans, scion of a junior line of the Bourbons descended from the brother of King Louis XIV. His 18-year reign, known as the July Monarchy, strengthened the power of the bourgeoisie politically and socially, and was marked by conspicuous consumption and a complacent society with strict, codified manners that would have repercussions for the artistic community. Given the soubriquet 'Citizen King', Louis-Philippe walked the streets of Paris carrying an umbrella rather than a sword, which had monarchical and aristocratic associations.

King Louis-Philippe followed his predecessors in stressing his association with the past glories of France. With the comte de Forbin continuing as director of museums, the major location for *troubadour* paintings continued to be the Musée Charles X in the Louvre where the pictures were meant to be complementary to the objects in the museum. Several collections of medieval and Renaissance art and artefacts were formed, and became accessible to a new generation of artists, including Alexandre-Marie Colin, Henri-Pierre Blanchard and Antoinette Haudebourt-Lescot. No collection was more extensive or atmospheric a place for Romantics than that of Alexandre Du Sommerand, located from 1832 in the Hôtel des Abbés de Cluny in Paris. Du Sommerand arranged his collection, in the tradition of Lenoir's Musée des Monuments français, with great sensitivity to the setting, which lent itself to an intense sense of the dramatic. After his death in 1842 the Hôtel and its contents were acquired by the French government and opened as a national museum, the Musée de Cluny in 1844. King Louis-Philippe also commissioned over the period 1833–37 a grand decorative scheme of large-scale paintings for the Musée Historique at Versailles, consisting of the Galerie des Batailles and the Salle des Croisades. He too was keen to be identified with his ancestor King Henri IV, and in order to reflect and legitimize his monarchy, baron François Gérard's *Entry of Henri IV into Paris*, 22 March, 1594 – an event seen as a national symbol of reconciliation following the 16th century's wars of religion – was hung in the Galerie des Batailles. Conceived as a national 'lieu de mémoire' ('place of memory'), the Musée Historique promoted 'toutes les gloires de la France'. It was during the July Monarchy that 'national history was redefined as the combined experience of the nation's people at large'. All classes of society were united to a collective history through the arts. 'Historic images, ranging from large-scale paintings to book illustrations, became an important part of the visual culture of the July Monarchy, and had a broad appeal ranging from the king to the man in the street, who found in history relevance, even justification, for their own existence.'[52]

Notwithstanding some brilliant *soirées*, the court of King Louis-Philippe and Queen Marie-Amélie was lacklustre, with the Queen 'not made to lead fashion'.[53] In her essay, 'Pop Culture in the Making: The Romantic Craze for History', in *The Popularization of Images: Visual Culture under the July Monarchy,* Petra Chu demonstrates how a preoccupation with history touched all cultural forms with a visual component in France at that time, especially art and fashion, reaching an exceptionally large part of the population, not just those close to court.[54] It was thus symptomatic of the emergence of a popular culture in France. Art and fashion were inextricably linked as cultures of consumption during the July Monarchy.

'History was everywhere in July Monarchy France: in Louis-Philippe's Musée Historique, in the Salon, the theatre, the opera, the library, the *cabinet de lecture,* the home. People's daily surroundings and the very clothes they wore were marked by the powerful historic consciousness of the time. Fashion prints of the mid-thirties show women dressed in Rococo-inspired fashions, seated on Renaissance chairs in interiors filled with Gothic bookcases. Typical of the July Monarchy, this historical eclecticism may perhaps be related to the contemporary stage, where props and costumes were 'recycled' from one historic play to another, without too much concern for historical accuracy. In a brief exposé on clothing during the July Monarchy, Henri Bouchot emphasizes the influence on women's fashions of the Romantic drama (to which we might add other histrionic events such as operas, masked balls, carnivals, etc.), which in turn were freely inspired by Renaissance and Baroque paintings. In the course of the 1830s those fashions moved from a Renaissance medley that combined leg-of-mutton sleeves (*manches à gigot*) à Francois I with ruffled millstone collars, to a clothing derived from the late seventeenth and eighteenth-century models, with toilettes à la Pompadour, à la Montespan or à la Lavallière.'[54]

A contemporary chronicler of the July Monarchy, Madame de Girardin, noted the continued popularity of *le style troubadour* in *Les Lettres parisiennes, années 1836–1840.* Indeed, leading French authorities on *le style troubadour,* such as François Pupil, believe that historians of today still underestimate the extraordinary influence of *troubadour* iconography on 19th-century historicist eclecticism in France, while Marie-Claude Chaudonneret cites the Restoration period, when a fascination for *le style troubadour* reached its zenith, as a time when there was a turning 'towards the past in order to understand the present'.[55] For fashion, the parallel of past with present was noted in periodicals, for example, *L'Illustration* in 1845 observed how 'women looked at the costumes of the past for ideas that could be adapted for modern attire'. This ubiquitous historical consciousness was aided by many factors, such as the mechanization of spinning and weaving, enabling large-scale production of garments sold at lower prices than the earlier hand-made clothing. New techniques could be admired by the public at the *Expositions des produits de l'industrie française* (Exhibitions of the products of French industry) held in Paris. With the organization of groups of shops into larger entities, such as the Galeries du la Commerce et de l'Industrie in 1838, followed by the Palais Bonne-Nouvelle in 1841, these precursors of department stores offered a range of articles that were within the reach of wider social groups than before. Improvements in transport in the 1830s facilitated both the movement of goods and the travel of customers. Vastly improved picture-printing techniques, such as lithography, enabled the cheap production of images, quickly finding their way into the expanding publishing industry. With the rapid growth of the women's press, a large group of fashion magazines sprang up, among the most notable being *Le Petit courrier des dames, Le Bon ton, Le Journal des demoiselles* and *La Mode,* which employed some of the best artists of the time to design the fashion plates. Improved literacy also had an impact on the increasing number of popular periodicals with some, like *Le Voleur,* being widely read for their fashion coverage. Catering for an unprecedented range of social strata, all these journals carried fashion plates, often done by, or after the works of well-known artists who exhibited at the *salons* or who had their paintings in museums such as the Musée Historique, thereby turning these venues from 'meeting grounds of the cultivated élite into places of popular entertainment'.[56] This growth of the art market saw the social and professional role of the artist enhanced, while the dramatic increase in the number of art exhibitions, especially those that included portraits of women adorned in their fashions, made going to see these works on display a popular pastime.

The close connection between popular visual culture and Romanticism's powerful sense of history under the July Monarchy was echoed in jewellery. To complement the dress, there was a corresponding historical revival in jewellery. With the unparalleled industrial expansion, vast quantities of jewellery were produced that were potent symbols of power and wealth not only for the traditional clientele of Parisian jewellers — royalty and nobility — but also for the burgeoning bourgeoisie — so much so that Madame de Girardin observed in *Les Lettres parisiennes* that 'the passion for ornament has been carried to the point of madness' and 'the style of the *troubadour*' was 'quite simply the love, the perfect love of the past'. 'Jewels and accessories were ornamented with Gothic fleurons, trefoils, ogival arches, lozenges, lopped tree trunks and romantic figures of knights in armour, pages and *châtelaines,* culled from this new golden age.'[57]

The *ferronnière* (the jewelled band encircling the brow) and gold chains draped across the bodice like those seen in Renaissance portraits, which had been so popular during the First Empire, also enjoyed a new vogue during the July Monarchy. Nostalgia for the past saw a fashion for the *bandeau berthe,* a chased (engraved) gold and coloured gem that was inspired by the headdress worn by medieval *châtelaines.* The leading Parisian jeweller of the period was François-Désiré Froment-Meurice, nicknamed by Victor Hugo the 'Cellini of Romanticism' because, like Benvenuto Cellini, he created sculptural jewels. To Théophile Gautier, Froment-Meurice imparted through his jewellery the eclectic nature of Romanticism as vividly as Delacroix did in his painting. Drawing on the literary source of the *romance,* he created scenes of courtly love featuring figures of knights and ladies cast in the round against a background of Gothic architectural ornament. 'The medieval style became so fashionable that a man about town complained that he could not escape kissing a lady's hand without having to embrace a knight in armour, a page or hound, nor could he raise his head without being greeted by the sardonic gaze of a hideous gargoyle.'[58]

The July Monarchy was the finest hour for *troubadour* developments in men's fashions, led by a group called *les Jeunes-France,* a term coined about 1831 for a coterie of young Romantic artists and writers that included Achille and Eugène Devéria, Victor Hugo and Théophile Gautier. In the ideological maelstrom that followed the July Revolution, this generation of younger Romantics adhered to the principle of freedom in the arts, and discussions in their circle included the deep affinities among all the arts. The visual arts played a central role in the writings of Gautier, who wrote a book on *les Jeunes-France* in 1833. The relationship of this group with dress was referred to by Delécluze in an essay of 1832, included as an appendix in his biography of David. Wanting to distinguish themselves from the bourgeoisie in their drab frock coats (caricatured so astutely by Honoré Daumier) and calling for costume reform, the counter-culture spirit of *les Jeunes-France* expressed itself in the colours and patterns of medieval and Renaissance-revival styles that included doublets with fur or gold trimmings. These were modelled on those found in *troubadour* paintings, such as those depicting Kings François I and Henri IV, or the hats seen in the paintings of Rubens, and gold-brocaded gowns featured by Titian. *Les Jeunes-France* also staged fancy-dress balls in Renaissance-style costumes, and their romance with historic costumes was felt especially in the theatre. At the première of Victor Hugo's *Hernani*, Gautier appeared in a pink waistcoat that the Goncourt brothers in their *Journal* said he insisted on calling a *pourpoint*, the 14th-century term for a doublet. Romantic elegance extended to their long, flowing hairstyles and beards, a reflection of many *troubadour* paintings, from depictions of Kings François I and Henri IV to the themes of Raphael. It was through their hairstyles that they made plain not only their allegiance to Romanticism in literature, painting and fashion, but also their criticism of the government and their belief in liberal politics.

The graphic arts in particular blossomed during the July Monarchy, and artists' series of fashion plates noted for their painstaking attention to the details of costume, such as those of Achille Devéria, were disseminated in large numbers, fuelling the dreams of a generation of Romantics. Devéria chronicled dress and taste in a series of 18 coloured lithographs called *Les Heures du jour* – which to Baudelaire epitomized 'the morals and aesthetics of the age' – and also compiled a vast series of 125 coloured lithographs (1831–39) entitled *Les Costumes Historiques*, and portrait lithographs that embraced the panache of *les Jeunes-France*. By the end of the July Monarchy beards and moustaches were common and the sartorial originality of *les Jeunes-France* was absorbed into the details of mainstream fashionable dress. The frock coat of the *flâneur* had a high, rounded roll-collar and a slim, curved waist, while the waistcoat, an item of singular importance in the wardrobe of *les Jeunes-France* as a canvas for bright hues and ornamentation, was the one garment to which the fashionable male could give free rein to his imagination and express his individuality of colour and design. Jewellery was an indispensable complement, especially to waistcoats. Precious stones mounted as buttons on waistcoats, and gold chains looped over waistcoats, were favourite types of jewels. One French wit wrote in 1836 that Romanticism consisted in not shaving and in wearing a waistcoat!

Modes de Paris, *engraved fashion plate (from* Petit Courrier des dames, 31 December 1836, Plate 1315). *The fashionable French male of the period used his waistcoat as the one garment to express his individuality of colour and design.*

Romanticism ☐

In 1848 the Second Republic was proclaimed in France, with Louis-Napoléon Bonaparte, the first Emperor's nephew, elected as President. By 1852 he was granted dictatorial powers under a new constitution and became Emperor Napoléon III (Napoléon II, the first Emperor's son, had never reigned and had died of tuberculosis in exile in 1832). During the Second Empire (1852–70) the dominant stylistic current continued to be a fascination with the past. The costume historian François Boucher has referred to a 'Second Empire Romanticism'. This manifested itself in a renewed interest amongst artists, writers and collectors of the Rococo, which had a direct influence on fashion. The Rococo Revival underpinned the social needs of the Second Empire.

> 'As capitalism and middle-class democracy triumphed decisively in politics and the economy, the affluent and well-born put increasing value on the aristocratic culture of the previous century: its arts, manners and costumes. Championing the Rococo was a way of contesting what was seen as an oppressive and stern bourgeois morality. To praise Antoine Watteau was to proclaim oneself for pleasure and the freedom of the imagination.'[59]

There was a renewed admiration for Watteau's art and, as part of this popularity, a vogue for Watteau-style dresses began to feature in the fashion plates of French fashion magazines of the later 1860s. Susan Grace Galassi, co-organizer of the exhibition *Whistler, Women and Fashion*, held at the Frick Collection, New York in 2003, notes that the artist who was in the vanguard of the Rococo revival of Watteau was Édouard Manet.

> 'A painting of the period which featured a young woman in a *robe d'intérieur* is *Manet's Young Lady in 1866 (Woman with a Parrot)*. It was shown privately to his friends and exhibited the following year in his solo exhibition at the Pont de L'Alma ... In *Woman with a Parrot,* the auburn-haired Victorine Meurent, accompanied by her parrot (the symbol of a confidante), wears a pink satin gown, which, in its loose shape, glossy fabric and colour evokes the style of dress seen in Watteau's paintings. Émile Zola noted that the garment 'succinctly characterises the innate stylishness of Édouard Manet.'[60]

Attention should also be drawn to the influence on Manet of Paul Gavarni (the pseudonym of Hippolyte-Guillaume-Sulpice Chevalier). One of the great graphic artists of the period, and an *artiste-flâneur* much admired by Manet, Gavarni was noted for his fashion plates, which appeared in magazines such as *La Mode, Le Journal des dames et des modes*, and *Le Petit courrier des dames*, and also for his images of *lorettes*. These were young women of easy virtue who frequented the new district in Paris around the church of Notre-Dame-de Lorette. His lithographs of these *femmes parisiennes* were widely circulated before the date of Manet's *Woman with a Parrot*, for example in Étienne de Neufville's *Physiologie de la femme* of 1842. Gavarni continued to produce lithographs of them throughout the

Paul Gavarni, Lorette in Dressing Gown with a Parrot *(c. 1865), lithograph (Chrysalis Image Library). Gavarni produced many lithographs of lorettes, who were young Parisian women of easy virtue.*

Second Empire. One entitled *Lorette in Dressing Gown with a Parrot*, dated about 1865, affords a wonderful back view of the garment worn by the *lorette* with an almost Watteauesque stance.

Among the great 19th-century collectors of French Rococo paintings were baron Dominique-Vivant Denon and Louis La Caze. They donated many paintings from their own collections to the Musée du Louvre. La Caze gave a bequest of 14 paintings by Watteau in 1869. The fashion plates of *La Gallerie des modes et costumes français,* which showed both the refined artistry of Sébastien-Jacques Le Clerc, Claude-Louis Desrais, Augustin de Saint Aubin and François-Louis Joseph Watteau, great nephew of Antoine Watteau, and the symbiotic relationship between art and fashion in late-18th-century France, were highly prized. The history of the Rococo was evoked by such writers as Théophile Gautier in his *Histoire du romantisme* and by the Goncourt brothers in their *L'Art du XVIIIe. siècle.* The two fashion leaders of the *ancien régime,* Madame de Pompadour and Queen Marie-Antoinette, enjoyed a rehabilitation. Madame de Pompadour's letters to her father and brother were published, but it was the Goncourt brothers who firmly placed her centre stage in the revival of the Rococo with their biography of her. Unable to forgive her bourgeois origins, they nevertheless accorded her a defining role as the greatest patron of the arts in the 18th century. They wrote of her advancing towards posterity, sitting on a cloud by Boucher, in the midst of a divine court of the family of Muses. This paean to Madame de Pompadour made objects associated with her sought after by 19th-century collectors, and there was a resurgence of interest in her fashions. 'In view of the intense nostalgia for Rococo luxury that characterized so many aspects of Second Empire life and style, it is also plausible to consider the late portrait of Madame Moitessier a full-scale resurrection of the style Pompadour.'[61] Ingres's portrait of *Madame Moitessier,* seated, dated 1856 (shown on page 82), is a veritable ode to the luxury and conspicuous consumption of the Second Empire. Located in the National Gallery, London, it can be compared to Drouais's portrait of Madame de Pompadour, also in the collection there, which was discussed in Chapter 1. Madame Moitessier's spectacular dress of Lyons silk, the bodice beribboned and the skirt supported by a crinoline, is akin to the Rococo pattern of Madame de Pompadour's dress in Drouais's portrait. The dazzling floral design of Madame Moitessier's dress was achieved by advances in technology in the textile industry. The invention of the Jacquard loom made possible the production of elaborate woven patterns in threads coloured by the new, bright aniline dyes. The Empress Eugénie began to wear this type of fabric in the mid-1850s at the request of her husband, who hoped to stimulate the silk-weaving industry in Lyons. With French superiority in dress and jewellery, the Emperor made his court the most brilliant in Europe, synonymous with *toutes les gloires de la France.* Madame de Moitessier shows her adherence to *le style troubadour* in her jewellery: a gold chain, a gold and enamel Renaissance-style brooch centrally placed on her bodice and gold bracelets studded with stones. As in his portrait of Madame de

Senonnes, Ingres again used the fashion-plate device of a mirror, which brings out the dense luxury of Rococo ornament in Madame Moitessier's drawing room as well as the details of her costume – for example, the exquisite lace and ribbon of her *cache-peigne* headdress – thus capturing the immediacy of fashion.

The leading patron of the Rococo Revival style and the new *doyenne* of fashion was the Empress Eugénie. Among items of furniture, she commissioned a Rococo *secrétaire* from Alphonse Giroux, while her favourite sculpture was designed by Jean-Baptiste Carpeaux, noted for his bronze monument to Watteau. Of Spanish origin, she liked to identify herself with another foreigner, Queen Marie-Antoinette. The Empress collected objects and memorabilia associated with the Queen, and housed them in the Petit Trianon, Marie-Antoinette's place of refuge at the château de Versailles. Her affinity for the Queen extended to dressing like her, and images of her in these styles were painted by Franz Xaver Winterhalter, whose smooth, shiny, glossy style was admirably suited to rendering the Empress's fashions. He, along with Achille and Eugène Devéria, Camille Roqueplan, Eugène Lami and Eugène Isabey, were the leading artists creating exquisite images of fashionable life in the Second Empire that revived the elegant world of their eighteenth-century ancestors. Winterhalter's portrait of *L'Impératrice Eugénie* (dressed as Queen Marie-Antoinette), painted in 1854 (shown left), situates the Empress, standing in profile, in a garden of lilacs, wearing a deep yellow taffeta gown trimmed with black bows and blue ribbons at the hem, ropes of pearls, fringes and tassels, with her hair powdered white and adorned with ribbons and a feather *aigrette* (a tuft of feathers worn as an ornament in the hair). Although there is no documentation, perhaps it is a direct representation of a costume worn by the Empress at one of her *bals costumés* held at the Palais des Tuileries. It is recorded that twelve years later she attended a ball wearing a gown copied from a portrait of Queen Marie-Antoinette painted by Madame Vigée Le Brun in 1787. The closest parallel to the Winterhalter portrait is *Queen Marie-Antoinette in the Park at Versailles* by Adolph-Ulrich Wertmüller, also painted in 1787. After meeting the Empress, the Goncourt brothers wrote: '...An empress of others, not the French, perhaps of some fairy place such as Baden. If you wish, Marie-Antoinette at the Mabille.'[62]

By the time of her ball in 1866, wearing the gown copied from the one worn by Queen Marie-Antoinette in the portrait by Madame Vigée Le Brun, the Empress had appointed Charles Frederick Worth (1825–95), often termed 'the father of *haute couture*', as her dressmaker. The Second Empire is often sartorially called the 'Age of Worth'. Although he did not have exclusive control over the Empress's vast wardrobe, he did have a monopoly on perhaps the most important pieces – ball gowns and state gowns. Worth survived the downfall of the Second Empire in 1870 and re-opened his *salon* in 1871, allying fashion to art until nearly the end of the century. Considering himself an artist, he adopted the bohemian style of dress worn by the artists of his generation, modelled after Rembrandt, which consisted of a velvet beret, a flowing cloak edged with fur and a scarf knotted at

Franz Xaver Winterhalter, The Empress Eugénie, (dressed as Queen Marie-Antoinette) *(1854), oil on canvas (Metropolitan Museum of Art, New York, Purchase, Mr and Mrs Claus von Bülow Gift). Empress Eugénie liked to dress like Queen Marie-Antoinette, and Winterhalter's smooth, shiny, glossy style was well suited to rendering the Empress's fashions.*

Jean-Auguste-Dominique Ingres, Madame Moitessier *(1856), oil on canvas (National Gallery, London/ www.bridgeman.co.uk). The bright floral design of Madame Moitessier's dress was achieved by advances in the textile industry.*

the neck. He considered his gowns works of art, and he plumbed artistic sources from the Renaissance to the Neo-classical and First Empire periods for his designs. Madame Carette, writing in 1889 in her book *My Mistress, the Empress Eugénie; or, Court Life at the Tuileries,* recognized his use of art in fashion, seen most clearly in his adoption of Aesthetic dress. 'We owe to the artistic taste of this great milliner, and to his intuition for aesthetic elegance, the revival of grace in dress.'[63] Aestheticism, one of the subjects covered in the next chapter, was one of the most pervasive reaffirmations of Romanticism.

3 Aestheticism, Realism and Impressionism

Aesthetics, the philosophy of the beautiful in art, derives from the Greek word *aisthesis*, meaning 'perception'. The term was first used by the German philosopher Alexander Gottlieb Baumgarten, who wrote a two-volume Latin treatise entitled *Aesthetica* (1750–58). It was taken up by the German philosopher Immanuel Kant, whose theory of Aestheticism, pioneered in his *Kritik der Urteilskraft* (1790), maintained that the philosophy of art is separate from any other form of philosophy, and that art can be judged solely by its own standards. Their pioneering views framed a keynote belief of the French Romantics – the autonomy of art and freedom of artistic expression. Théophile Gautier and Charles Baudelaire revived the concept of Aestheticism as *l'art pour l'art* – 'art for art's sake'. Originating as a literary movement, *l'art pour l'art* quickly echoed through many different artistic disciplines and forged close links with fashion in the second half of the 19th century, not only in France, but also in Britain and America. At a time of virtuoso *haute couture,* there was an awakening to the idea of dress as a means of self-expression, that it was possible to wear a style of dress unique to personality, and that one did not have to be a slave to mainstream fashion to be stylish.

In his book *Le Théorie de l'art pour l'art en France chez les derniers romantiques et les premiers réalistes,* André Cassagne focuses largely on the writings of Gautier and Baudelaire. The long preface to Gautier's supremely Romantic novel, *Mademoiselle de Maupin* (1835), maintaining the sovereignty of art and insisting on the importance of beauty, and the entire story itself, an exposition of his aesthetic attitude that expounded on his own worship of beauty, became the manifesto of the doctrine *l'art pour l'art.*

Gautier was famous for his verbal *transpositions d'art,* in which terms from one art from became metaphors for terms in another – for example, in his poetry, sonnets were called pastels, and vice versa. His best-known collection of poetry, *Émaux et camées,* published in 1852, contains many short, lyrical poems such as 'Symphonie en blanc majeur', with its images of snow, white sea foam and female swans. *Émaux et camées* also included the poem 'L'Art', an expression of his belief in art as the sole and supreme value. Gautier's ideas had an enormous impact on Charles Baudelaire, who in turn was a powerful influence on a whole generation, not only in Paris, but also in London where the young English poet Algernon Charles Swinburne was a great admirer. Baudelaire broke fresh ground with some of the most brilliantly written aesthetic treatises such as *Curiosités Esthéstiques* and *L'Art Romantique.* His principal claim to glory is his book of poems *Les Fleurs du mal,* with their evocative images and musical language, which were published first in 1857, and then again in 1861 in a new, augmented edition. From the poem 'Correspondance' came his eponymous aesthetic theme, the mixing of differing senses to fulfil artistic aims.

The writings of Gautier and Baudelaire were formative influences on the American painter James Abbott McNeill Whistler, when he arrived in Paris in 1855 to study. Gautier's *transpositions d'art* and Baudelaire's *correspondances* fascinated Whistler and would come to find parallels in the musical analogies he used to describe his paintings, suggesting that artistic quality lay in formal organization aimed at a decorative effect through a harmonious arrangement of line, colour and form where design was more important than likeness. Whistler first studied at the École Impériale et Spéciale de Dessin, where Degas was also a pupil, and then in the studio of Charles Gleyre, who stressed the primacy of personal expression. Although he had developed from the Realism of Courbet, Whistler turned away from Realism and chose the French avant-garde theory of *l'art pour l'art*. In 1859 he moved to London, but still maintained close ties with France, visiting Paris frequently. The French avant-garde artistic and literary circles in which Whistler moved can be glimpsed in Henri Fantin-Latour's painting, *Hommage à Delacroix*, dated 1864, which shows Fantin-Latour himself with Whistler, Baudelaire, Édouard Manet, Félix Bracquemond, Alphonse Legros and others, grouped around a portrait of Delacroix. Whistler has pride of place, standing prominently near the portrait wearing an impeccably tailored black frock coat and holding a bouquet of flowers.

The author and critic Émile Zola was much impressed by Manet, and wrote a piece in the paper *L'Evénement* (7 May 1866) about the *salon* of 1866, making a spirited defence of the artist, whose submissions for that year had been rejected. Zola followed this up with a longer article entitled 'Une nouvelle manière en peinture: Édouard Manet', in *Revue du XIXe. siècle* (15 January 1867). Full of gratitude, Manet painted a portrait of Zola in 1868. The portrait shows the impact on Manet of Japanese artefacts and Japanese prints, influences that were only just becoming known in Europe at that time, and which can be seen in his rejected works. Zola pointed out these features in Manet's art and argued that he was an artist who 'knows how to paint, and that is all'.[1] This defence of the representation of visual experience effectively aligned Manet and his circle to *l'art pour l'art*. Whistler became an important nexus between these artists in France and those in Britain who embraced 'art for art's sake'.

A flamboyant character, Whistler was the complete artist: not only a painter, but also a designer of interiors, picture frames and costumes, someone who assimilated the fashions of his time as an integral component of his art, such as the craze for everything Japanese that was sweeping Paris and London. With a keen sensitivity to his own appearance, already evident in Fantin-Latour's painting, he cultivated the image of a dandy as a way of attracting attention to his aesthetics, dressing-up in a tight-fitting black frock coat, dancing pumps, top hat and yellow tie, sporting a monocle and cane – as seen, for example, in Walter Greaves's painting of 1871, *James Abbott McNeill Whistler at His House in*

James Abbott McNeill Whistler, Symphony in Flesh Colour and Pink: Portrait of Mrs Frances Leyland *(1871–1874), oil on canvas (The Frick Collection, New York). A designer of costume and interiors as well as a painter, Whistler assimilated the fashions of his time as an internal component of his art. Here Mrs Leyland's dress harmonizes with her surroundings.*

Lindsey Row, Chelsea. With his impeccable dress and deportment, he appreciated beauty and style in women, and concentrated on them in his portraiture, painting images of beauty that could be appreciated on their aesthetic merit alone. On occasion, he designed dresses that his sitters wore in their portraits. His sitters represent a cross-selection of the fashionable world, including élite society women, actresses, artists, the aristocracy, members of his family and the *demi-monde,* which also help to shed light on the change in the status of women in this period and the role costume played in the presentation of the self and in laying claim to social position. As Susan Grace Galassi has noted:

> 'He had firm ideas and chose what his sitters should wear in order to reflect their character and persona ... [his] eye for fashion was so good that he could dictate what his subjects wore in order to enhance their figure, pose and costume ... Each painting was a design effect. Whistler was interested in its totality, its overall effect.'[2]

The details of costume in Whistler's portraits are subordinated to the overall arrangement of line, colour and form, as reflected in their titles, such as *Symphony in Flesh Colour and Pink: Portrait of Mrs Frances Leyland* (1871–1874). However, dress deeply absorbed and animated his work, with a strong undulation of the individual character and social milieu of his sitters. In his portrait of Mrs Leyland, the wife of the shipping magnate and art collector Frederick R Leyland, Whistler designed the costume and the interior as a *tout ensemble*. Mrs Leyland's dress harmonizes not only with her auburn hair but also with her surroundings. It consists of a soft pink chiffon gown with transparent silk sleeves, 'loosely classified as a tea gown', worn over a white underdress.[3] A panel from a mulberry-coloured collar floats down the back of her gown, terminating in a sweeping train, and dark pink ribbons decorate the gown. Mrs Leyland is standing with her back to the spectator, a device used in fashion plates, and which artists adopted, to focus attention on the elaborate style of the back of the dress and to demonstrate that the dress was designed to be as beautiful from the back as it was from the front. She is situated in Whistler's drawing room in his house in Lindsey Row, Chelsea in front of a white low-panelled dado. The pink walls and rush rug, with its abstract, basket-weave pattern (repeated on the frame) offset the naturalistic, flowering almond branches and reveal Whistler's taste for Japanese motifs. The calligraphic line of the blossoming almond branches, and the way they are asymmetrically composed and cut off at the left edge of the painting, are reminiscent of Japanese *ukiyo-e* prints. They serve to offset the exquisite floral decoration on Mrs Leyland's dress, the fabric and flowing lines of her tea gown also showing a Japanese influence. Whistler signed the portrait at the right with his emblematic butterfly, a pattern based on his initials JMW. Although never considered by Whistler to be totally finished, the portrait of Mrs Leyland, with its delicate harmony between the costume and the décor of the room, is imbued with the aesthetics of *l'art pour l'art* that he brought to the Aesthetic Movement.

The Aesthetic Movement is a 'term used to describe a movement of the 1870s and 1880s that manifested itself in the fine and decorative arts and architecture in Britain and subsequently the USA. Reacting to what was seen as evidence of philistinism in art and design, it was characterized by the cult of the beautiful and an emphasis on the sheer pleasure to be derived from it.'[4]

Algernon Charles Swinburne and Walter Pater are credited with introducing the phrase 'art for art's sake', the guiding principle of the Aesthetic Movement, in their writings in 1868, while the concepts of Aestheticism had been introduced to Britain from France around 1860 by Whistler and Swinburne. 'They became current in the tightly knit group of painters, poets and critics around Whistler and Dante Gabriel Rossetti and were controversial and avant-garde in the 1860s.'[5] Besides Swinburne, Pater, the Pre-Raphaelite artist Rossetti and Whistler, other prominent individuals associated with the movement were the actress Ellen Terry, and Oscar Wilde. During 1882–83, Wilde went on a lecture tour to the United States to 'to promote aesthetic values', and was photographed in New York wearing a jacket, decoratively frogged, with quilted silk collar and cuffs, a shirt with a turned-down collar, a large silk tie, 18th-century-style breeches and low-heeled shoes with ribbon ties. This style of dress of the male aesthetes, 'a modification of the French Romantic artist costumes described in Henry Murger's novel of 1845, *Scènes de la vie de bohème*', was satirized in the Aesthetic cartoons of George Du Maurier that appeared in *Punch* magazine from 1874 to 1882.[6] Wilde bore the brunt of most of the fun poked at male aesthetes, including being ridiculed as the central character, Bunthorne, in Gilbert and Sullivan's operetta *Patience*.

The member of the Aesthetic Movement who came closest to fulfilling its ideals was Whistler. Against the background of the sublime portrait of Mrs Frances Leyland, in which the setting and costume synthesize, his achievement of these ideals can be gauged. He led the movement in radically espousing a purely Aesthetic orientation in portraiture, creating a design rather than capturing an exact likeness. His pursuit of beauty, and understanding of its relevance to individual lives, led him to reform and simplify the decorative arts, creating an artistic environment in which the fine and decorative arts were in accord with costume. As his biographers E R and J Pennell pointed out in *The Whistler Journal,* 'every room was an arrangement and every sitter had to fit in'.[7] His views on the unity of the arts and costume stemmed from his study of the Japanese example. He was an important exponent of one of the central themes of Aestheticism, *Japonisme*, a term coined by the French critic, collector and printmaker Philippe Burty in 1872 to describe a range of European borrowings from Japanese art and the profound influence of Japanese aesthetics on Western art. It had been in fashion since the mid-1850s among a small French avant-garde artistic circle when the engraver Félix Bracquemond and the Goncourt brothers, and a little later Baudelaire, started to popularize Japanese prints.

Following the signing of the Kanagawa Treaty with the United States in 1854, Japan was opened to trade with the West. Public interest was fuelled by major

Above: Oscar Wilde, 1882. Photograph: Napoleon Sarony (National Portrait Gallery, London). The poet and writer is seen here in the style of dress of the male aesthetes, which is satirized in the Punch cartoon on the right.

Right: George du Maurier, Six-Mark Tea-pot (1880), engraved cartoon (from Punch, 30 October 1880)

exhibitions that featured the fine and decorative arts of Japan, such as the International Exhibition in London in 1862 and the Exposition Universelle in Paris in 1867 as well as by the addition of Japanese art to the collections of major institutions such as the South Kensington Museum (later the Victoria and Albert Museum) and the British Museum in London, and the Bibliothèque Nationale in Paris. The influx of Japanese prints and *objets d'art*, including porcelain, lacquerware and metalwork, as well as fabrics, fans and other accessories such as combs and parasols, was electrifying. Whistler came under the influence of Japanese prints as early as 1856. As a member of the restricted French avant-garde circle, he was shown, with Bracquemond, Katsushika Hokusai's *Hokusai manga* ('Hokusai's ten thousand sketches') by Auguste Delâtre, a printer of etchings and owner of a print shop.[8] 'By 1863, Whistler was avidly combing the junk shops of Amsterdam, Rotterdam and Paris for Oriental artifacts.'[9] Two of his early essays in *Japonisme* are *Symphony in White, No. 1: The White Girl (1862)* and *Symphony in White, No. 2: The Little White Girl* (1864). When Whistler submitted *No. 1* to the *salon* in Paris in 1863 it was rejected. Emperor Napoléon III invited avant-garde artists who had been denied official space to show their works in a *Salon des Refusés*, an exhibition that aroused enormous controversy. Whistler entered the painting in the *Salon des Refusés* where it joined Manet's *Déjeuner sur l'herbe* in a *succès de scandale*. Although Whistler's work was derided, a number of artists and critics praised it, including Paul Mantz. Writing in the *Gazette des beaux-arts*, he called it a *Symphonie en blanc* (symphony in white). In both pictures the model was Whistler's mistress, Joanna Hiffernan, painted in simple flowing white gowns without a crinoline, revealing the influence on Whistler of Pre-Raphaelite artistic dresses. The Pre-Raphaelites provided one of the first alternative vestimentary movements in 19th-century England to the fashion excesses of the Victorians. Whistler's dresses, echoing the beauty of the natural form, were similar to those worn by, for example, Elizabeth Siddal, herself a Pre-Raphaelite painter and poet, in Dante Gabriel Rossetti's drawings and paintings of her. The subdued colour appealed to the Aesthetes (the garish colours of fashion made possible by the new aniline dyes were anathema to them), as did the inclusion of Renaissance-style details such as the puffed, ruched sleeves, discussed in Chapter 2. The fan in the second painting (*No. 2*), while 19th-century Japanese (of a type made specially for the European market), is similar in shape to those carried by Renaissance women, seen, for example, in the *Venetian Noblewoman* from Vecellio's costume book, illustrated in the Introduction. The Pre-Raphaelites researched their costume by consulting works such as the *Costume Historique* of Camille Bonnard, which was published in Paris in two volumes in 1829–30. Pre-Raphaelite artistic dress allied with Whistler's own Aestheticism in its concern with colour and design, while the two dresses in Whistler's paintings 'seem a unique individual contribution, anticipating the way both high fashion *and* the principles of aesthetic dress ultimately developed'.[10]

In the first painting Whistler limits his palette to variations of white and skews the perspective in the manner of Japanese prints, while in the second, Whistler interprets the mood of Japanese art and culture with the fan, red pot, blue and white vase and pink azaleas. Their colour notes complement the neutral black and white. The mirror, used in the past by artists such as Boucher and Ingres, here reflects Miss Hiffernan's dress and contemplative mood and also the hanging pictures, whose frames create right angles that are repeated by the fireplace and the mirror itself, segmenting the painting like a Japanese print.

With an increasing demand for things Japanese, specialist shops in London and Paris were established that catered for artists, writers and other enthusiastic *japonistes*. Farmer and Rogers Oriental Warehouse opened in 1862 in Regent Street, London and its Oriental Manager, Arthur Lasenby Liberty, who shared the ideals of the Aesthetes, opened his own renowned firm in May 1875, also selling Japanese goods and also located in Regent Street. E W Godwin, the architect, designer and advocate of dress reform, wrote in *The Architect* in December 1876, only 19 months after the opening of Liberty's, of the excitement occasioned by the rumour that a new consignment of Japanese fans had been delivered. While the waiting crowd was disappointed when the cases were delayed, it left Godwin free to explore Liberty's, which he found was crammed with 'carpets, matting, embroideries, bamboo and lacquered furniture, porcelain, bronzes, dress fabrics'.[11]

In an interview he gave to the *Daily Chronicle* later in life, Liberty told how

> 'famous artists got the idea that I took a real interest in what we sold and my knowledge and appreciation of art were extended by prolonged visits to their studios, where I was always made welcome. The soft, delicate coloured fabrics of the East particularly attracted these artists because they could get nothing of European make that would drape properly and which was of sufficiently well-balanced colouring to satisfy the eye.'[12]

Godwin, who had been one of the first in England to start collecting Japanese prints in the early 1860s and was prominent in the Aesthetic Movement by 1870, was, according to Oscar Wilde, 'the greatest Aesthete of them all'. He studied historic dress and was honorary secretary of the Costume Society, founded in 1882, whose members included Oscar Wilde and Whistler. Liberty later recalled that he and Whistler 'had a feeling of sympathy on the Japanese impressionist side of things'. But it was Godwin from whom Liberty took advice and encouragement to join the crusade for Aesthetic dress. This led to the establishment of the Costume Department at Liberty's in 1884, directed by Godwin. It had its own studio and workroom where dresses would be made and designed in Liberty fabrics. Liberty and Godwin visualized the Costume Department as

> 'an almost missionary project ... to initiate a renaissance that should commend itself artistically to leaders of art and fashion ... The introduction of the new department had been easier because from the earliest days of the Firm, garments from the East had formed part of the stock ... such as Japanese kimonos and ... Japanese embroidered coats ... and soon it became very much the *mode* among artistic people and their imitators to wear a 'Liberty' gown at any special function – such was, in fact, recognisable at a glance.'[13]

A magnificent example is the Liberty tea gown of 1891, made of pale pink and white China silk and embroidered in pink silk floss, which is in the collection of the Costume Institute at the Metropolitan Museum of Art in New York.

> 'The origin of the tea gown is not entirely certain, but it is generally believed to be derived from the French *peignoir* or *robe d'intérieur* with which it shared a loose shape, soft lines and often a train. In as early as 1873 Watteau pleats and a loose centre from panel appeared in gowns labelled *robe d'intérieur* and became standard features of the tea gown, often mixed with other revival styles.'[14]

Such a French *peignoir* or *robe d'intérieur* was featured in Manet's painting, *Young Lady in 1866 (Woman with a Parrot)* and Paul Gavarni's lithograph, *Lorette in Dressing Gown with a Parrot,* discussed and illustrated in Chapter 2. At the Exposition Universelle in Paris in 1889 Liberty's exhibited some of their Aesthetic gowns and, on the success of the orders taken, *Maison Liberty* opened in 1890, reflecting the style and spirit of the mother shop, and becoming 'the centre of a Parisian social craze'.[15] Parisian *haute couture* made further significant gestures towards Aesthetic dress entering mainstream fashion when the *couturier* Worth, who considered himself an artist and who relied on artistic sources to promote his fashions (see Chapter 2), began to make tea gowns, which 'allowed full expression of his artistic principles'. One of the most beautiful of these artistic dresses appeared as a carefully detailed black-and-white engraved fashion plate in the 12 December 1891 issue of *Harper's Bazar,* much the finest fashion magazine for high fashion for this period, with this insightful caption:

Charles Frederick Worth, Tea Gown, *engraved fashion plate from* Harper's Bazar, *12 December 1891, (from* Victorian Fashions & Costumes from Harper's Bazar: 1868–1898, *Dover Publications, New York, 1974). For high fashion,* Harper's Bazar *was by far the finest fashion magazine of the period.*

> 'This gown is a masterpiece, unique in design and materials. It is a long flowing caftan of beige-coloured cloth, draped over a velvet gown which fits the slender figure with sheath-like closeness. *Velours frappé* (stamped velvet) with maroon design on lighter ground, is used for the front of the close gown; it is fitted by darts and extends far back on the sides, fastening invisibly on the left. The fronts frame the slight figure with wide revers of white plush; their fullness is narrowly massed on the shoulders, with ends carried thence to the middle of the back, and knotted there above full back breadths that fall in Watteau-like pleats. A high collar has velvet at the back, and is covered in front with white lace extending lower in a pointed plastron. Deep cuffs and lace on the sleeves.'[16]

The fashion innovations of Mariano Fortuny relate to the dress of the Aesthetic Movement and Liberty's. As Guillermo de Osma points out, Fortuny achieved what he did 'in a completely personal way as a result of a highly inquisitive mind and a strong desire to do everything by himself'. Yet he acknowledges that 'a few shops, like Liberty's and the Aesthetic Gallery, were channels for the diffusion of new ideas'.

'With their superior knowledge of the human form, artists were perhaps the most suitable people to design the beautiful 'rational' dress of the Aesthetes. As Walter Crane remarked, 'regarding dress as a department of design, we may consciously bring to bear upon it the results of artistic experience and knowledge of form'. And the first thing that the study of the human body teaches one is the need to respect it, which is why these painters and sculptors adorned the 'sacred' forms of their models with simple garments, showing, many years before Poiret, that a dress should adapt to the shape of the body without hiding, altering or deforming it.'

Fortuny, a painter, photographer, inventor, alchemist, architect and theatre designer, achieved international fame though his innovative textile processes and fashion designs. His early years were spent largely in Paris as a painter, where Théophile Gautier wrote of him that 'as an etcher he is the equal of Goya and close to Rembrandt'.[17] In 1889 he settled in Venice, where his contemporaries called him the 'Magician of Venice', the personification of the Renaissance man with his prodigious talent and wide-ranging interests. The catalyst for his interest in costume and fabrics was the theatre. For a production of the play *Francesca da Rimini* in 1901, for instance, he meticulously copied the costumes from the drawings of Pisanello. He turned his attention to textile and fashion design in 1906 with his Knossos scarf. Made of silk, it was inspired by Cycladic art and perfectly complemented his most celebrated creation, the Delphos dress, which appeared around 1907. Named after the ancient Greek city, it had initially been conceived as a tea gown for Henriette Negrin, his muse who became his wife. Made of finely pleated silk by a process that he patented in 1909, the gown draped from the shoulder and elegantly sculpted the body. His costume design focused on the unrestrained, natural body in the classical sense. Fortuny's fondness for the Italian Renaissance and the great painters of Venice led him to experiment with historic woven patterns. Venice, as we saw in the Introduction, had been one of the great centres of the European textile industry. Fortuny combined his colour effects with stencils, designing exquisite heavy brocades and velvets in the style seen in portraits by Botticelli and Titian. Fortuny's interest in the exoticism of Japan was also apparent in his designs of kimonos, which he freely appropriated and recombined to create original works.

In Paris, the literary and artistic apostles of *l'art pour l'art* found specialist shops in which to purchase Japanese artefacts; they also used these establishments as meeting grounds. The most popular was Madame Desoye's shop in the rue de Rivoli, opened in 1862, a haunt not only of Whistler, but also of Gautier, Baudelaire, the Goncourt brothers, Émile Zola, James-Jacques-Joseph Tissot, Manet, Monet, Degas and Alfred Stevens, who were all collectors. Alfred Émile-Léopold Stevens, a Belgian painter who had settled in France in 1844, was one of the first enthusiasts and connoisseurs, already collecting Japanese porcelain by the 1850s. His paintings record with a spectacular Realist precision every decorative detail, such as in *The Porcelain Collector* of 1868. This shows a chic Parisian lady, dressed probably by Worth,

Alfred Stevens, The Porcelain Collector
*(1868), oil on canvas (North Carolina
Museum of Art, Raleigh, Gift of Dr and
Mrs Henry C. Landon III). Stevens, a friend
of Manet and his group, was one of the
first enthusiasts for Japanese artefacts.*

comparing the vase in her hands to printed sources in the book lying open before her. Endowed with a meticulous painterly touch, Stevens was called the 'ter Borch of France'. He delineated the materials and colours of each unique curio in the lady's elegant interior – the various other vases, the screen, the print, the carpet and the fan – creating a Japanese environment and imparting a graphic sense of time and place. A great friend of Manet and a member of his group, Stevens's work was admired by Monet, Degas, Baudelaire and Gautier. Gautier likened his work to visual 'poems' of the modern woman, while for Camille Lemonnier, another 19th-century writer and art critic, they were 'rare perfume concentrated within a scent bottle'.[18]

In a letter of 12 November 1864, Dante Gabriel Rossetti told his mother that he had visited a shop in the rue de Rivoli where Madame Desoye sold Japanese items, 'but found all the costumes snapped up by a French artist, Tissot, who, it seems, is doing three Japanese pictures, which the mistress of the shop described to me as the three wonders of the world, evidently in her opinion, quite throwing Whistler into the shade'.[19] Tissot was in the artistic milieu of both Paris and London, where he lived from 1871 to 1882. A friend of Manet, Degas and the Goncourt brothers, he 'was drawn into discussions about "art for art's sake" over Whistler's dinner table'.[20] As the son of a *marchand de nouveautés* and a *modiste*, he had the fashion pedigree that distinguished his work for his passionate observation of stylish women. He rendered their costumes and accessories very accurately and tactilely, combining this with a masterful understanding of Japanese aesthetics. In his book, *Vulgar Society: The Romantic Career of James Tissot 1836–1902*, James Laver noted that 'to the eyes of cultivated French people, familiar with the paintings of Manet, the canvases of Tissot seemed like coloured photos'.[21] His photographic reality and pervasive understanding of Japanese art was such that when Prince Akitake of Japan came to Paris in 1867 to represent his country at the Exposition Universelle and stayed on for further education, he received drawing lessons from Tissot. Tissot delighted in portraying the four seasons in the Japanese tradition of *bijin-e*, portraits of beautiful, serene women. He translated this theme into his portraits of his beautiful mistress, Kathleen Newton. One of his most joyous portraits of her is entitled *Summer* (1878), where she wears an elegant black hat and dress accented with a small bouquet of vivid red blossoms (shown on page 94). Silhouetted against an open Japanese golden-yellow paper parasol, which effectively suggests the season, she is the very embodiment of refined taste and composure. *Summer* also shows Tissot's flawless assimilation of Japanese prints. He uses the graceful, wide vertical format of *hashira-e*, derived from the 18th-century artist Utamaro. Some three years after *Summer*, Manet also made a series of four portraits of women to represent the seasons that are reminiscent of Tissot. 'However, this is where the comparison ends, as Tissot's interpretation is bolder and more avant-garde. Tissot's *Summer* is as innovative as any work by the Impressionist painters, more modern than Manet, and one of the most daring and beautiful compositions that Tissot had ever produced.'[22]

James-Jacques-Joseph Tissot, Summer, oil on canvas (Sotheby's, New York). In this painting of Tissot's mistress, Kathleen Newton, Tissot used the Japanese tradition of bijin-e, portraits of beautiful, serene women.

In 1880 the critic of the *Gazette des beaux-arts*, Arthur Baignières, wrote of 'une épidémie d'éventails' ('an epidemic of fans'), and it is recorded that in 1891 the combined total of folding and rigid fans exported from Japan was 15,724,048.[23] Hélène Alexander points out in her book *Fans* that the Aesthetic Movement did much to promote Eastern influence, in particular Liberty's 'where fans from the East and objects with fan motifs could be purchased ... In fact all the artistic manifestations of the time found an expression, either on the leaves of fans or in their shape and composition'.[24] French artists played a part in this 'epidemic', seizing on the vogue for fans by making extensive use of them in their paintings, such as Manet in his *Dame aux éventails (Lady with fans)* (1873–74). Artists were also inspired to design fans. Indeed, in 1882 when Pissarro was experiencing financial difficulties, the art dealer Paul Durand-Ruel recommended that he 'make some small gouache paintings on taffeta and some fans; they sell well and have been very successful'.[25] Fans were also a point of crossover between art and fashion. At the Exposition Universelle of 1878, the critic of *La Gazette rose* compared fans to paintings.[26] As well as Manet, fans inspired artists such as Gustave Caillebotte, Berthe Morisot, Pierre-Auguste Renoir and Edgar Degas to paint fan leaves. Degas in particular was fascinated by the artistic challenge of the fan leaf: constructing, colouring and decorating, in the manner of a Japanese fan, an arc-shaped format within which is a precise, unified composition. *The Ballet*, his fan leaf of 1879, was strongly influenced by Japanese lacquers. The stage at the left is sprinkled with silver powder and painted with thin washes of tin, and the outlines of the dancers are drawn in a gold-coloured paint that is made from brass powder. When Degas painted this fan leaf, he wished to organize a room at the *Salon des Indépendants* devoted exclusively to the fan paintings of Félix and Marie Bracquemond, Jean-Louis Forain, Berthe Morisot, Pissarro and himself. To Degas's chagrin, the room never came into being, but 21 fan paintings by himself, Pissarro and Forain were exhibited that celebrated the use of the fan as an art form. One of the great masters of Post-Impressionism, Paul Gauguin, also painted fan leaves, and he was 'certainly inspired by many fan paintings of the "father figure" of the Impressionist and Post-Impressionist artists, Camille Pissarro'.[27]

For many, the image of a woman dressed in a kimono and holding a fan embodied the exoticism of Japanese aesthetics. A most glorious example is Claude Monet's *La Japonaise (Camille Monet in Japanese Costume)*, a portrait of his wife, painted in 1876. Madame Monet wears a boldly coloured and patterned kimono and holds open a folding fan. Standing on a flooring of *tatami* matting, she is framed by an array of no less than 15 colourful Japanese fixed fans mounted on the wall behind her and strewn at her feet. Throughout his life, Monet was attracted to all things Japanese, especially prints, which he collected and which are on display in his house at Giverny. The sinuous outline and flowing line of Madame Monet's kimono, creating a floating, swaying silhouette, is similar to that of courtesans in Japanese prints.

Claude Monet, La Japonaise (Camille Monet in Japanese Costume) *(1876), oil on canvas (Museum of Fine Arts, Boston/www.bridgeman.co.uk). A woman in a kimono holding a fan was seen as the height of the exoticism of Japanese aesthetics.*

Japonisme was understood by its followers to have a powerful element of modernity. It was the Japanese approach to form, expressed through asymmetrical line and bold silhouette, that most stamped its influence on art and fashion during this period, and later had its greatest impact when it became such a fundamental aspect of Art Nouveau, whose variety of names included Modern Style, *Modernisme* and *Stil'modern.* In her book, *The Aesthetic Movement: Prelude to Art Nouveau*, Elizabeth Aslin wrote that *'Japonisme* and the Aesthetic Movement were virtually synonymous'.[28] Together with other characteristics of Aestheticism in Britain and France discussed in this chapter, it had become one of the contributory elements in the search for modernity. Aestheticism in both Britain and France had been an important cultural movement, informing and reforming taste, focusing on the role the arts and fashion played in people's lives and in society. It had occurred at a time of great expansion in the fashion industry: technological developments in textiles, industrial production and the rise of *haute couture. Haute couture* had encountered a challenge and an alternative – Aesthetic dress, which articulated ideas of the beautiful while asserting its modernity – evolved and entered the mainstream of fashion. In the continuing debate on modernity in painting and literature during the 19th century, fashion came to play a key role.

Writing in 1848 to his parents, the French painter Gustave Courbet felt himself 'on the point of success because I have all around me very influential people in the press and in the arts who are enthusiastic about my work'. With them, he hoped 'to constitute a new school, of which I shall be the representative in painting'.[29] Courbet coherently outlined the theory on which he based his ambitions in his manifesto entitled *Le Réalisme.* Published for an exhibition of his works, held in the purpose-built Pavillon du Réalisme in Paris in 1855, the manifesto emphasized the dual concepts of personal independence and of objective representation based on the impartial observation of contemporary life.[30] While writers such as Émile Zola and the Goncourt brothers were preoccupied with the issue of Realism in painting and literature, it was Baudelaire who loomed large in Courbet's reference to the influential people around him. In his *Salon de 1846*, Baudelaire had already identified the crucial concepts of 'Romantic individualism, with an art that reflected its own epoch', and, 'in its demands for a modern style Realism continued the aims of the Romantics'.[31] Baudelaire fully and profoundly adumbrated the theme of *modernité* in *Le Peintre de la vie moderne,* a long study published in *Le Figaro* in 1863. An eloquent affirmation of his ideas on art, beauty and life, *Le Peintre de la vie moderne* exhorted young contemporary artists to take their subjects from modern life, and presented the artist Constantin Guys as its model. Over 60 years old when Baudelaire singled him out, Guys had the advantage of belonging to the first generation of artists who had produced a vast pictorial record of the contemporary scene for the rapidly expanding magazine industry. His drawings of Parisian society, sketched from life, such as women in fashionable dresses and crinolines and men in black

Constantin Guys, Meeting in the Park, *pen-and-ink drawing and watercolour (The Metropolitan Museum of Art, New York, Rogers Fund). Guys sketched from life and his work was used by the rapidly expanding magazine industry.*

frock coats and top hats, horse-drawn carriages in the Bois du Boulogne and balls and carnivals, earned him the admiration of artists such as Delacroix and Manet, who owned some of his drawings, and art critics, especially the Goncourt brothers, Gautier and Baudelaire. The latter, marvelling at his ability to capture the moment and draw with rapid strokes a dress or a frock coat, gave him the soubriquet 'the painter of modern life'. In an earlier piece of criticism, his *Salon de 1845,* Baudelaire had already urged artists to consider the 'mysterious grace of fashion'. 'The painter, the true painter, will be he who can wring from contemporary life its epic aspect and make us see and understand, with colour or in drawing, how great and poetic we are in our cravats and our polished boots.'[32] In *Le Peintre de la vie moderne,* Baudelaire proposed a concept of beauty suitable for the modern age:

'The beautiful consists of one eternal, unvarying element – the proportion of which is extremely difficult to determine – and another relative element that is shaped by circumstances, which, if you will, can be the epoch, fashion, morals, or passion, one after another or all at once. Without this second element, which is like the entertaining, titillating and appetising icing on the divine cake, the first element would be indigestible, imperceptible, unsuitable to human nature and inappropriate.'[33]

Hajo Düchting in *Édouard Manet: Images of Parisian Life* clarifies Baudelaire's concept of the dual nature of beauty in art in terms of contemporary fashion:

> For Guys, it was a question of 'capturing the poetic element in the ephemerality of fashion, of extracting an eternal quality from the transitory'. The exemplary art of the *peintre moderne* ... discovers in ephemeral and accidental phenomena an element of eternal beauty and sets free the poetic quality in both fashionable and historical appearances. 'Modernity is the transitory, the ephemeral, the contingent, one half of art, the other half being the eternal and immutable' – this was the essence of Baudelaire's message. Baudelaire saw this new artistic ideal as being realised in Constantin Guys's watercolours and drawings, but his requirements for modernité were far better met by the work of Manet.[34]

Manet was a close friend and disciple of Baudelaire and engraved his portrait in 1862, the same year in which the poet wrote a quatrain to the painter's *Lola de Valence*. It is thought that Baudelaire may have been too ill (he died in 1867) to reflect on his close association with Manet, the painter who most clearly carried out his instructions to young artists in *Le Peintre de la vie moderne*. Manet's celebrated painting of 1862, *Music in the Tuileries Gardens*, showing a fashionable crowd gathered to listen to a band playing, was his first major work depicting modern city life and it ushered in a new era of contemporary urban subjects. During the Second Empire, baron Georges Haussmann, the Prefect of the Seine, directed the modernization of Paris. His urban renovations, creating a network of wide, tree-lined streets, squares and parks, such as the Tuileries Gardens, a popular place for fashionable society to assemble and be seen, gave Paris a new look. *Music in the Tuileries Gardens* is a visual statement of Manet's *dictum*, quoted in the memoirs of his childhood friend, Antonin Proust, that 'il faut être de son temps et faire ce que l'on voit' – 'one must be of one's time and draw what one sees'. The idea behind the painting derived 'from Manet's discussions with Baudelaire on the duties of the *peintre moderne*'. For, as early as 1846, Baudelaire had included in his review of the *salon* a section entitled 'De l'Héroïsme de la vie moderne' – 'On the Heroism of Modern Life', where he discussed the '"modern beauty" of dandydom and the spectacle of elegant life'. In *Music in the Tuileries Gardens,* by including himself, as well as his brother Eugène, Fantin-Latour, Gautier, the art critic Jules Champfleury (a close friend of Courbet's and a staunch defender of Realism), the composer Jacques Offenbach

Édouard Manet, Music in the Tuileries Gardens *(1862), oil on canvas (National Gallery, London/ www.bridgeman.co.uk). Manet included himself in this painting of fashionable Parisians.*

and Baudelaire, all dressed in the contemporary fashion of black coats and top hats, Manet 'identified himself with the dandy in pursuit of the "heroism of modern life"'.[35] Fashion had a central role in the lives of Baudelaire and Manet. Baudelaire designed his own clothes and, according to Champfleury, drove his tailor to distraction in his quest for perfection in his dress, demanding fitting after fitting until he thought his tailor had got it absolutely right.[36] For Manet, 'dress represented, in the sense of Baudelaire, the outward aspect of modern life, that transient envelope that both veils and reveals its unchanging essence'.[37] Manet took great care with his appearance and was noted for his elegance and refined deportment by those who knew him. This is evident in Fantin-Latour's portrait of him of 1867 in which he wears an impeccably cut black coat, black waistcoat adorned with a gold chain, top hat, immaculate white shirt, cravat, gloves and walking stick, in his fashion and pose the epitome of Baudelaire's chic Parisian dandy, the perfect *artiste-flâneur*, the painter of modern life. *Music in the Tuileries Gardens*, in its images of men and women of fashion, encapsulates the delight Manet felt in looking at the world around him. One of his visual excitements was the use of black in his depictions of those contemporary gentlemen's fashions, the ubiquitous coats and top hats. The intensity of the black Manet achieved was strongly reminiscent of Velázquez. *Hispagnolisme*, a love of things Spanish, owed a great deal to the Romantic poets and writers such as Victor Hugo, Prosper Merimée and especially Théophile Gautier, whose *Voyage en Espagne*, published in 1843, did much to introduce Spanish painting to French artists. Little-exhibited in France before the Revolution, Spanish paintings, including the works of Murillo, Ribera and Zurbarán, entered the Musée du Louvre after Napoléon's Spanish campaigns (1808–14). However, a deeper French appreciation of Spanish painting came with King Louis-Philippe's installation of the Galerie espagnole in the Musée du Louvre from 1838 to 1848, featuring some four hundred paintings that he had acquired, by such masters as El Greco, Zurbarán, Velázquez, Murillo and Goya. Although the King's collection was sold in 1853, the Emperor Napoléon III's marriage in that year to the Spanish beauty Eugénie saw the fashion for Spanish culture rekindled in Parisian social life, and the Musée du Louvre acquired more Spanish paintings, which became accessible to French artists to study and appreciate. They also travelled to Spain to see the masterpieces in the Museo del Prado. Manet's *Hispagnolisme*, both before and after his trip to Spain in 1865, was largely inspired by his great artistic hero, Velázquez, 'the painter of painters'. As the exhibition, *Manet/Velázquez: The French Taste for Spanish Painting* (held at the Musée d'Orsay in Paris and the Metropolitan Museum of Art in New York during 2002–03) showed, it was Velázquez's extraordinarily modern quality of realism and directness, above all his use of paint, that Manet admired and sought to emulate, in order to better depict the realities of life, including fashion.[38]

The two women in the foreground of *Music in the Tuileries Gardens*, Madame Lejosne and Madame Loubens, are similarly dressed and posed close together to show off as much of their clothing as possible, a device borrowed from fashion plates. Manet was one of the generation of young artists who benefited from the explosion of fashion literature and fashion plates that had occurred during the July Monarchy. The imagery of fashion illustration continued apace during the Second Empire, with the editors of fashion magazines again commissioning artists to contribute fashion plates, a notable example being Jules David, the painter and lithographer who had a unique association with *Le Moniteur de la mode*.[39] Manet is known to have enjoyed chatting about painting and fashion with his women friends. He was also an inveterate letter-writer. Several letters to Isabelle Lemonnier, sister-in-law of the publisher Georges Charpentier, and to Madame Jules Guillemet, wife of the painter, are illustrated with drawings in watercolour and ink of female accessories such as handbags, boots, hats and umbrellas that have the registrative quality of fashion plates seen in his paintings.[40]

It was Baudelaire who had furthered the dialogue between fashion and painting when he recommended the study of fashion plates in *Le Peintre de la vie moderne*. He was inspired by the fashion plates of the late-18th and early-19th centuries, particularly those from the most widely subscribed and influential fashion magazine, La Mésangère's *Le Journal des dames et des modes*.

> 'I have here in front of me a series of fashion plates ... which have a double kind of charm, artistic and historical. They are very often beautiful and wittily drawn, but what to me is at least as important, and what I am glad to find in all or nearly all of them, is the moral attitude and aesthetic value of the time. The idea of beauty that man creates for himself affects his whole attire ... and even in the process subtly penetrates the very features of his face. Man comes in the end to look like his ideal image of himself.'[41]

According to Baudelaire, fashion plates reveal how our notion of beauty changes over the passage of time, and that every dress style is beautiful *in its own time*. This theme was taken up by the painters who came to be called the Impressionists. They were inspired by the huge range of fashion plates available to them encapsulating scenes of modern Paris and the dress of its inhabitants. Their paintings of women show this influence, calling to mind Baudelaire's characterization of the *parisienne* whose 'beautifully composed attire ... is inseparable from the beauty of the woman wearing it, thus making of the two, the woman and the dress, an indivisible whole'.[42] Calling themselves the *Société Anonyme des Artistes, Peintres, Sculpteurs, Graveurs* (Anonymous Society of Artists, Painters, Sculptors and Engravers), they opened an exhibition in April 1874 independent of the official *salon*. Manet, the recognized leader of the avant-garde, never participated in their eight exhibitions, but his style and modern urban subject-matter inspired these younger artists. The poet Stéphane Mallarmé 'wrote a profound appreciation of Manet in 1876 that acknowledged his historic connection with Impressionist painting and his engagement with the contemporary world'.[43]

A relationship with fashion plates can be seen in the paintings of the young Claude Monet, the leading member of the Impressionist group of French painters; indeed, the movement's name, Impressionism, derived from his painting *Impression, Sunrise* (1872–1873). Following the lead of Manet, they shared a commitment to contemporaneity of vision, in which their depiction of dress was a salient sign of their determination to be modern. 'Fashion and art shared certain features ... and for the Impressionists there was an underlying association of contemporary life with fashion'.[44]

Eugène Boudin was also a great influence on Monet, whom he introduced to the idea of *plein-air* painting. Regarded as one of the most important precursors of Impressionism, and who exhibited in the first Impressionist exhibition in 1874, Boudin was noted for his paintings of the French seaside resorts of Deauville and Trouville, which the Empress Eugénie made fashionable holiday towns. He painted her at Trouville in 1863 promenading on the beach with her ladies-in-waiting, all

Claude Monet, The Beach at Trouville *(1870), oil on canvas (National Gallery, London/ www.bridgeman.co.uk). Images of fashionably dressed women by the sea was one of the most popular subjects in the fashion plate magazines of the 1860s.*

fashionably clad and wearing that most distinctive and ubiquitous garment associated with the Second Empire, the crinoline. It has been written that 'perhaps his greatest seascapes are the crinolines which he painted':

'What fascinated Boudin at Trouville and Deauville was not so much the sea and the ships but the group of people sitting on the sand or strolling along the beach: fine ladies in crinolines twirling their parasols ... In the elegant clothes he found contrast to the delicacy of the skies ...'[45]

Pierre-Auguste Renoir, La Parisienne (1874),
oil on canvas (National Museum of Wales, Cardiff).
With an elegance in dress and deportment,
La Parisienne is the female counterpart of the
Parisian dandy.

Boudin's inspiration for undertaking this subject was Baudelaire, who visited the artist's studio and wrote about him in his *salon* review of 1859. In the way he observes the figures in his seaside paintings, paying close attention to their costumes, gestures and poses, Boudin made adroit use of fashion plates to capture the 'indivisible whole' so dear to Baudelaire. Not even in *The Beach at Trouville – the Empress Eugénie* 'can we be sure which, among the fashionably dressed women, is the Empress herself'.[46] Beach scenes of stylishly clad women strolling or sitting along the edge of the sea were one of the most popular contemporary subjects that featured regularly in the fashion plates of magazines from the 1860s. With consummate skill, Boudin treats the holidaymakers according to the rituals of the fashion plate, with their pose, gestures and dress all corresponding to the norms of fashion display.

Monet's painting *The Beach at Trouville* (1870) reveals his affinity with his 'master', as he called Boudin, to whom he wrote 'I haven't forgotten that you were the first to teach me to see and understand'.[47] The figure on the left in white is probably Monet's wife Camille, and the woman on the right in black may be Boudin's wife. The painting is a *pochade* or sketch, probably for a larger, picture that was never realized.[48] Yet even with his free handling, Monet captures the fashionable vacationers according to fashion-plate convention, and also the essence of their fashions, the pork-pie-shaped hats tilted forward at a jaunty angle, the indispensable parasols, and the emphasis on the new vertical line of their dress.

It was Pierre-Auguste Renoir that the art dealer Paul Durand-Ruel was describing when he wrote that 'of all the Impressionist painters, he was the most delicate, the most feminine'.[49] It is significant that Renoir's parents were a tailor and a seamstress, that he began work as painter in a porcelain factory in Limoges, his birthplace, and that this led him to paint fans. Early on, he developed the light palette that was to distinguish his painting in the Impressionist group, of which he was a founding member, and he also learned the importance of good design, which he brought to his fashion work. As we have seen, the proliferation of fashion plates, the development of ready-made clothing and the establishment of department stores where the sale of fashionable clothes could be seen to advantage displayed on mannequins, made fashion a large sector of the French economy in its own right. Department stores were nothing less than shopping paradises, as Émile Zola described them in his novel of 1883, *Au Bonheur des dames (The Ladies' Paradise)*. Set in a Parisian department store, it tells the story of women falling prey to their passion for fashion. Renoir made engravings for publication in Zola's novel. Paris offered Renoir a rich source. Renoir's *La Parisienne* of 1874 is someone purely delineated by her clothes, face, gesture and pose, as in a fashion plate. The model was most probably Henriette Henriot, a young actress at the Odéon theatre, but by giving his painting the generic title *La Parisienne,* Renoir implies that this fashionable young woman is typical, that she is representative of a new kind of urban woman, causing Paul Cézanne to remark that 'he has painted *the* woman of Paris'.[50] Wearing a *capote* (hat), gloves, a high-neckline dress with an S-shaped silhouette, she is the quintessential image of the fashionable *Parisienne*, the female counterpart to the Parisian dandy, with an elegance in dress and deportment. Fashion illustration was of continual interest to Renoir, and its influence can be seen, among many other examples, in his pastels for *La Vie moderne (The Modern Life)*, a weekly magazine devoted to art and fashion, founded in 1879 by Georges Charpentier.

The final Impressionist exhibition, in 1886, featured Georges Seurat's masterpiece, *A Sunday Afternoon on La Grande Jatte,* in which the central female figure in profile, slender and elongated, is clearly derived from fashion illustration. The fashionable silhouette of the 1880s required a corset and a bustle (*tournure*), which was tied around the waist. The *tournure* was a small pad (or overlapping frills) of horsehair cloth bound with braid and stiffened with steel bands, or a frame of wires that supported the fullness of the large folds of the skirt and created a sharp, shelf-like projection. The bustle of Seurat's figure, together with her jacket with its cuirass bodice that extends over the waist and hips and her small, high hat shaped like an abbreviated cone, shows Seurat's graphic flair for contemporary fashion. He used the imagery of advertising found in department stores, where fashionably dressed mannequins in profile were placed in a garden or park setting – venues, as we have seen, where sartorial exhibition was important. Seurat's fashionable lady wears a costume like the one designed by Worth that was issued as a fashion plate in *L'Art et la mode* for 26 April 1884.[51]

L'Art et la mode, founded in 1880, featured not only black-and-white fashion plates, but had the distinction of publishing the first half-tone illustration ever printed in a fashion magazine (in its first issue), and of experimenting early on with publishing photographs, making it an essential source for studying art and fashion.[52]

When John Ruskin, the influential 19th-century English art critic, saw Tissot's paintings, he called them 'mere coloured photographs', such was the astounding accuracy with which he painted the *minutiae* of the *toilettes* of female sitters. The Japanese made some of the finest hand-coloured photographs during the 1860s and 1870s, mainly for the substantial market in Paris and London. Since Tissot was a pioneering *japoniste* (as discussed earlier in this chapter), celebrated for his 'Japanese studio', art historians think it reasonable to assume he was *au fait* with Japanese hand-coloured photographs and was an early advocate of the use of photography in his painting.[53] Although Ruskin in England and Baudelaire in France at first accepted photography for its utility as documentation, they became hostile to it when it began to intrude on the sphere of fine art. Writing a piece entitled 'Le Public moderne et la photographie' ('The modern public and photography') in his review of the *salon* of 1859, Baudelaire maintained that Louis Daguerre – the inventor twenty years before of the most widespread early form of photography, the daguerreotype – had been sent as his 'Messiah' by 'a revengeful God' to a multitude which believed that art was 'the exact reproduction

Georges Seurat, A Sunday on La Grande Jatte *(detail) (1884–1886) oil on canvas (The Art Institute of Chicago, Helen Birch Bartlett Memorial Collection). Seurat's fashionable lady wears a costume similar to the one designed by Worth seen in the fashion plate in L'Art et la Mode, 26 April 1864.*

of nature', and hence that 'Photography and Art are the same thing'. He went on to 'expose the false logic of this syllogism', denying photography any artistic value.[54]

Notwithstanding the reverence in which Baudelaire was held, many of the Impressionist painters, most notably Degas and Gustave Caillebotte, were by the very nature of their adherence to the Realists' ideology drawn to the use of photography in their work as a facet of modern life, and saw that contemporary costume could be framed in new and exciting ways. Degas asked Caillebotte to participate in the First Impressionist Exhibition; however, it was only at the time of the second exhibition in 1876 that Caillebotte joined the group. He 'was involved in the search for a new Realism that was to a great extent the catalyst of the Impressionist revolution ... He was considered one of the painters most responsive to the ideas of the French Realist writers.'[55]

Caillebotte lived in the heart of Paris so recently transformed by the urban planning of baron Haussmann, and was therefore particularly able to interpret the atmosphere of the Parisian scene. His painting *On the Europe Bridge* (1876–1877), with its restricted, cool palette of blacks, blues and greys, looks like a gigantic snapshot, especially in its composition: all three figures are bunched over to one side, and one is cropped by the edge, as if the painting is a photograph that has been snapped without being framed in the viewfinder first. On this famous bridge he emphasizes its rising perspective, and the figures in their top hats – two seen from the back and one framed in between them – convey the visual rhythm of Parisian modernism.

Gustave Caillebotte, On The Europe Bridge *(1876–1877) oil on canvas (Kimbell Art Museum, Fort Worth). Caillebotte was 'one of the painters most responsive to the ideas of the French Realist writers'.*

Edgar Degas, The Millinery Shop (1884–1890), oil on canvas (The Art Institute of Chicago/www.bridgeman.co.uk).
Degas frequented fashionable shops, studying in particular the shop assistants and customers totally absorbed in
the act of choosing items of clothing.

Edgar Degas, a painter as well as a photographer, was one of the founding members of the Impressionist group and a champion within it of the movement's Realist tendency, with a strong interest in modern Parisian life. He was passionately interested in dress and even suggested to the publisher Georges Charpentier that Zola's novel *Au Bonheur des dames* have real samples of the items of fashion attached to the pages in place of illustrations.[56] His sculpture of *The Little Fourteen-Year-Old Dancer* of 1881 wearing a real tulle *tutu*, a satin ribbon and a wig caused a shock when exhibited at the Sixth Impressionist Exhibition. Degas was especially noteworthy for his series of paintings on women such as *modistes*. He frequented their shops and captured their customers totally absorbed in the act of trying on a hat, unaware of the viewer, as in his painting *The Millinery Shop* (shown on page 107). With its cropping and perspective, Degas conveys the sense of space and movement of snapshot photography, and also the sense of leisure that was indispensable in the important art of selecting just the right hat – an important accessory in the late 19th century and a virtual status symbol in the first decade of the 20th century, at the height of Art Nouveau. What began as a painting about fashion became a metaphor for artistic creation.

Mariano Fortuny, Pleated silk satin Delphos dresses *and* Printed silk velvet evening coats, *1915–1935, (Cincinnati Art Museum, Gifts of Patricia Cunningham and Mrs James Marjan Hutton). Fortuny, a painter, photographer, architect and theatre designer of the late 19th and early 20th century, pioneered innovative textile processes and fashion designs. In 1907, inspired by Cycladic art, he created the Delphos dress.*

4 Art Nouveau and Art Deco

At the end of the 19th century, 'new' seemed to be the buzz word. Articles in newspapers and magazines referred to the 'new woman', the 'new fiction', the 'new journalism' and the 'new art'. The key date for the 'new art' was 1884. This was the year *Les XX* was founded in Belgium, and the term 'Art Nouveau' was coined by the supporters of this avant-garde group, Octave Maus and Edmond Picard, in their periodical *L'Art moderne,* in which they proclaimed: 'we are believers in Art Nouveau'.[1] Maus and Picard had founded their publication in 1881 and its chief purpose was 'to introduce art into every aspect of everyday life', with the editors calling themselves 'the Art Nouveau faithful'. *Les XX,* a group of 20 artists who sought to show their work outside the official *salon,* held their first exhibition in Brussels in 1884. The dissolution of *Les XX* in 1893 led to the foundation in its place of another progressive group, *La Libre Esthétique.* Those invited to exhibit with *La Libre Esthétique* included Georges Seurat and Henri de Toulouse-Lautrec.

> 'Of singular importance to the development of Art Nouveau was the fact that [William] Morris's and [Aubrey] Beardsley's book illustrations and objects designed by [C.R.] Ashbee were given equal prominence to the paintings. With Claude Debussy playing his music at the opening, the exhibition was seen as an attempt to establish a relationship between all the arts.'[2]

Art Nouveau was the first concerted attempt to create a modern international style based on decoration.[3] The aim of the style was to produce an art form appropriate to the new age: one that could be employed across all the visual arts. All would work in harmony and be part of a 'total work of art', or *Gesamtkunstwerk,* conforming to the principle of Art Nouveau of unification by the same design. The idea of the all-embracing work of art afforded a unique opportunity for the leading exponents of Art Nouveau to take an interest in fashion and for the visual arts and fashion to interact and stimulate one another. Art and fashion intertwined in Vienna and would come to make a mark on the international fashion scene, influencing the *couturier* Paul Poiret. The Austrian architect Josef Hoffmann, a co-founder in 1903 of the Wiener Werkstätte (the 'Viennese Workshop'), an avant-garde group of architects, artists and designers that was closely associated with the Vienna Secession, created jewellery and clothing to complement his architectural designs. The leading painter and draughtsman in Austria, Gustav Klimt, who was the first President of the Vienna Secession, designed dresses – some of which were executed by the Wiener Werkstätte – and a series of ten of his dress designs was commissioned by and illustrated in *Deutsche Kunst und Dekoration* in 1906. It was Klimt's practice to insist that his sitters wore a dress from the Wiener Werkstätte. A superb example is his picture of Hermine Gallia, dated 1904. She was the wife of Moritz Gallia, an adviser to the Austrian government. They were leading patrons of the arts who commissioned interiors from the Wiener Werkstätte. Klimt painted her in a sumptuous chiffon dress that was probably a creation of the Wiener Werkstätte, and it may have been designed by Klimt himself. With it she wears a luxurious feathered boa, which softens the angularity of her silhouette. Klimt has skilfully used the creative power of fashionable dress, and especially the chic elements of the forward-tilted stance and celebrated S-bend so characteristic of Art Nouveau fashion, to conjure up a portrait of a modern 'new woman', someone who would be comfortable in her avant-garde environment.

Klimt also collaborated on dress designs with one of the great trend-setters of turn-of-the century Vienna, the fashion designer Emilie Flöge, who founded her own fashion house, Schwestern Flöge, in 1904, with her *modesalon* entirely designed and decorated by the Wiener Werkstätte. Klimt was also a strong influence on the young Austrian artist Egon Schiele. Schiele designed men's suits – often serving as his own model – which were intended for, but never used by, the Wiener Werkstätte. Nevertheless, they were fully realized fashion drawings and Schiele had several of them made up for himself to wear. The Czech artist Alphonse Mucha designed posters, magazine covers, book illustrations, sculpture, jewellery and textiles. Mucha's graphic work inspired motifs for one of the most

Gustav Klimt, Hermine Gallia *(1904), oil on canvas (National Gallery, London). Klimt was a designer of dresses as well as a painter. His designs were executed by the Wiener Werkstätte.*

Lace Tulips, tortoiseshell fan, French, c. 1900. (Fan Museum, Hélène Alexander Collection). The early 20th century saw interest in fan design at a high point.

Above: Paris Model from Autumn Reception Costume, *engraved fashion plate from* Harper's Bazar, *17 September 1898 (From* Victorian Fashions and Costumes from Harper's Bazar: 1867–1898, *Dover Publications, New York, 1974).*

Right: Jacques Doucet, La Robe Rose, *fashion plate (pochoir process) from* La Gazette du bon ton, *May 1913 (Private Collection). Doucet's dresses, with airy fabrics and intricate floral details, reveal the influence of the Art Nouveau strong interest in nature.*

popular accessories of Art Nouveau, the fan, examples being the 'hand-out' publicity and advertising fans, such as 'Edmond Rostand' and 'The Carlton London'.[4] This was an exciting period for fan design, with the great fashion designers like Jeanne Paquin commissioning fans from artists such as George Barbier and Paul Iribe, both noted graphic artists closely connected with fashion design, the theatre and the cinema. The leading French Art Nouveau jeweller, René Lalique, also designed metalwork and glass. The prodigious output of the Belgian architect, painter and designer Henry Van de Velde include interior furnishings, dresses and metalwork. He recognized early on the power of clothing as an aid to artistic expression when he used the term *Künstlerkeid* at his exhibition in Germany in 1894 to signify clothing worn by an artist.[5] The French *couturier* Jacques Doucet was a patron and collector of art and a bibliophile. He built up an outstanding collection of 18th-century French Rococo art that included works by Fragonard and La Tour, which he housed in an 18th-century style *hôtel* in Paris. Doucet commissioned a number of young artists, including Paul Iribe, to design furniture and fittings for his Parisian apartment. He compiled a scholarly library of books, prints and drawings that from 1911 became the basis for the *Répertoire d'art et d'archéologie (Repertoire of Art and Archaeology)*, and in 1917 he donated his library to the University of Paris, the magnificent Bibliothèque Doucet.

Art Nouveau was an essentially urban creation of sophisticated artists and designers, and reflected a diversity of trends. The natural world was the single most important source. Nature was widely used to achieve a modern look, so much so that in Art Nouveau circles, nature and modernity came to mean almost the same thing. Dresses designed by Doucet made of beautiful light, airy fabrics such as lace with intricate floral details; gossamer lace fans shaped as flowers produced by the Maison Duvelleroy; and jewellery such as hair-combs, necklaces, brooches and buckles designed by René Lalique, Alphonse Fouquet and the Maison Vever using gemstones, enamelling and metals for lustrous motifs based on the observation of nature, were major vehicles for artistic expression. Art Nouveau borrowed from several historical and cultural styles, including the Rococo and, as discussed in Chapter 2, *Japonisme*. The exhibition *Art Nouveau 1890–1914*, held at the Victoria and Albert Museum, London, and the National Gallery of Art, Washington, in 2000, featured a portrait of Madame de Pompadour, the great patron of Rococo, painted by François Boucher. Typical features of Rococo, discussed in Chapter 1, were its use of rich materials and curvilinear forms, and its harmonious integration of painting, the decorative arts and fashion – all elements of seminal importance to Art Nouveau. The decorative motifs and patterns of *Japonisme*, with their use of asymmetrical line, bold, flat colours and stylized organic forms, had a tremendous impact on Art Nouveau.

Art Nouveau was also an offshoot of Symbolism, an influential literary and visual-arts movement that originated in France and flourished from about 1885 to about 1910. As a literary movement, it goes back at least to Baudelaire's poem 'Correspondance', from *Les Fleurs du mal,* and was continued by Arthur Rimbaud's *Saison en enfer* of 1873 and *Illuminations* of 1886, in which year a manifesto, 'Le Symbolisme', was published in *Le Figaro*. Symbolism's painters included Odilon Redon, Gustave Moreau and Pierre Puvis de Chavannes. Both writers and painters were inspired by the same kind of imagery. One dominant theme was the female figure, which, allied to nature, endowed Art Nouveau with a sense of mysticism and eroticism that informed the work of, for example, Lalique and Mucha.

Art Nouveau flourished in most of the countries of Western Europe and North America from the 1890s to World War I. The variety of names by which it was known across these countries attests to its eclectic character: Glasgow style (Scotland); *Modern style, Style nouille, Style coup de fouet* (Belgium); *Style Jules Verne, Style Métro, Style 1900, Art fin du siècle, Art belle époque* (France); *Jugenstil* (Germany and Austria); *Sezessionstil* (Austria); *Art joven* (Spain);

Modernisme (Catalonia); *Stile floreale, Stile Liberty* (Italy); and Tiffany style (United States). A large number of attractive periodicals published in these countries promoted and mirrored Art Nouveau. Among the best-known were *The Yellow Book, The Savoy, La Plume, Jugend, Dekorative Kunst, Deutsche Kunst und Dekoration* and *La Revue des arts décoratifs*.

In England, Aubrey Beardsley was the quintessential Art Nouveau artist, with his stylized black-and-white illustrations exuding the influence of Japanese prints and highly wrought Rococo ornament. It was, however, the outstanding writings on Aestheticism of the designer William Morris, championing the unity of the arts, and also of John Ruskin, that were so influential for the flourishing of Art Nouveau in England. When Europeans spoke of *le style anglais* they meant the bold, flowing designs and vivid colours of the textiles, wallpapers, embroideries, jewellery, stained glass and furniture produced by William Morris and members of the Arts and Crafts Movement. In 1877, William Morris gave his first public lecture, entitled 'The Decorative Arts'. It was later published as *The Lesser Arts*, with Morris's purpose being to reawaken the applied arts to a creative engagement with the fine arts. John Ruskin believed that the decorative arts should reclaim the central place in artistic importance that they had occupied during the Renaissance. The two leading members of the Aesthetic Movement in England, James Abbott McNeill Whistler and Oscar Wilde, exported the idea that a work should be judged by its formal criteria. For Whistler, discussed in Chapter 3, there was no aesthetic distinction between the beauty of a dress, a vase, a painting and an interior décor. In Austria, Art Nouveau made its appearance in the form of *Sezessionstil* – dominated by the figure of Gustav Klimt – and in the Wiener Werkstätte, co-founded by Josef Hoffmann and Koloman Moser.

Although Art Nouveau was flourishing in Belgium and growing elsewhere in Europe and the United States, the epicentre of the style was Paris. Pioneering work in the neo-Gothic revival by the French architect, designer and writer Eugène-Emmanuel Viollet-le-Duc had a considerable influence on contemporary design. The importance of his *lampas néo-Gothique*, shown at the Exposition Universelle in Paris in 1855, was documented in the exhibition *L'Art de la soie, Prelle 1752–2002*, held at the Musée Carnavalet, Paris, during 2002 and 2003.[6] His scholarly *Dictionnaire raisonné du mobilier français de l'époque carlovingienne à la Rénaissance* of 1858 had a significant impact on French attitudes to Art Nouveau. As well as furniture, it contained sections on goldsmiths' work, jewellery and clothing, with numerous accurate drawings by Viollet-le-Duc that perfectly complemented his writing. While his inspiration came from medieval models, the objects created, he argued, should be beautiful and modern. His preference for individually designed and hand-crafted work, and his advocacy of a total work of art, anticipated the theories of William Morris and the medieval-inspired guilds, such as C R Ashbee's Guild of Handicraft. The *Dictionnaire* eventually extended to six volumes, the last being published in 1875. Although Siegfried Bing did not invent the term Art Nouveau, it only came to be widely adopted when he chose to call his gallery/shop *La Maison de l'Art Nouveau,* which opened in Paris in 1895. This venue became 'the rallying-point for the creators and devotees of Art Nouveau'.[7] Henry Van de Velde designed the rooms and Louis Comfort Tiffany designed the stained glass for Bing's establishment, which promoted the work of a number of artists and designers. Paris was the centre of the art and fashion trade and the Exposition Universelle of 1900 held there, where Bing's pavilion brought together a number of artists and designers displaying furniture, textiles, jewellery and decorative objects as part of a total work of visual art, made Art Nouveau a French force. Bing's pavilion was greeted with great enthusiasm, with the *Revue des arts décoratifs* declaring 'nothing is superior to this exhibition of Art Nouveau'. 'An article such as this and the enormous success of the exhibition led Parisians to believe that Art Nouveau was a typically French style.'[8]

At the beginning of the 20th century advances in printing technology made it possible for fashion photographs to begin replacing fashion plates as both a means of mass communication and as an individual expression of the latest styles. The new, elegant French fashion magazine *Les Modes* tapped photography's potential for linking fashion to its immediate environment. Founded in Paris in 1901, it sold as well in London, Berlin and New York. Publishing half-tone photographs and tipped-in pages of colour photographs on high-quality glossy paper, in a substantial format measuring 11 by 14 inches (28 by 36cm), *Les Modes* featured *haute couture* and the arts, thus making it an excellent medium for the Art Nouveau notion of the all-encompassing work of visual art and the response to modern needs. The *beau monde* could see the latest fashions in an interior through the camera's lens. The fashion photographs of *Les Modes* reflected clearly the decorative element and sweeping lines of Art Nouveau that dominated women's fashions. Jacques Doucet was the *couturier par excellence* of this period, which came to be known in France as the *belle époque.* The photograph of his *Robe de diner en dentelle Venise* for the January 1903 issue of *Les Modes* picked up every flowing flounce and surface ornamentation of the lace. The pose of the model in the period chair, whose designs echo that of the dress, showed off the outline of the dress with its softly undulating curves in the S-shaped bend mirroring the sinuous line and the movement that were such important themes of Art Nouveau. Even the detail of the train of the dress was carefully arranged for the camera to draw the eye's attention to the intricate and lustrous quality of the Venetian lace. The photograph captured the ornate gossamer dress in a way that was reminiscent of Watteau, while the shimmer of the reflected light recalled an Impressionist portrait. Doucet was clearly stimulated by artistic developments and adapted his work to the design forms of the new art. This photograph, with its dazzling display, conveyed a totally new aesthetic of *le grand couturier.*

A major transformation in fashion in early-20th-century France was an elevation in the status of the *couturier*. Following the example of Charles

Jacques Doucet, Robe de diner en dentelle de Venise
(1903), photograph (from Les Modes, *January 1903).*
Fashion photography began to replace fashion plates
in the early 20th century and French magazine Les
Modes *featured* haute couture *and the arts.*

Frederick Worth, discussed in Chapters 2 and 3, the *couturier* shed his identity as
a tradesman and came to be regarded as an artist. A number of new fashion
houses were established by fashion designers – both male and female – who, in
the light of avant-garde art, came to be respected as artists themselves. In addition
to Doucet, their numbers included Madame Paquin, the Callot sisters and
Madeleine Chéruit, who had their fashions photographed by some of the leading
Parisian studios, such as Mlle Reutlinger and Boyer.[9] Their originality and flair for
exquisitely designed, glamorous, romantic clothes and accessories – especially
hats, scarves and boas, which described the Art Nouveau curve while reflecting the
features of the dress itself – made this an era of great refinement in *haute couture*
and confirmed Paris as the pre-eminent centre of fashion. Madame Paquin, for
example, was appointed President of the Fashion Section of the Exposition
Universelle held in Paris in 1900, and two years later opened branches of her
fashion house in London, Buenos Aires and Madrid. A number of artists worked
for her, including Léon Bakst, who designed dresses, and Paul Iribe and Georges

Lepape, who both contributed images for a deluxe album entitled *L'Éventail et la fourrure chez Paquin*. Her importance in the annals of French fashion and art was confirmed when she was awarded the Légion d'Honneur in 1913.[10]

However, the most exciting new *couturier* to emerge in the early years of the 20th century, both as a liberating force for fashion, and as a major influence on the interaction between art and fashion, was Paul Poiret. In his autobiography, Poiret maintained that his designs arose not from a desire to release women from the tyranny of the corset – the undergarment by which fashionable dress achieved the writhing line of Art Nouveau – but from a passionate search for a new form of beauty. It is significant that the great exhibition held at the Palais Galliera in Paris in 1986 devoted to Paul Poiret and his sister Nicole Groult should have as its sub-heading 'Maîtres de la Mode Art Déco' ('Masters of Art Deco Fashion'). Indeed, Poiret 'marked the beginning of a new era, not only in fashion but in its illustration too, heralding the birth of the style which is known today as *Art Deco*.'[11]

The term Art Deco has been used only since the late 1960s, when there was a revival of interest in the art and fashion of the early 20th century sparked by the 1966 exhibition held at the Musée des Arts Décoratifs in Paris entitled *Les Années '25': Art Déco/Bauhaus/Stijl/Esprit Nouveau*. It was a retrospective of works designed in the style that had been shown in Paris in 1925 at the Exposition Internationale des Arts Décoratifs et Industriels Modernes, which is the basis for the term, for this exhibition was known simply as the 'Les Arts Décos'. A weighty two-volume catalogue of the landmark 1966 exhibition was produced, of which volume one was entitled *Art Déco*. Art Deco identifies an aesthetic that was 'essentially French in origin.'[12]

Like its predecessor Art Nouveau, Art Deco was eclectic in character, encompassing a wide variety of the arts, and committed to creating a modern style based on a revitalized decorative language. Art Deco both emanated from Art Nouveau and reacted against it.

> 'Like Art Nouveau the decorative repertory of Art Deco was based on nature, but, whereas the former often derived its formal language from exotic flowers and plants whose twisting and climbing stems were usually integrated into the structure of an object, the latter was much more restrained, rejecting running motifs and climbing stems for stylised and geometricised flower blossoms, often roses, gathered up and tied into bouquets or in baskets.'[13]

Art Nouveau fell out of favour in the years preceding World War I. With an increasingly conservative political climate, Art Nouveau was deemed 'decadent' and 'over-elaborate', and was accused of failing to meet the demand for a modern national style in France. Indeed, a stipulation of the programme of the great Exposition Internationale des Arts Décoratifs et Industriels Modernes in 1925 was that everything included had to be 'modern' –

by implication ruling out objects in an Art Nouveau style. As early as 1912, a veteran of Art Nouveau in France, the decorator Paul Follot, recognized the need to modernize tradition and adapt designs to the machine age. He designed a dining-room ensemble with a motif of geometric baskets of fruits and flowers, which was exhibited that year at the *Salon d'Automne*. He also jettisoned the pale tones of Art Nouveau for bright, vivid colours – an influence stemming from the Fauves ('wild beasts'), a term coined by the French art critic Louis Vauxcelles to describe a group of young painters, including Henri Matisse (generally regarded as the leader) and André Derain, who showed their paintings featuring bold colours for the first time in Paris at the *Salon d'Automne* in 1905. Art Deco drew on many other sources, such as the pictorial conventions of contemporary avant-garde art – not only of Fauvism, but also of Cubism, Futurism and Constructivism. In addition, tradition was not abandoned altogether, and historical styles such as ancient Greek sculpture and the Neo-classicism of the *Directoire* period (see Chapter 1) in France, non-European cultures such as Africa and the archaeological discoveries of the tomb of Tutankhamun by Howard Carter in Egypt in 1922, which fuelled a romantic fascination with all things Egyptian, were all pivotal in the development of Art Deco. Of seminal importance across the Art Deco period were the performing arts. The arrival of the Ballets Russes in Paris in 1909 introduced the exotic and rich colours of the costumes and sets designed by Léon Bakst, which were conceived as a complete visual unit. The following year their season included performances of *Schéhérezade* (Rimsky-Korsakov), for which Bakst produced a Persian-inspired design that resulted in an absolute mania for all things Oriental, influencing painting, architecture, interior design and fashion.

A study of the development of Art Deco shows how closely it was linked to transformations in fashion and how art and fashion nurtured each other. Indeed, the exhibition *Art Deco 1910–1939*, held in several museums around the world in 2003–05, placed fashion at the heart of the exhibition. The exhibition curators could have pushed back the date in its title to at least 1907, when the great Exposition Internationale des Arts Décoratifs et Industriels Modernes was first conceived, and when Paul Poiret was 'waging war' on the *gache sarraute* or corset, and perceptibly shifting the S-bend silhouette of Art Nouveau to a vertical line, raising the waistline above its natural level and introducing a narrower, straighter outline.

Poiret had served an apprenticeship under Jacques Doucet from 1898 to 1900, and had worked at *La Maison Worth* in 1901, before opening his own fashion house in 1903. By getting rid of the *gache sarraute* he was, in effect, reflecting a movement in fashion away from the softness of Art Nouveau taste in the fine and decorative arts and looking towards the geometric shapes of Cubism, which Pablo Picasso was already developing in close association with Georges Braque.

Jettisoning the *gache sarraute* was his first great 'revolution', as he called it in his autobiography:

'The last representative of this abominable apparatus was called the *Gache Sarraute*. It divided the wearer into two distinct masses: on the one side there was the bust and bosom, on the other, the whole behindward aspect, so that the lady looked as if she were hauling a trailer. It was almost a return to the bustle. Like all the great revolutions, that one had been made in the name of Liberty – to give free play to the abdomen: it was equally in the name of Liberty that I proclaimed the fall of the corset and the adoption of the *brassière* which, since then, has won the day.'[14]

The silhouette Poiret developed was inspired by the high-waisted dresses in the Neo-classical taste of the *Directoire* period, and is referred to in France as the *Directoire* Revival. Poiret related in his autobiography how his father, a cloth merchant, had sent him to work for an umbrella-maker. Poiret hated the work but was often able to escape to the Musée du Louvre to study paintings and ancient sculpture.

'While studying sculptures of ancient times, I learned to use one point of support – the shoulders, while before me it had been the waist. All my gowns flowed from that point of support at the extremity of the shoulders and were never fastened at the waist. This new basic principle caused fashion to evolve toward classical antiquity ... Fabrics flowed from this ideal point like water from a fountain and draped the body in a way that was entirely natural.'[15]

Among Poiret's precocious gifts was that of a painter. Having an affinity with painters, he was the first *couturier* to relate fashion successfully to the other arts. Among the many artists with whom he was associated and whose works he collected were Paul Iribe, Georges Lepape, Edouardo Benito, Man Ray, Edward Steichen, Raoul Dufy, Erté, Constantin Brancusi, Kees van Dongen, Boutet de Monvel, Pierre and Jacques Brissaud, André Dunoyer de Segonzac, Henri Matisse, Amedeo Modigliani, Francis Picabia, Jean Metzinger, Jean-Louis Boussingault, Bernard Naudin, Marie Laurencin, Robert Delaunay, Roger de la Fresnaye, Luc-Albert Moreau, André Derain and Pablo Picasso. He recalled in his autobiography his reception of artists and his creation around him of a 'movement'. 'Am I a fool when I dream of putting art into my dresses, a fool when I say dressmaking is an art ... For I have always loved painters and felt on an equal footing with them. It seems to me that we practise the same craft and that they are my fellow workers.'[16]

Another of Poiret's innovations was the rejuvenation of fashion illustration, with the help of artists, demonstrating his belief in the interaction of art and fashion. As we saw in Chapters 1 and 2, fashion illustration had reached its apogee in the fashion plates of Pierre de La Mésangère's *Le Journal des dames et des modes*. The hand-coloured plates were noted for their accuracy and aesthetic appeal, directly relating fashions to the *beau monde* through the use of contemporary settings drawn by a small group of artists who were outstanding draughtsmen. However, as the 19th century progressed, fashion illustration degenerated with the closure of *Le Journal des dames et des modes* and the application of photography. Poiret must have studied the fashion plates of the *Directoire* period with their elegant interiors in *Le Journal des dames et des modes* when he was serving his apprenticeship with Doucet. The setting of Doucet's *maison de couture,* Poiret recalled, 'was composed of engravings and pictures of the 18th century, and of rare and ancient furniture'.[17] Doucet's library, now in the University of Paris, is the only institutional library in France with a complete set of *Le Journal des dames et des modes* for the *Directoire* period. So important was this period to Poiret that the Russian artist Erté noted in his autobiography that when he came to work for Poiret, 'all the *salons* in his fashion house were in the *Directoire* style'.[18] Poiret had relocated his fashion business in 1906 from the rue Auber to the rue Pasquier, but when Erté came to work for Poiret in 1913, he was ensconced in yet another *couture* house, to which he had moved in around 1908–09, a majestic 18th-century *hôtel* on the Avenue d'Antin in the Faubourg Saint-Honoré where he would remain for the next 20 years. He had had it renovated in the *Directoire* style, with Neo-classical interiors by the architect, interior decorator, furniture and textile designer Louis Süe. Süe's aim was the same as that of the Atelier Français, which he went on to found in Paris in 1912 – namely, to create a modern style that evoked French design traditions. This is suggested by the following description of Poiret's new *couture* house:

'The walls [of one of the *salons* on the ground floor], decorated with panels of Nile green, are enriched by frames threaded with dark green and antiqued gold. On the floor, a raspberry-coloured carpet, on the windows, taffeta curtains in the same tone. The very clear opposition of these colours, the one neutral and the other hot, produced a bizarre atmosphere, at once soft and vibrant, and which must harmonise happily with the fresh and buoyant colours from which Poiret likes to take his effects. The furnishings belong to that delicious *Directoire* period that recalls the scarcely vanished graces of the Louis XVI era, and does not yet do more than presage the severe correction of the Empire. The chairs, covered in strawberry and green striped velvet, correspond to the general tonality, while here and there Oriental embroideries and marquetries play and change lustre.'[19]

With his artistic flair Poiret recognized the need to renew fashion illustration along the lines of *Le Journal des dames et des modes*. He commissioned two magnificent albums of his designs: *Les Robes de Paul Poiret racontées par Paul Iribe* in 1908 and *Les Choses de Paul Poiret vues par Georges Lepape* in 1911. The importance accorded to the artists is immediately recognized in the titles of the publications: the gowns of Paul Poiret 'as related by Paul Iribe' and the things of Paul Poiret 'as seen by Georges Lepape'. These were luxurious albums produced by the *pochoir* process.

'In *pochoir,* stencils separated the colours for reproduction. The colours, both opaque and transparent, were applied by hand, by daubing, spraying, stippling or sponging to achieve various effects. Sometimes black outlines were first printed in lithography. The concept of *pochoir* is simple, but the application can be very complicated and time-consuming. However, the result is stunning: vibrantly rich colours, often indistinguishable from original watercolours and gouaches.'[20]

In 'Three Directoire Gowns by Paul Poiret', Iribe has grouped the mannequins in a sparse *Directoire*-style interior imparting distinctly modern overtones, and has left large areas of the background empty, thus showing the high quality of the handmade paper, a technique reminiscent of the fashion plates of the *Directoire* period in La Mésangère's *Le Journal des dames et des modes*. The Poiret gowns are made in either plain, bold colours akin to the palette of the Fauve painters or with small geometrical designs, and are very simple with the waistline high and the skirt long and tubular in shape. The models also suggest the *Directoire* period in their hairstyles of loose curls set off by Grecian-style fillets. Iribe was an artist who was also a fashion designer and illustrator and an interior decorator. Particularly fond of the *Directoire* era, his album fuelled much contemporary interest in these historical styles of dress and décor.

While evolving his *Directoire* style, Poiret had also been developing his other passion, Orientalism. Long before the arrival of the Ballets Russes in Paris in 1909 with their exotic colours and themes, Poiret was innovating in fashion with Eastern-inspired clothing. While still working for the House of Worth he designed a cloak which he called 'Confucius' (1901–02), and at his own fashion house in the rue Auber in Paris he designed a kimono coat which he called 'Révérend' (1905). As a painter himself, Poiret went back to artistic sources to achieve his own particular interpretation of Oriental themes in fashion. The richly decorated hats of Art Nouveau were an anathema to his style, and so he revived the wearing of turbans, a popular accessory of the original *Directoire* period, influenced by the Egyptian campaigns of the Emperor Napoléon and delightfully illustrated in *Le Journal des dames et des modes* from 1797 to 1799. In addition to studying fashion plates, Poiret also visited the Victoria and Albert Museum in London to view the fine collection of Indian turbans. Both in his dress and headwear designs, Poiret anticipated many elements of the pared-down style of the 1920s. The results of his contribution to the development of fashion, as well as to other aesthetic areas, can be seen in 'The Cushions' from *Les Choses de Paul Poiret vues par Georges Lepape*. The angular model emphasizes perfectly the elongated line of Poiret's plain *Directoire* gown with its simple ornamentation of blue beads outlining the high waistline and set off by a turban with a design of small blue circles. The geometrical precision of their scheme echoes the interior itself. What is also interesting is the way Lepape, who had studied at the École des Beaux-Arts under Fernand-Piestre Cormon (whose former pupils had included Matisse), anchored the figure in her environment, and so exquisitely harmonized the clothes with the beautifully conceived interior. More than just showcasing Poiret's fashions, Lepape interpreted his ideas, successfully implementing the Art Deco shapes and motifs of furnishings, clothing and accessories into a unified whole.

Right: Three Directoire Gowns, *fashion plate (pochoir process) from* Les Robes de Paul Poiret racontées par Paul Iribe, *1908 (Chrysalis Image Library). Paul Poiret rejuvenated fashion illustration, acknowledging the importance of the artist.*

The inspiration Poiret derived from the simplicity of *Directoire* and Oriental clothing contributed to more physical freedom in women's fashionable dress – which is usually attributed to the social impact of World War I – and ultimately to the establishment of the foundations of modern fashion. In January 1911, Poiret launched a collection in which he introduced the 'pantaloon gown'. Other names given to this fashion were the *jupe-culotte*, the 'trouser skirt' and the 'harem skirt'. They were included again in his August collection and proved so popular that he was inundated with orders. The pantaloon gown enabled women to walk properly, to enjoy the growing popularity of sports such as tennis and to dance the new craze, the tango. In his *Les Choses de Paul Poiret*, Lepape included a drawing of four different pantaloon gowns (shown on page 122). Perceptively called 'Celles de demain' ('Fashions of Tomorrow'), Poiret's design and cut shows not only the harmony of the bold colours of Fauvism and the linear vision of Cubism, but also the creation of a real style for the modern woman, years before it entered the mainstream of clothes design. Poiret's two albums had a decisive impact on Art Deco illustration. 'The success of these books stimulated interest in, and extensive use of, the [*pochoir*] process in all fields of graphic arts at the time.'[21]

A more immediate impact on the world of art and fashion was made when Poiret was instrumental in getting Iribe's album exhibited at the *Salon d'Automne* in 1909. In 1910 a commercial gallery, the Galerie Barbazanges, was founded on Poiret's premises, and he exhibited the original drawings of Lepape's album in 1911 together with works by the notable graphic designers Bernard Boutet de Monvel and Pierre and Jacques Brissaud. Poiret's reputation as an important patron of contemporary art, especially of its avant-garde tendencies, as well as an innovator in art and fashion, was confirmed in 1916 when he sponsored at the Galerie Barbazanges an exhibition organized by the critic and poet André Salmon entitled *Salon d'Autin: L'Art Moderne en France*. It featured a veritable 'who's who' of the contemporary art scene: Amedeo Modigliani, Henri Matisse, André Derain, Fernand Léger, Gino Severini and André Lhôte. It also included two of his closest collaborators in art and fashion, Raoul Dufy and Kees van Dongen, as well as Pablo Picasso, who first unveiled there his groundbreaking Cubist work *Les Demoiselles d'Avignon* (1907), which Jacques Doucet bought directly from the artist in 1924.[22] Poiret's innovations also led in 1920 to an exhibition at the Musée des Arts Décoratifs of artists who were also fashion illustrators, followed by an annual *Salon de la mode*.

In addition, a whole host of artistic fashion magazines were launched, such as *La Gazette du bon ton, arts, modes et frivolités* sponsored by a group of seven of the most important *couturiers* in France of the pre-World War I period, including Doucet, Paquin and Poiret. It used the same style and printing method as Poiret's albums and furthered his idea of using fresh artistic talent that included not only Iribe and Lepape but also of others in his circle such as Bernard Boutet de Monvel, George Barbier, André Marty, H Robert Dammy, Erté, Pierre Brissaud, Étienne Drian, Charles Martin and Eduardo Benito.

Paul Poiret, Evening Coat, lithograph by Raoul Dufy, Croquis No. VII from La Gazette du bon ton, No. 1, January/February 1920 (Chrysalis Image Library)

Paul Poiret, Fashions of Tomorrow, *fashion plate (*pochoir *process) from* Les Choses de Paul Poiret vues par Georges Lepape, *1911 (Private Collection)*

'The *pochoir* illustrations in particular were presented not simply as renditions of existing or imagined garments but as 'veritable portraits of dresses by the most subtle artists of our time'. *La Gazette du bon ton* thus embodied Poiret's strategic and theoretical alignment of contemporary fashion and art under the sign of late eighteenth and nineteenth-century French design traditions.'[23]

When Poiret held a party in 1914 to celebrate the first 18 months of *La Gazette du bon ton*, the writer Henry Bidou, in an article with drawings by André Marty, stressed 'the enduring nature of transitory fashion, whose memory survives, even when historical events have been forgotten'. Nancy Troy has demonstrated in her book *Couture Culture* how Bidou's ideas linking the ephemerality of fashion to the timelessness of art 'clearly recall the terms in which Charles Baudelaire had written of fashion more than fifty years earlier in "The Painter of Modern Life".'[24] In 1920, *La Gazette du bon ton* also published 11 watercolour drawings by the Fauve artist Raoul Dufy of fashions designed by Poiret. Meanwhile, a newly revitalised *Le Journal des dames et des modes* had made a comeback in 1912, with fashion plates *au pochoir* designed by such artistic luminaries as Léon Bakst, George Barbier and Paul Iribe. Other innovative magazines included *Art-Goût-Beauté, L'Art et la mode, Les Élégances parisiennes, Vogue* and *Femina*, which produced some of the most stylish Art Deco covers.[25]

Improvements in techniques meant that fashion photography would continue to be a commanding platform for artistic expression. The Ballets Russes, for example, commissioned the pioneering photographer baron Adolph de Meyer – noted for back-lit photographs that gave his sitters and their dress a luminous glow worthy of romantic portraiture – to make a photographic series of their most famous dancer, Nijinsky, which were published in art magazines. Poiret saw fashion photography as another exciting medium through which to express his ideas. Many of the photographers he worked with were also painters, such as Edward Steichen and Man Ray, and the influence of Poiret's interest in fashion plates and his work in fashion illustration, especially with Lepape, was clear. An outstanding example is Poiret's collaboration with Steichen, one of the most prominent fashion photographers of the 20th century, in 1911. They worked out a soft-focus technique and Poiret supervised the backgrounds and the poses of his models. Steichen photographed them as in a *tableau*, as seen for instance in 'Robe Strozzi' (seen on page 124) which appeared in *Art et décoration* in April 1911, a well-respected magazine devoted to the fine and decorative arts. The gown was overlaid with two tunics in differing lengths and colours, and edged with shimmering diamonds. The turban topped with an *aigrette* complements the elongation of the *Directoire* ensemble and harmonizes with the decorative scheme of the room. The backdrop was a *salon* in Poiret's *maison de couture*, and Steichen shows to advantage one of the beautiful *Directoire* interiors that so impressed Erté. Steichen's photographs were accompanied by an article entitled 'L'Art de la robe' written by Paul Cornu, a friend of Poiret's, who was librarian of the Union

Costumes Parisiens 64

use de satin blanc brodée. Jupe drapée de cachemire de soie

Fashion plate (pochoir process) by A. Vallée from Le Journal des dames et des modes, *1913, Plate 64 (Private Collection)*

Centrale des Arts Décoratifs in Paris, and who edited, about 1912, a reproduction of *La Gallerie des modes* (1778–87), printed in the exact hues of the original.

As the title of Cornu's article suggests, he was addressing Poiret's interaction of art and fashion. In particular, he was drawing attention to the influence of contemporary graphic designers on the fashion photography of Steichen by featuring ink drawings made specially for the purpose by Lepape, as well as several of his drawings from *Les Choses de Paul Poiret vues par Georges Lepape*.

During 1911–12 Poiret made a fashion tour of European capitals and in 1913 his fashion business took him to the United States. He was the first *couturier* to promote fashion through tours accompanied by models trained in their profession, and his whirlwind peregrinations through Europe were nicknamed 'Poiret's Mannequin Circus'.[26] While in Rome he went to the International Exhibition and 'when he saw the Klimt room … he sensed a remarkable harmony between Parisian and Viennese designs'.[27] Vienna, which had emerged at the turn of the century as a great cultural centre with international repercussions, was a major stop in Poiret's tour. The success of Klimt and the Vienna Secession, and the achievements of the Wiener Werkstätte, were heralded by Berta Zuckerkandl, a member of the artistic and literary milieu of Vienna:

> 'It was logical that the spirit of the Klimt group should lead to the creation of the Wiener Werkstätte dress. The leading artists of Vienna have raised the frippery of fashion to a noble craft. They have even created outstanding fabrics, unique in colour and ornamentation, for their original designs. They have utterly changed the concept of accessories through the batik sashes, knitted belts and novel passementerie. They have taught us to realise that design determines the character of the dress. These dresses, coats, sashes and hats work because they are decorative distillations of an idea of our time. Through careful, conscious design, fashion has become style.'[28]

Poiret paid a visit to the Wiener Werkstätte, which had opened a fully fledged textile division in 1909 and a fashion department in 1910 under the direction of Eduard-Josef Wimmer-Wisgrill. 'I went to all the exhibitions of the decorative arts. It was then that I made the acquaintance of the chiefs of the schools, such as Josef Hoffmann, the creator and director of the Wiener Werkstätte … and Gustav Klimt.'[29] What interested Poiret about the Wiener Werkstätte were the hand-printed silk floral designs and, as someone committed to the idea of fashion as part of the artistic creation in general, the emphasis on the environment, from furnishings to dress, as a total work of art. The Wiener Werkstätte 'followed the general stylistic trends of the times … and … put the brake on Art Nouveau exuberance and introduced a more restrained geometric inventiveness.'[30]

Elements of the Art Nouveau visual language of naturalistic decoration were adapted to the linear, geometric variant characteristic of Art Deco. This was the beginning of a cross-fertilization in fashion design between Paris and Vienna, where the pure lines and exceptional artistry of the Wiener Werkstätte began to

Paul Poiret, Robe Strozzi, *1911, photograph: Edward Steichen (from* Art et Décoration, *April 1911). Steichen was one of the prominent fashion photographers of the early 20th century. Here designer Paul Poiret has supervised the background and the pose of the model.*

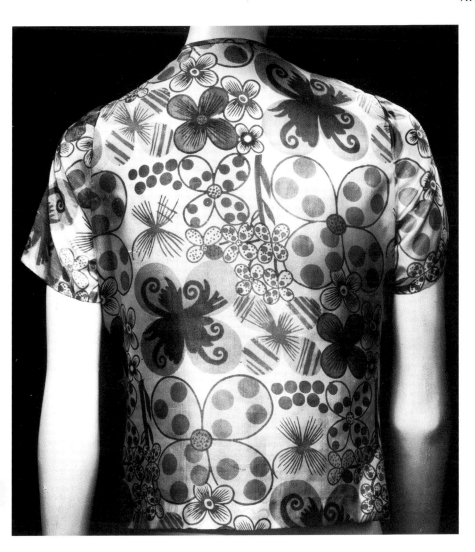

Lady's Printed Silk Blouse from the Wiener Werkstätte *(c. 1918)*, *(The Metropolitan Museum of Art, New York, Gift of Mrs Federica Beer-Monti). Paul Poiret was particularly interested in the silk floral prints of the Wiener Werkstätte, which had opened a textile division in 1909.*

affect international fashion. The development of textile design during this period is fundamental to subsequent changes in fashion and interior design.[31]

Berta Zuckerkandl attests that Poiret was so impressed with the Wiener Werkstätte hand-printed silks that he not only ordered them in large quantities but also used them in *haute couture*.[32] A coat of Poiret's, lined with Wiener Werkstätte material designed by Dagobert Peche, was an eloquent testament to the influence of Vienna on Paris. And Poiret's dramatic theatre coat of 1912, based on the loose, unstructured drapery of the kimono, had an influence on the robes and kimonos of Hoffmann and Peche. The Vienna/Paris axis also included an invitation from Poiret for an exhibition of Viennese fashions in his *maison de couture*.[33] It was Zuckerkandl, in fact, who had introduced Poiret to Hoffmann, Klimt and the Wiener Werkstätte circle. 'Very soon the close connection between the

Fashion plate (pochoir *process) by George Barbier
from* Le Journal des dames et des modes, *1913,
Plate 84 (Private Collection). Le Journal had been
revitalized in 1912 and, like the new, innovative
magazines, produced some of the most stylish Art
Deco covers.*

style of Poiret and that of the Klimt group became obvious ... Through Paul Poiret the Austrian taste was once again brought into contact with the French tradition.'[34]

Shortly after his return to Paris, Poiret called on Madame Sérusier, the wife of the painter Paul Sérusier, to help him realize his dream of 'creating a new fashion in decorating and furnishing in France'.[35] Paul Sérusier had met Gauguin in Pont-Aven in 1888 and became the principal theorist of the Nabis, a movement of painters that included Pierre Bonnard, Maurice Denis and Édouard Vuillard. Sérusier blended the ideas of Symbolism with Paul Gauguin's theory of expressive colour. He rejected any distinction between the fine and decorative arts, and emphasized surface pattern and decoration in his work. Madame Sérusier taught in schools in Paris and recommended to Poiret a group of working-class girls, whom she proceeded to teach in his house. When she gave up the project Poiret did not replace her but scoured the working-class districts of Paris himself for girls who had finished their schooling.

> 'I set aside several rooms in my house for them, and I put them to work copying nature without any teacher. Naturally, their parents soon discovered they were wasting their time, and I had to promise them stipends and prizes. I rewarded the best designs. Free to do as they liked, I discovered all the spontaneity of their natures.'[36]

The École Martine and the Atelier Martine (named after his daughter) were founded, with the girls providing naïve, stylized floral designs in bold colours that were sold as textiles, fans, wallpapers and curtains. Poiret also diversified into make-up and was the first *couturier* to launch a perfume, which he called Rosine (named after another daughter). With Raoul Dufy, he established a workshop for printing textiles, which they called La Petite Usine (The Little Factory). Dufy's talent lay essentially in the decorative arts, something Poiret recognized when saw his woodcuts, with their flat stylization, in the edition of Guillaume Apollinaire's *Le Bestaire ou Cortège d'Orphée (The Bestiary or Parade of Orpheus)* that was published in 1910. With the aid of a chemist proficient in 'colouring matters, lithographic inks, aniline dyes, fats and acids', Poiret and Dufy printed textiles in graphic designs that were incorporated into *haute couture*.[37] Dufy often worked with the Martines, as Poiret called his girls, on specific commissions, with Dufy in overall charge of the projects. Although he continued to collaborate with Poiret, Dufy's great success at La Petite Usine led to his employment between 1912 and 1928 with the great silk firm Bianchini-Férier in Lyons. The astounding range of his output was displayed in the exhibition *Raoul Dufy 1877–1953* at the Hayward Gallery, London in 1983–84, and at the sales of his works at Christie's, London in 2001 and 2003.

Poiret was at the centre of art and fashion in Paris when World War I broke out. After the war, he resumed his fashion designing, and a synthesis of his work was presented at the Exposition Internationale des Arts Décoratifs et Industriels Modernes in 1925, the criteria for which, as discussed earlier, stressed the need for 'modern' inspiration and showcased France's leading artistic talents over a sixth-month period. French fashion had reached such a peak of excellence that it was accorded its own exhibition area, with the catalogue stating: 'this superiority [of French fashion design] rightly entitles fashion to a privileged showing'.[38]

With the Pavillon de l'Élégance featuring creations by *couturières* such as Jeanne Lanvin, Jeanne Paquin, the Callot sisters and Madeleine Vionnet, and *haute couture* by Poiret presented in three barges moored on the banks of the River Seine at the Quai d'Orsay, fashion was assured a prominent role. The barges were sumptuously decorated by Dufy and the Martines. The barge named for the occasion *Amours* (Loves) was devoted to interior design; *Délices* (Delights) housed a magnificent restaurant; and *Orgues* (Organs) exhibited 14 *tentures* or wall hangings designed by Dufy, depicting Poiret's fashions in settings found in the artist's paintings such as racecourses and regattas. The organizers of the Exposition were fulsome in acknowledging their debt to Poiret. 'It is possible to hold this event only because of the impetus that Poiret has given to modern decorative arts by founding the Martine School and Shop and encouraging professional interior decoration.'[39]

The Exposition brought together thousands of designs from all over Europe and beyond. More specifically, it was a government-sponsored event with the precise aim of showcasing Paris as the most internationally fashionable of cities, and of establishing the pre-eminence of French art and fashion in the aftermath of World War I. Millions of Americans and Europeans and hundreds of international manufacturers visited the Exposition, which has often been called a 'shoppers' paradise'. French department stores ('museums for people') and a 'rue des Boutiques' ('shopping centres for modern women') along the Pont Alexandre III were represented, with carefully orchestrated window displays intended to underline Paris's position as a world centre for shopping.

One eye-catching boutique contained the work of the painter, designer and printmaker Sonia Delaunay. In 1924 she had established her Atelier Simultané with four directors, among them the distinguished *courturier* Jacques Heim, who shared her 'inclination for interesting juxtapositions of geometrics and colours'. Producing textiles, interior decoration and clothing, she was of the belief that there should be 'no differentiation between the artistic merit of her paintings and her textile and fashion designs'.[40] At the *Salon d'Automne* in 1924 she displayed her textiles on rotating devices. These exhibits of her fabrics 'in motion' were the smash hit of the *Salon*. Next she designed a range of textiles, accessories and stunning clothes for her Boutique Simultané, in collaboration with Jacques Heim, which was a highlight of the fashion section of the Exposition Internationale in 1925. Her models wore her striking fashion designs that combined the geometrical language of the avant-garde with short, modern, flexible cuts. They posed before appropriately modern settings, showing the close harmony of her work with decorative symbols of the day, such as Cubist concrete trees designed by the sculptors Joel and Jan Martel in collaboration with the architect Robert Mallet-

Jeanne Lanvin, Silk Taffeta Robe de Style (1927), (Cincinnati Art Museum, Gift of Mrs Raymond M. Lull). Lanvin's creations were featured at the Pavillon de l'Élégance, an Exposition that aimed to prove that Paris was the most fashionable city in the world.

Stevens, or a car she herself had painted in her 'simultaneous' pattern. She was a celebrated exponent of Orphism, a term coined in 1913 by Guillaume Apollinaire to describe a form of abstract painting with Cubist affinities and originally inspired by the work of Robert Delaunay, her husband, which advocated colour as the primary means of artistic expression. Their geometric designs in brilliantly coloured hues were based on the theory of the simultaneous contrast of colours formulated by the 19th-century French chemist Michel-Eugène Chevreul and published under the title *De la loi du contraste simultané des couleurs (The law of the simultaneous contrast of colours)* (1839). It was the kinetic element of the visual flow created by contrasting blocks of colour that fascinated Sonia Delaunay. Her originality lay in her concept of *tissu patron*, or fabric pattern, whereby the cut of the garment was conceived simultaneously with its design. The cut of the garment and the decoration, suited to the shape, were both printed on the same fabric. Perfectly complementing the newly planar forms and cylindrical, waistless silhouette of women's fashions of the 1920s – as well as the spirit of the time in the terms critics used to refer to it, such as 'Style Moderne', 'Jazz Moderne', or 'Zigzag Moderne' – Sonia Delaunay made a significant impact on how art and fashion could overlap and influence each other. 'She was a pioneer of the new painterly style, in which fashion fabrics were covered in careful combinations of different colours in ingenious primary shapes.'[41]

As a testimony to her renown in art and fashion, she was in 1925 the subject of an album of twenty plates made by the hand-stencilling technique, *pochoir*, entitled *Sonia Delaunay, ses peintures, ses objects, ses tissus simultanés, ses modes (Sonia Delaunay, her paintings, her objects, her simultaneous fabrics, her fashions)*. It was edited by the artist André Lhôte, and he wrote this tribute to her creative spirit as an artist and as a fashion designer:

> 'We must thank Sonia Delaunay for her constant inventiveness, the discreet gaiety which she brought to women's fashion, the agreeable way in which she covered the soft undulations of the human body with a geometrical architecture, and the rightness and unexpectedness of her colour contrasts. But at a time when the Exposition des Arts Décoratifs appears to more attentive observers as a homage from all the countries of the world to the Cubist School, we must give her our special thanks for having, in a pleasantly roundabout way, obliged the public to take an interest, against its will, in the most generous painterly manifestations of our time.'[42]

Sonia Delaunay's fame continued to spread: her silk fabric was printed for Chanel in 1925, and she designed clothes for the film and theatre actresses Gloria Swanson, Gaby, Paulette Pax, Gabrielle Dorziat and Lucienne Bogaert, as well as Nancy Cunard, an icon of the 1920s. She was invited in 1927 to give a lecture to the Visual Art Department of the Sorbonne; she entitled her lecture 'The Influence of Painting on Fashion Design'. She spoke about the liberation of fashion from 'academic *couture*' and, in her discussion of her concept of fabric pattern,

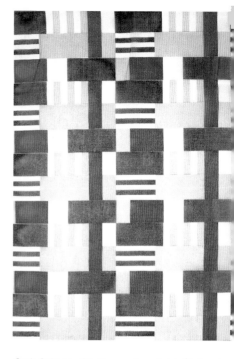

Sonia Delaunay, Silk Organza Dress Fabric (designed 1925–1927), screen-printed by Ascher Ltd of London, 1967 (V & A Picture Library, London). A painter, designer and printmaker, Delaunay had an inclination for interesting juxtapositions of geometrics and colour.

introduced the idea of *prêt-à-porter* ('ready to wear'), which she had inaugurated with her husband. She also foresaw the future trends in art and fashion.

> 'A movement is now influencing fashion, just as it influences interior decoration, the cinema and all the visual arts, and it overtakes everything that is not subject to this new principle which painters have spent a century seeking; we are only at the beginning of the study of these new colour relationships, still full of mysteries to unravel, which are at the base of a modern vision.'[43]

Sonia Delaunay remained active in her support for the theoretical underpinnings of the relationship between art and fashion in a substantial number of publications, including 'Tissus et tapis', which appeared in *Art d'aujourd'hui, art et architecture* in 1929 and *Sonia Delaunay: Compositions, Couleurs, Idées (Compositions, Colours, Ideas)*, an album she produced in 1930.

Themes of the exhibition *Souvenirs muscovites 1860–1930*, held at the Palais Galliera in Paris from October 1999 to February 2000, included fashion in Russia under the last three czars, its influence on Parisian fashion, and the role of Russian *emigrés* in Parisian *couture* during the 1920s. The artist Natalia Goncharova was one of the *emigrés* who had considerable influence in Paris. Famed for her costumes for the Ballets Russes, she also turned to fashion design and from 1922 to 1926 she worked for the Maison Myrbor, which exhibited at the Exposition in 1925. Her vibrant designs for Myrbor were described as a 'changing exhibit of modern art'. The arrival of the Russian Constructivists Varvara Stepanova, Liubov-Sergeevna Popova and Alexander Rodchenko, whose clothing was also displayed in 1925, while not having the impact of Natalia Goncharova because of their lack of experience in fashion, nevertheless astonished those who saw their work, and they were an influence on the *Abstraction-Création* group in France. The aim of the Constructivists, as described in their *Realist Manifesto*, was to 'construct' art by conceiving a purely geometric, abstract art that reflected modern machinery and technology, and by applying this to the social and industrial needs of the time, integrating it with architecture and with the design of clothing.[44]

One of the chief characteristics of the 1925 Exposition was the dominance of women fashion designers in the revitalization of Parisian elegance. Jeanne Lanvin, Jeanne Paquin, the Callot sisters and Madeleine Vionnet, who was to occupy centre-stage in art and fashion, all had their glamorous designs mounted on Siégel mannequins especially made for the exhibit by André Vigneau. Critics noted the particular influence of Cubism on their work:

> 'But short, flat, geometrical, rectangular, women's clothing took the parallelogram as its template, and 1925 will not welcome the return of a fashion of soft curves' ... Colette wrote in *Vogue*. Reduced to its most basic lines, this vision was quite precise, and provided a good definition of *couture* as it appeared to the astonished viewers in certain paintings by Braque or Picasso.'[45]

Richard Martin, in the catalogue of the exhibition *Cubism and Fashion* held at the Metropolitan Museum of Art in New York from December 1998 to March 1999, demonstrated how the fundamental traits of Cubism in art translated into fashion and in particular how Madeleine Vionnet's fashion forms and silhouettes exemplified Cubism's interpretation of the body.[46] Freedom of movement was her priority, and this dovetailed with the increasing social emancipation of women and the general trend towards liberalism that were hallmarks of the 1920s, and pivotal to the evolution of Art Deco fashion. Vionnet's interest lay in classical dress and she experimented with its characteristics of simplicity and draping, so much so that her fashions were often likened to the sculpture of Cubism. Her clothes were illustrated by the Futurist artist Thayaht (Ernesto Michelles) in *La Gazette du bon ton*, who brought out the fluid movement and geometry of her designs.

As well as his importance in fashion illustration, Thayaht was also an artistic influence on fashion designers. He arrived in Paris after World War I and worked with Madeleine Vionnet from 1921 to 1925. Futurism was an Italian avant-garde movement founded in 1909 by the writer and poet F T Marinetti. Although originating as a literary movement, the dominant figures were visual artists, most notably Gino Severini, Giacomo Balla and Umberto Boccioni. Futurism also embraced sculpture, architecture, music, the cinema, photography and fashion. Their primary aim, outlined in a series of manifestos, was the celebration of modern technology, and the rendering of movement was a key concern of the Futurist painters, whose emphasis was on giving the impression of speed and the representation of successive phases of movement and, like Cubist painting, on the interpretation of shifting planes. Thayaht was one of this group, along with Giacomo Balla and Fortunato Depero, who also designed clothing. Futurist theories extending visual ideas previously explored in paint and sculpture – such as diagonals and spirals – to dress, proved ideal for the interaction of art and fashion, especially when imparted to a *couturière* of the stature of Madeleine Vionnet. For her method involved the draping of fabrics such as muslin on an artist's lay doll that was mounted on a revolving piano stool. Those who observed her at work likened her to a sculptress moulding her designs to achieve a modern Grecian silhouette that took its shape from the body. Madeleine Vionnet's style came to fruition with her development of the bias cut, a cut across the grain of the fabric. This allowed the material to cascade in vertical, graceful folds, thus aligning her technique (of cutting cloth on abstract lines with diagonal seaming) to classical Greek sources, Cubism and Futurism. She had begun experimenting in the early 1920s with cutting a dress in the bias of the material, a method until then only used in the making of collars, sleeves, gores and borders. Vionnet's bias-cut dresses were figure-hugging and moved sensuously with the body's contours. French bias-cut dresses were a great influence on the American cinema, and the bias-cut dress featured in Hollywood films of the era, for example, those designed in slinky silver-satin by Gilbert Adrian for the actress Jean Harlow. The influence of fashion in the cinema also worked in the opposite direction.

Madeleine Vionnet, Silk Velvet Bias-Cut Evening Dress (1927), (Cincinnati Art Museum, Gift of Dorette Kruse Fleischmann in Memory of Julius Fleischmann). When designing clothes, Vionnet's priority was the freedom of movement given to the women wearing her clothes.

Romantic images of fantasy and illusion, in time of political turmoil and the Great Depression, were escapist entertainment for women who yearned for the supple bias-cut dresses worn by the film stars, while at the same time showcasing fashion to a wider audience than ever before. Bias-cut dresses became so widely popular in the 1930s that *Vogue* reported in 1934 that a fashionable woman's profile would have to be 'the windswept, fleet lines of a speed boat or airplane'. *Vogue* was referring to streamlining, a hallmark of Art Deco throughout the 1930s that was a great influence on American design. Streamlining lent style and glamour to fashion, and it was the bias cut that shaped the streamlined effect referred to by *Vogue*.

The Art Deco period had witnessed the triumph not only of Madeleine Vionnet but also of Gabrielle (Coco) Chanel. This is reflected in some of the alternative names by which the Art Deco style was known, including *Style Poiret* and *Style Chanel*.[47] 'He [Poiret] was not dethroned until the 1920s, when Coco Chanel became the leader of fashion trends with a totally new look that anticipated what is now recognized as the second phase of the development of Art Deco style: streamlining and a shift towards mass production'.[48]

In 1910 Coco Chanel was licensed as a *modiste* and put over her boutique at 21 rue Cambon, Paris a plaque with the words *Chanel Modes*. Always her own best advertisement, she appeared in the issue of *Comoedia Illustré* for 1 March 1911 wearing her hats. Her career as a *modiste* flourished when her hats were worn by the actress Gabrielle Dorizat in F Nozière's play *Bel Ami* at the Théâtre de Vaudeville, Paris, in 1912; Dorizat then modelled them in *Les Modes*.[49] From 1913 to 1915 she established a boutique in Deauville, the fashionable seaside town on the Normandy coast, where she expanded her repertoire to include loose, casual clothes suitable for this luxurious resort with its emphasis on leisure and sports. She was launched on a career as a fashion designer with her next boutique, Chanel-Biarritz, which opened in 1915. Biarritz was another fashionable resort, where her lightweight clothes made in jersey, a fabric that had previously been reserved for men's underwear, enabled her, as she said, 'to give a woman comfortable clothes that would flow with her body'.[50] In 1919 she was officially registered as a *couturière*, and established her *maison de couture* at 31 rue Cambon, an address just a few doors away from her first boutique, and one which still bears her name.

Coco Chanel's designs reduced the silhouette of women's clothes to a geometric purity of line in plain colours that drew comparison with Cubism, particularly the art movement's Analytic phase, which ennobled humble materials and muted colours. She devised the basic constituents of the modern women's wardrobe: knitwear, shorter skirts, trousers, the three-piece suit, the little black dress and costume jewellery to complement her fashions. When the little black dress, adorned only with simple pearls, appeared as a fashion plate in the issue of American *Vogue* for 1 October 1926 with the caption, 'here is a Ford signed Chanel – the frock that all the world will wear', the magazine recognized the

Coco Chanel, Little Black Dress *(1926), fashion plate from American* Vogue, *1 October 1926 (Courtesy American* Vogue *© 1926 (renewed 1954) by Condé Nast Publications, Inc.). Chanel's fashion ascendancy anticipated the second phase of the Art Deco style, namely streamlining and a move towards mass production.*

beginning of standardization in fashion.[51] Even the bottle of her perfume, Chanel No. 5, launched in 1921, reflected the glamorous angularity of the time with its cube-shaped design made of plain, clear glass. In her book *Art Deco Graphics*, Patricia Frantz Kery wrote eloquently on Chanel and fashion entering the new age:

'Coco Chanel was the incomparable enigmatic leader of international fashion in the 1920s, rivalled only by Elsa Schiaparelli in the 1930s. In 1922 Cocteau asked her to create the costumes for *Antigone* (with sets by Picasso) 'because she is the greatest designer of our day'. No one understood more clearly, or earlier, than Chanel that a major shift in design concepts was about to occur, with strong movements toward clean lines and mass production. She anticipated the emancipation of women and avoided designing only for the elite, as Poiret did. Like Diaghilev, whose later ballets (which she financially supported) embraced the avant-garde, Chanel drew inspiration from modern art movements. Her designs reflected the streamlining and functionalism found in modernist architecture, Constructivism and the Bauhaus, and she often gave her suits a boxy shape, rather like simplified Cubism. Slim, classic, graceful, elegant and often sporty, Chanel's signature fashions were styles that could be produced easily in large numbers by post-World War I manufacturers.'[52]

Fred Astaire and Ginger Rogers in the musical Top Hat *(1935), photograph (Chrysalis Image Library). French bias-cut dresses, pioneered by Vionnet, greatly influenced the costume of American cinema of the era.*

5 From Surrealism to Fashion in the Art Museum

In his book *The Glass of Fashion*, Cecil Beaton wrote that 'sandwiched between two world wars, between Poiret's harem and Dior's New Look, two women dominated the field of *haute couture* – Schiaparelli and Chanel'.[1] Poiret fared no better with Coco Chanel than he had with Cecil Beaton. In a celebrated exchange, Poiret, likening her designs to the 'pauvreté de luxe' ('poverty of luxury'), enquired 'who are you in mourning for, Mademoiselle Chanel?' She retorted 'for you, monsieur'.[2] It was Elsa Schiaparelli who, in her autobiography *Shocking Life* acknowledged her debt to Poiret. The first collection she had ever seen in Paris was Poiret's of 1922 and she marvelled at his sheer invention. She acknowledged the 'ideas which she had borrowed from him and which had contributed to her success', and described him as 'the Leonardo of Fashion'.[3] Poiret had been the first modern fashion designer to collaborate with artists of the avant-garde. It was partly through his endeavours that an avant-garde visual culture advanced in Paris in the early 20th-century. As André Salmon, the French writer and critic and a leader of the Surrealists put it, 'Poiret had put an end to the many powerful forces hostile to modern art'.[4] For the 15 July 1925 issue of *La Révolution Surréaliste*, it was a mannequin dressed in a Poiret creation photographed by Man Ray that appeared on the cover. Poiret's initiatives served as a template for the two great *couturières* and arch rivals, Coco Chanel and Elsa Schiaparelli, who dominated fashion between the two world wars and who plunged into the world of Surrealism. They found a new and exciting canvas on which to articulate their ideas, by translating Surrealist art into clothing.

Surrealism was the leading and most controversial movement in literature and the arts between the world wars. Centred mainly in Paris, it grew out of Dada, an anarchic literary and artistic movement that had sprung up during World War I. Both movements jettisoned rationalism, to which was attributed the wholesale carnage of the War. While the Dadaists were purely negative in their stance, the Surrealists gave positive expression to their views. While perceiving a crisis in Western culture, they reacted with a review of values at every level of society, inspired by the psychoanalytical theories of Sigmund Freud.

The term *surréalisme* was coined in 1917 by the French prose writer, poet and art critic Guillaume Apollinaire, in connection with the ballet *Parade* (by Jean Cocteau, Erik Satie and Pablo Picasso), and also with his own 'surrealist' play, *Les Mamelles de Tirésias*. 'Although Apollinaire had left the term's meaning quite vague, he seems to have understood not only a form of expression exceeding realistic effects (sur-real) but also one that involved a strong element of surprise.'[5]

It was the French poet André Breton who laid claim to the term. Called the 'Pope of Surrealism' because of his strong leadership and dictatorial organization, Bréton issued the first *Manifeste du surréalisme* in 1924, which launched it as a movement. He defined Surrealism as 'the dictation of thought, in the absence of all control exercised by reason, beyond all aesthetic or moral preoccupation'[6] Surrealism aimed 'to change life' and 'to transform the world', and drew its subject matter from the imagination, dreams, the unconscious mind, visions and obsessions and fantasies. Through means such as automatism, meditation and mysticism, the Surrealists explored underlying desire, which was 'the authentic voice of the inner self'. As the exhibition *Surrealism: Desire Unbound* (held at Tate Modern, London in 2001) showed, 'desire drove man to imagine and struggle for a better world ... that the Surrealists celebrated in their art and writings.'[7]

To this end, a 'Bureau of Surrealist Research' was established in Paris and it was from there that the journal *La Révolution Surréaliste* was published. The periodical ran from late 1924 until 1929, the year of *Le Second Manifeste du surréalisme,* and was replaced in 1930 by *Surréalisme au service de la Révolution.* Among the French men of letters associated with Surrealism were Paul Éluard, Louis Aragon and Jean Cocteau, who was also an artist, film-maker and stage, textile and jewellery designer. Surrealism embraced many of the ideas of Romanticism and, like Romanticism, began as a literary movement that quickly encompassed the visual arts. Among the artists associated with Surrealism were Marcel Duchamp, Max Ernst, Joan Miró, Giorgio de Chirico, René Magritte, Salvador Dalí, Christian Bérard, Edouardo Benito and Marcel Vertès. Gathering momentum as a cultural force, Surrealism also branched out into cinema, photography and fashion. The exhibition *Fashion and Surrealism*, held at the Fashion Institute of Technology, New York and the Victoria and Albert Museum, London from 1987 to 1988, examined the substantive participation of fashion in Surrealism. Richard Martin, in his book to accompany the exhibition, wrote that the 'metaphor and meaning of fashion were at the heart of Surrealist visual language'.[8] In one review of this book it was stated: 'While Coco Chanel, her greatest rival, was designing fashionable dress for the new emancipated women, and adhered to the philosophy of the Bauhaus School of Design, "Form Follows Fashion", Schiaparelli was creating fashion inspired by, and in collaboration with, the avant-garde artists of the day, Dali, Cocteau ...'[9]

It is often assumed that Surrealism's application to fashion was the sole domain of Elsa Schiaparelli. However, Coco Chanel played a very active role in the circles connecting art and fashion in Paris, including Surrealism, and her contribution in this respect has yet to be fully acknowledged or documented. She was a friend of the artist Tamara de Lempicka, the subject of an exhibition at the Royal Academy of Arts in London in 2004, whose portraits captured the fashion and glamour of the Parisian elite in the 1920s and 1930s. Her friend Misia Sert, a notable figure in the world of Parisian high society and avant-garde artists, wrote that 'Coco came to know Diaghilev at my house, as well as the whole group of artists who gravitated around the Ballets Russes'.[10] Coco Chanel was a friend and colleague of, among others, Picasso, Diaghilev, Igor Stravinsky, Jean Cocteau, Christian Bérard, Eduardo Garcia, Marcel Vertès and Salvador Dalí. She designed the costumes for Cocteau's play *Antigone* (1922), Diaghilev's and Cocteau's *Le Train Bleu (The Blue Train)* (1924), Stravinsky's ballet *Apollo Musagètes* (1929), Cocteau's plays *Oedipe roi (King Oedipus)* (1937) and *Les Chevaliers du table ronde (The Knights of the Round Table)* (1937) and Dalí's ballet for the Ballets Russes of Monte Carlo, *Baccanale* (1939). It was inevitable that Chanel would venture into Surrealism, and, during the last years of the 1930s she brought about a fascinating interplay between art and fashion.

One of the major themes of Surrealism was, like that of Rococo, a preoccupation with the natural world, albeit now with a more provocative stance. Aquatic and marine life was a favourite motif. Max Ernst, the German artist who settled in Paris in 1922 and was associated with the Surrealists from 1924, made collages and *frottages* (rubbings) and wrote collage-novels. His two-volume collage-novel, *Une Semaine de bonté (A week of kindness),* was published in Paris in 1934. The second volume has a particularly striking plate entitled *Eau.* He placed a shell on a woman's head and both the shell and the head merge into a female personification of water. Coco Chanel, who had begun her career as a *modiste,* took this Surrealist image and transformed it into a chic fashionable accessory. 'Chanel's Immaculate Shell of White Grosgrain' appeared as a fashion plate in *Harper's Bazaar* in January 1938. Drawn by Marcel Vertès, one of the major graphic artists of Surrealism, the imagery of the shell had a striking influence on Chanel. She chose the tactile fabric, grosgrain, a variety of silk which has cord running from selvedge to selvedge. The plain white grosgrain gave fluidity while the cord echoed the sinuous, organic lines of a shell. Just as the shell provides a protective covering in the natural world, so Chanel has done the same for the lady of fashion with her charming shell hat, redesigning nature, like Ernst, in a most inventive way. In the 1930s Coco Chanel was photographed on the Côte d'Azur with Serge Lifar of the Ballets Russes. Her sporty outfit worn with pearls was unheard of at the time, and she furthered her avant-garde image, merging fashion and Surrealism, with her turban-style hat of twists and lines that embody the spirit of a shell. Fish were another source of images that fascinated the Surrealists and pervaded their literature. The very first issue of *La Révolution Surréaliste* (1 December 1924) featured on the cover a picture of a fish with the word *surréalisme* written across it. The words 'Nous sommes à la vielle d'une Révolution. Vous prenez y prendre part' ['We are at the eve of a Revolution. You can take part'] were placed next to the image[11]. And as late as 1945–46, the announcement for the exhibition *Surréalisme,* held at the Galeries des Éditions La Boétie in Brussels, featured a stylistic extension of the fish. A fish and a mermaid were illustrated, with each having the properties of the other.

Chanel imbued her garments and accessories with this Surrealist motif in a most imaginative and stylistic way. About 1938–39 she designed a dress and cape

Marcel Vertès, Chanel's Immaculate Shell of White Grosgrain, *fashion plate from* Harper's Bazaar, *January 1938 (National Magazine Company). Aquatic and marine life were favourite motifs of the Surrealists.*

of black satin embroidered with glistening black sequins arranged in a fish-scale pattern. Added drama was provided by the scarlet silk satin panels and sashes, the colour combination serving to reinforce the more decorative component of this aspect of Surrealism. The same could be said of her colourful enamelled seahorse brooches, designs that interpreted Surrealism in a witty and elegant way.

To the Surrealists, the female figure was ripe for exploitation. In their quest for a metaphor for the human body, they found it in another of their favourite themes, the statuary mannequin. As Richard Martin put it:

> 'The Surrealist striving for an analogue to the human body found fulfilment in the mannequin and dress form as well as in classical statuary. These comparable sets of bodies afforded possibilities for both fashion and the fine arts to represent the figure and to demonstrate the transmutation into art of the form found in nature.'[12]

Jean Cocteau was obsessed with classical Greek statuary. In his film *The Blood of a Poet* (1930), Cocteau was gripped by what he saw as 'living drapery', 'the classical form that becomes a kind of body, and the statue, the structure that extends the life of the real body, setting off a play in transitions between the real and the artificial'.[13]

Salvador Dalí is the artist *par excellence* who explored the imagery of classical drapery, his most compelling painting on this theme being *Shades of Night Descending* of 1931, where an apparition of drapery assumes a living, moving form in a fallow landscape. This haunting Surrealist theme was taken up at the Exposition Internationale held in Paris in 1937, where the Pavillon d'Élégance featured an installation whose designer, Étienne Kohlmann,

> 'worked in an artistic 'surrealist' mode to dramatise a display of Parisian fashion. Faceless figures, gesturing elaborately, were adorned with the latest gowns and accessories. Their limbs were frozen in positions similar to the sculpted drapery and foliage of the stark scenery against which they were displayed. Sparse lighting created an atmosphere of mystery more usually evoked by surrealist writing, revealing a layer of meaning beyond uncanny human resemblance: the mannequin as mysterious muse, catalyst for the human imagination.'[14]

One of the fashion designers featured in the exhibition was Germaine Émilie Krebs, better known as Madame Grès, but in the 1930s also known as Alix, the name of her first shop. Wanting originally to be a sculptor, her trademark style was inspired by ancient Greece. Using white silk jersey, she draped the fabric directly onto her model. Her mannequin, thus clothed, was often photographed next to a piece of classical statuary and the deep pleating and folds of the fabric complemented the flowing drapery of the classical sculpture, recapturing some of its timeless beauty. An outstanding example is her 'Grecian Column Gown', which was photographed by Man Ray for *Harper's Bazaar* in 1937. The previous year

Alix (Madame Grès), Grecian Column Gown,
photograph: Man Ray, From Harper's
Bazaar, 1937 (Chrysalis Image Library).
The Grecian Column Gown was Madame
Grès's most famous design, exemplifying
her trademark style that was inspired by
Ancient Greece.

Harper's Bazaar had proclaimed that 'Alix stands for the body rampant, for the rounded, feminine sculptural form beneath the dress'.[15] This exhibition inspired the Exposition Internationale du Surréalisme held in Paris in 1938, the last major Surrealist exhibition held before World War II. Organized by André Breton, Paul Éluard and Marcel Duchamp, and with contributions by all the important Surrealist artists working in France, it presented a suite of mannequins as *apparitions d'êtres-objets* (phantom object-beings).

> 'On arrival, the visitor was invited to walk down a corridor of 'mannequins de la maison', fashion house mannequins, each posed in front of an imaginary Parisian street sign, presenting her as an available night walker. The mannequins were dressed by surrealist artists with a variety of accessories, each suggesting new sexual or social roles for the artificial women.'[16]

Eduardo Benito, another of the great graphic masters of Surrealism, made the two rival fashion designers, Coco Chanel and Elsa Schiaparelli, collaborators in the evocation of Surrealist mannequins placed within a barren Surrealist landscape for his fashion plate that appeared in the 15 July 1938 issue of American *Vogue*. His acute drawing of two statuary mannequins carrying their own heads, one attired in a Chanel signature sleek black lace evening gown and the other in a Schiaparelli curvaceous wine crêpe evening suit with leg-of-mutton sleeves, was also a seminal example of Surrealism as art and fashion merchandise. During the 1930s fashion illustration enjoyed a special relationship with Surrealism. The main visual record for sartorial commerce were the fashion magazines, in particular *Harper's Bazaar* and *Vogue*. It was Surrealism's mysterious but tactile ability to juxtapose the real and the unreal that made it so successful at expressing itself in fashion illustration. As Richard Martin pointed out: 'when these works were achieved in 1938, when many of the Surrealist artists had embraced disciplines related to fashion, this suggests the possibilities that Surrealism had embraced fashion phenomena as the experience of art and that art had the attributes of fashion'.[17]

Benito was also noted for his imaginative vignettes. Perhaps he may also have seen that the two different fashions were perfect foils for each other – redolent of the personalities of Chanel and Schiaparelli, one rather stark and the other more capricious – as well as a sign of their mutual dislike. Chanel called Schiaparelli 'that Italian artist who's making clothes' and Schiaparelli vilified Chanel as 'that dreary little bourgeoise'.[18] Be that as it may, the two fashion designers were not above keeping an eye on each other's fashions – an activity made easier by the fact that some of the Surrealist artists, including Dalí, Bérard and Cocteau, worked in both camps. Cocteau, for example, designed textile motifs for Chanel and often sketched her fashions while overlapping with Schiaparelli, for whom he designed embroideries, fabrics and jewellery.

Coco Chanel was right. Elsa Schiaparelli saw her work as art, as she herself described it in her autobiography. While perhaps not appreciating Chanel's

Edouardo Benito, Chanel Black Lace Evening Gown and Schiaparelli Wine Crêpe Evening Suit, *fashion plate from American* Vogue, 15 July 1938 *(Courtesy of American* Vogue © *1938, 1966 by Condé Nast Publications, Inc.)*

characterization of her, she would have been pleased with that of others. To Cristóbal Balenciaga, the great Spanish *couturier* for whom, like Chanel, nothing but perfection would do, Schiaparelli 'was the only real artist in couture'. 'Anaïs Nin, in a diary entry for October 1935, described Schiaparelli's *salon* presentation as a "magnificent work of art", writing that she could "well believe she was a painter and a sculptress before she designed dresses".[19]

As *artiste-couturière* pursuing the mixture of art and fashion, she not only evoked the major themes that relate to Surrealism but also excelled at the wit and surprise effects at the heart of the movement, realizing 'that the act of shocking was part and parcel of any new idea'. 'Schiaparelli was drawn to Surrealism by her natural fancifulness, and her 'shocking pink' colour and 'Shocking' perfume, with the bottle designed by the Surrealist painter Leónor Fini in the shape of a dressmaker's dummy based on the hourglass figure of Mae West (whom she dressed along with a host of other Hollywood stars), 'summed up her whole approach of elegant outrage'.[20] She was unrivalled in her exploitation of this device, something often reported in the captions to illustrations of her designs in fashion magazines. For example, the caption to the fashion plate of a group of her suits that appeared in *Woman's Journal* in January 1938 read:

> 'The suit with that air of being just off to the Ritz is the suit that Madame Schiaparelli does to perfection. She gives to her wearers a look of unstudied leisure, and amuses them with foolish buttons – those pleasant conceits which are in keeping. Her black suit is trimmed with velvet, hides a bold red blouse and shows cupid clips.'[21]

This Surrealist posture was echoed in fact from the very beginning of her career, in her fashion debut in 1927. It launched her sweaters with a *trompe-l'oeil* effect. Flirting with transparency and turning the body inside out, her skeleton sweater, as she put it in her autobiography, gave 'women wearing it the appearance of being seen through an X-ray'.[22] To underpin the surprising effects of Surrealism she experimented throughout her career with a variety of unconventional materials such as rayon, cellophane, rough silk, newspaper print, Rhodophane and plastic zips. Schiaparelli is also credited with introducing thematic collections and fashion shows as performance art: 'models in the "Circus" show of 1938 swung out of the windows of the Place Vendôme *salon*, their surreal coat-buttons fashioned by Dalí, and the manic event captured in a Bérard painting'.[23] It was with Christian Bérard, Jean Cocteau and above all Salvador Dalí that her most striking and memorable fashions were created. With her close friend Cocteau, she used two drawings he made for her in her 1937 collection. Cocteau was a brilliant draughtsman with a distinctive outline-drawing style that was simple and elegant and could also challenge visual perceptions. This was evident in his asymmetrical design that appeared in the July 1937 issue of *Harper's Bazaar* entitled 'Robe de Schiaparelli – 1937 – ornée par Jean Cocteau'. The jacket of the ensemble features a woman's head in profile with her long hair cascading down one of the sleeves

Schiaparelli Evening Suit Embroidered with a Design by Jean Cocteau, from Harper's Bazaar, 1937 (National Magazine Company)

JAN 1938

No paper patterns are obtainable of the models on this and the opposite page.

The suit with that air of being just off to the Ritz is the suit that Madame Schiaparelli does to perfection. She gives to her wearers a look of unstudied leisure, and amuses them with foolish buttons—those pleasant conceits which are in keeping. Her black suit is trimmed with velvet, hides a bold red blouse and shows cupid clips.

You see the favourite fitted jacket in the brown suit with fur buttons, and you realize the new vogue for woollen braiding on the black ensemble with the uncommon cut.

43

SCHIAPARELLI

Ladies' suits designed by Elsa Schiaparelli, *fashion plate, Woman's Journal, January 1938 (Chrysalis Image Library)* of the jacket. This was offset by a hand clasping the waist of the jacket. Of all the parts of the female body that the Surrealists disembodied, perhaps the most vulnerable to fantasy was the hand. For the Surrealists, the hand was obliquely sexual and functional, made up of parts of its own. The design creates a disharmony between the apparition on the jacket and the actual wearer of the garment, confusing the spectator who tries to place the parts of the body in direct relationship to the figures, but at the same time achieving an accurate placement of the waist. Schiaparelli made up the design in coarse grey linen, with Cocteau's imagery translated into gold embroidery by Maison Lesage. It was previously unheard of to mix linen and gold embroidery, and this was another illustration of how a collaboration between art and fashion could overturn the conventions of the time. In April 1937 Cocteau had written in *Harper's Bazaar* how literally Schiaparelli had taken the expression '*Théâtre de la mode*'.

It was probably her work with another close friend, Christian Bérard, in which her sense of theatricality was most brilliantly reflected. Like Cocteau, Bérard was masterful in many artistic media. He designed costumes and stage sets for many of Cocteau's plays. Also like Cocteau, he had a drawing style that was immediately identifiable, a free, elliptical line imbued with rich colours. He likened fashion to theatre, and he endowed the drawings he did for *Vogue* from 1935 to 1949, which were defined as romantic expressionism, with this characteristic. For Schiaparelli he designed some equally lush motifs such as the sun-ray embroideries for her 1938 Astrology/Zodiac collection. The idea was already being given a trial run by Schiaparelli in her claret silk velvet jacket, the gently curving front heavily embroidered with gilt metal thread and sequins and applied with blue and pink faceted glass decoration, the perfect design to frame the two large sunburst buttons. The jacket was paired with a plain claret gown in her winter 1937 collection.

Schiaparelli's most rewarding partnership was the one she had with Salvador Dalí. Such was the force of Dalí's inspirations that *Vogue* commissioned him to make 'photo-paintings', describing fashion's relationship with Surrealism, that ran in American *Vogue*. During his sojourn in America from 1941 to 1948 he delved into every aspect of contemporary fashionable life. He especially immersed himself in the commercial side, making window displays for the chic Bonwit Teller department store in New York and a series of advertisements for Bryans Hosiery that were illustrated in American *Vogue* and *Harper's Bazaar*. The ads were especially well received, being imbued with 'Dalí's characteristically witty Surrealist imagery and technical prowess'.

> 'Each image presents a wholly realised composition which happens to include, among its other inhabitants, a disembodied leg or a diaphanous, fetishistic stocking. Here the stockinged leg is heralded in a spirit, worshipful celebration, with adoring mannequins, waving butterfly wands [a favourite Surrealist object] leading the procession.'[24]

A classic Dalí/Schiaparelli design is the group of 'Surrealist' suits and coats of 1936 with numerous real and fake pockets in the form of miniature drawers, complete with handles. Dalí had been experimenting with this Surrealist theme of 'body and parts' since 1934, and for him it was 'a sort of allegory in which each drawer corresponded to a smell emanating from the body of a woman'. [25] Dalí's verve is again evident in the 'Shoe Hat' shown in Schiaparelli's Winter 1937 collection, where the Surrealist subject of 'displacement and illusion' is eloquently reflected. Altered by its removal from its conventional domain, it causes disruption both in scale and role association.

> 'The idea evolved from a 1933 photograph Gala Dalí had taken of her husband in Port Lligat, in which the artist wears a woman's shoe on his head and another on his right shoulder. Gala was photographed wearing Schiaparelli's ensemble, but it was agreed that only Daisy Fellowes managed to carry it off successfully.' [26]

Dalí and Schiaparelli also collaborated on two of the most iconic dresses of the 1930s, the 'Organza Dress with Painted Lobster' of 1937 and the 'Tear Dress' of 1938. In the Surrealists' theme of the 'Natural World' the most celebrated, if not preferred, category of fish was the lobster, inspired in part at least by Apollinaire, who walked a lobster on a lead in Paris! Some of Dalí's most famous works of this motif are *New York Dream – Man Finds Lobster in Place of Phone* (1935) and *Lobster Telephone* (1936). Instead of giving it a pre-historic appearance, the Dalí/Schiaparelli lobster is very sedate, an edible amid sprigs of parsley cooked to a *cordon bleu* standard, signifying gracious living. But, as always, nothing is what it seems with Surrealism. For Dalí, the lobster had sexual connotations, and his strategic placement of it on the front of the garment was charged with erotic tension. The lobster dress was worn by Mrs Wallis Simpson, A-list celebrity customer, captured in a mood of elegant grandeur by Cecil Beaton. In her review of the exhibition, *Shocking! The Art and Fashion of Elsa Schiaparelli*, held at the Philadelphia Museum of Art in 2003, and in particular of this image, Suzy Menkes wrote: ' ... the lobster print climbing toward the thighs of Wallis Simpson, the future Duchess of Windsor ... with its mixture of elegance and graphic sensuality ... still gives out a sexual frisson today'. [27]

The Surrealist theme of 'displacement and illusion' reached its zenith in the 'Tear Dress'. Janet Flanner had written in *The New Yorker* as early as 1932 that 'a frock from Schiaparelli ranks like a modern canvas'. The 'Tear Dress' was inspired by one of Dalí's paintings of 1936, *Three Young Surrealist Women Holding in Their Arms the Skins of an Orchestra*, where torn fabric is indistinguishable from flayed skin, thus dissolving the parameters between body and garment. An evening gown of luxurious silk crêpe meant to be worn at the most formal of functions and presented in Schiaparelli's Circus Collection, the 'Tear Dress' gives the illusion of tatters and violence. In the collection of the Philadelphia Museum of Art the 'Tear Dress'

> 'is printed with an illusion of torn animal flesh, with the *trompe-l'oeil* effect given a third dimension in the appliquéd fabric applied to the 'tent' veil. On the pale blue

Schiaparelli Tear Dress and Cape in a Fabric Designed by Salvador Dalí *(1938)*, *photograph: Cecil Beaton (Chrysalis Image Library). The Tear Dress was inspired by Dalí's 1936 painting* Three Young Surrealist Women Holding in Their Arms the Skins of an Orchestra.

Salvador Dali, Three Young Surrealist Women Holding in their Arms the Skins of an Orchestra, *1936, oil on canvas (Collection of the Salvador Dali Museum, St Petersburg, Florida, © Gala-Salvador Dali Foundation, Figueres (Artists Society [ARS] New York © Salvador Dali Museum, Inc.)*

fabric, now faded to white, the 'skin' is slashed and peeled back to reveal a magenta underlayer, the hanging pieces printed to look like fur, as if the gown were made from an animal skin turned inside out.'[28]

When the 'Tear Dress' appeared in 1938, it caused a furore.[29] At the time of the Spanish Civil War, the 'Tear Dress' must have made a powerful visual statement not only for the art and fashion worlds, but the political world as well – and a harbinger of worse to come. Richard Martin called the 'Tear Dress' 'a *memento mori* ... in a state of destruction even when it was new'.[30]

Surrealism had a long heyday, spanning World War I and World War II, and its spirit has lived on. 'Surrealism's longevity had ensured its place within wider cultural currents, becoming as much of a seedbed of inspiration as the unconscious and suppressed part of the psyche it had exposed.'[31]

Its 'machine to capsize the mind' ensured that the appropriation of its themes by art and fashion would continue. 'Almost every fashion and art movement has its roots in Surrealism, including the obsession with sewing tools, as in the avant-garde's last twenty years of visible seaming, edges left raw and clothing deliberately turned inside out to show its construction – or deconstruction.'[32]

In 1946 the Italian painter and sculptor Lucio Fontana issued his *Manifesto Blanco* where he introduced a new concept of art, Spatialism, which he felt was in keeping with the spirit of the post-war age. For Fontana, art could only go forward and develop through new media such as plastic and light. His most characteristic works in this vein are his paintings of plain surfaces that are lacerated in the canvas, thereby allowing him to escape 'symbolically but also materially from the prison of the flat surface'.[33] Along the same principle, he designed dresses with Bruna Bini in 1961 that represented 'the boundary between the interior and the exterior, between the fabric and the skin it covers, between dress and nudity'.[34]

Surrealism also breathed new life into fashion photography. In addition to the photographs of Man Ray,

> 'Horst P. Horst, Cecil Beaton, George Hoyningen-Huene, Erwin Blumenfeld, Maurice Tabard and several others all repeatedly indulged in disconcerting imagery such as metaphysical perspectives, the play of mirrors or enigmatic simulacra, etc. They eluded photographic convention and the camera's objectivity enriching it with new discoveries, poetry and surreal symbols.'[35]

Horst, a friend of Cocteau and Dalí, preferred to work in a studio, where he specialized in elegant settings and props which, combined with dramatic light effects, created images that imposed an unreality on his models. His photographs were likened to poems in light and deep shadow that produced a glamorous ideal. Erwin Blumenfeld, who particularly admired and photographed the work of the fashion designers Cristóbal Balenciaga and Charles James, had a penchant for letting parts of the body exemplify the whole, as in his image of lips and eye for the January 1950 cover of *Vogue*.

It was this display of 'imagination, initiative and daring', qualities Schiaparelli alluded to in *Shocking Life*, nurtured by an artistic awareness, 'that inspired new generations of designers, from Geoffrey Beene to Zandra Rhodes, to Yves Saint Laurent, and continues to influence today's *enfants terribles*, among them John Galliano and Jean-Paul Gaultier'.[36] She can be seen as a precursor of Punk, an anarchic style that intentionally set out to shock, which emerged in London in the mid-1970s in the fashions of Zandra Rhodes and also of Vivienne Westwood, the surrealist soul *par excellence* of the Punk-style era. Vivienne Westwood's crucial business partnership was with Malcolm McLaren (manager of the Punk rock group the Sex Pistols), with whom she had opened the Let it Rock boutique in 1970. It was subsequently re-named Too Fast to Live, To Young to Die (1972), Sex (1974), Seditionaries (1976), and finally World's End (1981). It became *the* place for the young generation interested in fetishism and bondage, as seen in Westwood's

Left: Vivienne Westwood/Malcolm McLaren Pirate Shirt, Trousers and Leather Boots *(early 1980s); Right:* Tartan Bondage Trousers with Anarchy Bum-Flap, *English (c. 1980), Vivienne Westwood/Malcolm McLaren* 'Anarchy in the UK' T-shirt *(c. 1980) and Vivienne Westwood/Malcolm McLaren* Canvas and Leather Bondage Boots *(c. 1980) (Sotheby's, London). Like Schiaparelli, Westwood's designs challenged conventions and reflected anxieties and concerns.*

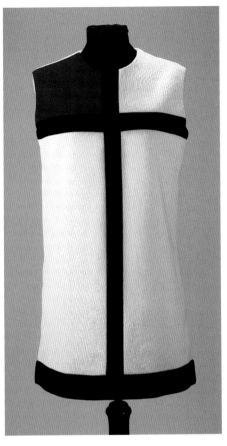

Yves Saint Laurent, Wool Jersey Mondrian Tunic Dress *(1965–1966), (Sotheby's, London). In 1965 Saint Laurent's 'Mondrian look' was described as 'the dress of tomorrow'.*

leather and rubber clothing and T-shirts. Like Schiaparelli, she expressed her avant-garde ideas on fashion with an artistic vision that was also unsettling, challenging conventions and reflecting anxieties and concerns.

> 'Of the punk years Westwood said: "It changed the way people looked. I was messianic about punk, seeing if one could put a spoke in the system in some way. I realised there was no subversion without ideas. It is not enough to want to destroy everything."... She paved the way for the next generation – John Galliano and Alexander McQueen – to reinterpret fashion history. She created a new language of clothes.'[37]

Alexander McQueen's Spring/Summer 2004 show in Paris was like performance art. An extravaganza of art and fashion that paid homage to the film *They Shoot Horses, Don't They?*, it featured twenty dancers and twenty models, choreographed by Michael Clark. The fashion show included themes such as racial discrimination in America in the 1930s, emotion, distress and the collapse of physical beauty, with the audience rising to their feet in a resounding ovation.

Mention has already been made of both Yves Saint Laurent and Cristóbal Balenciaga, who were both considered to be geniuses by Schiaparelli. They are discussed here because 'it was during the post-war years that the full scale of [Balenciaga's] genius became apparent', while 'Saint Laurent marks the transition between yesterday's fashions and today's'.[38] Schiaparelli purchased from the collections of both Balenciaga and Saint Laurent, and some of the latter's sketches of designs he had made for her were shown in the exhibition *Hommage à Elsa Schiaparelli,* held at the Palais Galliera in Paris in 1984. They were the two *couturiers,* that for her, had the imagination to follow their 'dream' and 'dared' to do what they liked.[39]

In 1992 Saint Laurent declared 'I am a failed painter'.[40] Yet, like Schiaparelli, it was his sublime fusion of art and fashion, creating designs involved with paintings from the 1960s through to the 1980s, which was highlighted at the exhibition devoted to him in 1983. 'The retrospective exhibition held of Yves Saint Laurent organised by the Metropolitan Museum of Art is not just a collection of clothes. For twenty-five years, Saint Laurent has fully exemplified Jean Cocteau's phrase: "In every landscape or still life, a painter always portrays himself".'[41]

Art that incorporated an element of movement continued to fascinate fashion designers because of its direct relationship with the body. Among the forerunners of this type of art were the Constructivists and also Alexander Calder, who began making mobiles in the 1930s. Greatly impressed by the work of the Dutch artist Piet Mondrian, he said he wanted to make 'moving Mondrians'. Kinetic energy came to full prominence in 1955 when an exhibition entitled *Mouvement* was held in Paris. Among the artists exhibiting was Victor Vasarely, whose works contrasted black and white and explored optical effects, making a leading figure of Op Art, a term that was coined in 1964 by *Time* magazine. The graphic character of optical illusions, and the belief of its practitioners that clothing moved with the body, made it ideal for fashion design. Getulio Alviani, for example, produced moving materials and dresses that were a 'constantly changing picture because of their many colour combinations and variations of line'.[42] The American dress manufacturer Larry Aldrich commissioned the textile designer Julian Tomchin to create fabrics for dresses derived from the paintings of Bridget Riley, another leading Op artist.

The welding of art and fashion, however, found its most vivid expression in the Mondrian dresses of Yves Saint Laurent. One fashion magazine reported that 'the Mondrian style in fashion has existed precisely since August 2, 1965. On this day, Yves Saint Laurent showed his Winter Collection in Paris for the first time.'[43]

Saint Laurent designed a group of wool jersey tunic dresses consisting of intersecting black lines and blocks of bold primary colours based on the abstract paintings of Mondrian. His application of these geometric-shaped silhouettes to his dresses, dubbed the 'Mondrian Look', brought a new elegance and sophistication to *haute couture*. But they were also designated by *Harper's Bazaar* in September 1965 as 'the dress of tomorrow'. Saint Laurent's Mondrian concept of treating these dresses like canvases was a phenomenon, and manufacturers made cheap copies for the mass market. Saint Laurent had an uncanny ability to predict the changes taking place in fashion. In 1966 he showed his Pop Art collection of dresses and opened his first *prêt-à-porter* (ready-to-wear) boutique in Paris, called Rive Gauche. As he put it, he conceived his *prêt-à-porter* designs 'in terms of machine fabrication'.

Art as inspiration for Saint Laurent was again the subject of an exhibition on the occasion of the opening of the Pierre Bergé–Yves Saint Laurent Foundation in Paris in 2004. Yves Saint Laurent Dialogue with Art (10 March–18 July 2004) featured a group of the *couturier*'s creations and paintings, by, among others, Piet Mondrian, Henri Matisse, Pablo Picasso and Andy Warhol. 'But I never compared myself to these artists – that would be pretentious,' said Saint Laurent. 'I just tried to be an artist in my own *métier*.' For Saint Laurent, Warhol 'was inspiring in everything he did', and the exhibition included two of the fashion designer's Pop Art dresses.[44]

As the art historian Marco Livingstone stressed in his book *Pop Art: A Continuing History*, Pop Art was never a clearly defined movement with manifestos, but rather an art that, emerging in the 1950s and becoming rampant in the 1960s, made use of the imagery of mass culture and consumerism, such as comic strips, billboards and packaging – in other words, the imagery of art and the everyday, which fashion quickly embraced and played an important role in disseminating.[45] Pop Art, reacting against Abstract Expressionism (which Surrealism had influenced), heralded a return to representational art, whether that be in comic strips, advertising or magazines. It was an international movement in painting, sculpture, printmaking and fashion.

'The term originated in the 1950s at the ICA [Institute of Contemporary Arts], London, in the discussions held by the Independent Group concerning the artefacts of popular

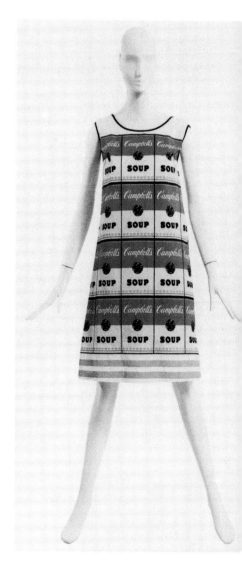

The Souper Dress, *paper A-line dress printed with the Campbell's Soup logo, 1966–1967 (FIT Museum, New York/Irving Solero). These paper dresses were meant as throwaways, a comment on consumerism.*

culture. This small group included the artists Richard Hamilton and Eduardo Paolozzi (a latter-day Surrealist) as well as architects and critics. Lawrence Alloway (1926–1990), the critic who first used the term in print in 1958, conceived of Pop Art as the lower end of a popular-art to fine-art continuum, encompassing such forms as advertising, science-fiction illustrations and automobile styling'.[46]

Pop artists in the United States included Roy Lichtenstein, Claes Oldenburg, James Rosenquist and the most celebrated of all, Andy Warhol. Andy Warhol began his career as a fashion illustrator for fashion magazines such as *Mademoiselle, Vogue* and *Harper's Bazaar.* Like Salvador Dalí, he produced window displays for department stores in New York such as Bonwit Teller and Tiffany's. His advertisements in *The New York Times* for the shoe manufacturer I Miller & Sons from 1955 to 1959 were highly acclaimed, having the same simplicity of line that Dalí had with his similar advertising commissions, 'helping to earn him major awards from the Art Directors Club'.[47] A compulsive shopper who was acutely aware of the relationship of art and fashion with the commercial and advertising, he embraced music and films from the early 1960s, dressing up in leather jackets and satin shirts that rock stars wore and sporting a silver-sprayed wig. He used the actresses in his films to model paper dresses printed with his Banana paintings, while his paintings of Campbell soup cans influenced, in 1966–67, a series of paper dresses in an A-line mini-dress style under the title 'The Souper Dress'. These paper dresses were throwaways, a comment on consumerism, and played an important role in the dissemination of Pop Art. The catalogue of the exhibition *The Warhol Look: Glamour/Style/Fashion,* held at various venues in the United States, Canada, Europe and Australia from 1997 to 1999, stated that in the work of Warhol 'fashion is the connective tissue joining what previously appeared as disparate elements'.[48] Indeed, Andy Warhol can be said to have played the 'Jean Cocteau role' during the brilliant years of Pop Art.[49] He transposed his paintings into dresses, while his friend, the fashion designer Halston, created dresses with large floral prints based on Warhol's series of flower paintings. The 'Warhol look' extended to Paraphernalia, the New York boutique resembling an art gallery, where his friend Betsey Johnson and several other women designers displayed youth-inspired fashions such as dresses made from plastic, paper and metal that could be purchased. With the Velvet Underground, the cult rock band that he managed, Warhol organized the opening event at Paraphernalia, conceived as a continuous 'happening', a term that had been coined in 1959 by the American artist Allan Kaprow to describe a form of entertainment in which an artist directs a multimedia event. *The Warhol Look* exhibition catalogue proclaimed that 'today's merging of art and fashion is in large measure the legacy of Andy Warhol'.[50] The 1990s witnessed an *hommage à Andy Warhol* when Stephen Sprouse acquired exclusive rights to use Warhol's images, Jean-Charles de Castelbajac designed dresses printed with Warhol motifs, and Gianni Versace created his 'Marilyn Monroe' dress. January 2003 saw the designer Philip Treacy

L'AMPLEUR EN ARRIÈRE est sensible dans certaines robes du soir. Celle-ci légèrement drapée aux hanches est agrémentée d'une draperie de satin rose pâle.

Cristóbal Balenciaga, Suit of Navy Woven Wool and Silk (c. 1964), (V & A Picture Library, London). In contrast to the fun in Pop Art, Balenciaga continued in his austere fashions that had a powerful architectural dimension.

Reinolo, Dior Evening Gown, fashion plate from Femina, October 1947 (Private Collection).

Liberty of London, Peacock Feather Silk Scarf (detail), 1975. *Originally designed by Rex Silver, c. 1900 (Private Collection). Liberty was a textile manufacturer who, along with Ascher, made textiles designed by artists. These textiles were supplied to fashion designers and influenced fashion trends.*

team up with the Andy Warhol Foundation in a limited-edition collection of hats and bags with Warhol's iconic images.[51]

While the fun and excitement of the Sixties Pop Art/fashion scene was taking place, the purist Cristóbal Balenciaga, in complete contrast, was continuing to produce his austere fashions. In *The Glass of Fashion*, Cecil Beaton wrote: 'If Dior is the Watteau of dressmaking — full of nuances, chic, delicate and timely — then Balenciaga is fashion's Picasso. For like that painter, underneath all of his experiments with the modern, Balenciaga has a deep respect for tradition and pure classic line.'[52]

In his later work, *Self-Portrait with Friends*, Beaton referred to the 'depth of thought' and the 'intense concentration' that went into the work of the master of precision. How Balenciaga pictured the female shape, and how he related it to fabric and scale, gave his fashions a powerful architectural dimension.

Balenciaga's *protégé,* Hubert de Givenchy, called him the 'architect' of the *haute couture*. His modern vision was recognized by *Harper's Bazaar* as early as 1938 when the magazine reported that 'Balenciaga abides by the law that elimination is the secret of chic'.[53] As a Spaniard, he had a feeling for the sombre colours seen in the paintings of Velázquez, Zurbarán and Goya. Allied to his perfect balance between line and proportion was his palette of rich, dark colours. His two-piece suit of navy woven wool and silk of about 1964 is an ensemble of shapely simplicity which, with its stark colour and elongated tunic line drawing the eye away from the waist, could be worn by women with a slim or a curvaceous figure. It is an example of his combining an elegant harmony of cut and construction with an understanding of the female body's architecture. Balenciaga created his timeless fashions in an air of secrecy for an exclusive clientele that included the Duchess of Windsor, Pauline de Rothschild and Diana Vreeland. Disillusioned with trends such as mass production and youth fashion, he closed his *maison de couture* in Paris in 1968. His designs are often compared to those of Charles James, whom Balenciaga said was the 'world's best and only dressmaker', who had raised *haute couture* from an 'applied to a pure art form'.[54] An extreme purist and classicist, James, who died in 1978, was noted for his exquisite evening gowns, for which he worked obsessively on the cut and construction. He twisted and spiralled their seams — characteristics of architecture — creating 'sculptural garments regarded as "human architecture" due to the robust construction principles that reinforced their shapes'.[55]

An exhibition celebrating the taste and acumen of a small group of post-war textile manufacturers, such as the firms of Ascher and Liberty, was held at the Fine Art Society, London, in 2003. Entitled *Artists' Textiles in Britain 1945–1970,* it was a groundbreaking assessment of the contribution made by a broad range of artists including Pablo Picasso, Jean Cocteau, Eduardo Paolozzi, Henri Matisse and Victor Vasarely to British textile production in this period. Because the textiles were designed by artists, the overall effect was pictorial, and showed the interaction of art and fashion. The textile company founded by Lida

Charles James, Silk Faille and Velvet Evening Dress *(1956),*
(Cincinnati Art Museum, Gift of
Mr and Mrs J G Schmidlapp, by
exchange). James, a consummate
dressmaker, twisted and spiralled
the seams of his evening gowns,
creating sculptural garments.

and Zika Ascher, for example, contracted leading French and British painters and sculptors such as André Derain, Henry Moore and Graham Sutherland to design printed textiles for scarves and dresses, which were supplied to fashion designers and influenced fashion trends. The impressions gleaned from the exhibition were a sense of dazzling colour, and of how contemporary the designs of these artists still seem today. An elegant headsquare designed by Sonia Delaunay in 1969, when she was 84, 'in the abstraction of its design ... and the subtlety and painterly qualities of the nuances and delicate colouring of Delaunay's work, is in many ways ... a summation of textile design as a 20th-century medium, perfectly translated in a *tour de force* of silk-screening by Liberty.'[56]

An art and fashion trend of the 1970s that took place in Paris was a distinctive type of performance art. It was carefully programmed, unlike the happenings of the 1960s.

> 'The term *créateur* emerged and was subsequently applied to the designers who represented the avant-garde of ready-to-wear. Créateurs et Industriels was set up, on a fee-paying basis, to promote a group of stylists assembled over a period of five years, a task that had been accomplished with unparalleled commitment and inventiveness. A utopian scheme, the initiative injected new life into ready-to-wear and constituted an investment in the future of a distinctively Parisian brand of fashion.'[57]

One of these *jeunes créateurs* was Jean-Charles de Castelbajac, a collector of contemporary art who 'liked to draw parallels between his designs and avant-garde movements'.[58] Under the Créateurs et Industriels scheme, he held his first fashion show in the Palais Galliera in Paris in 1972, a spectacular, full-blown performance art with special direction, lighting and music that interacted immediately with the audience.

The 1980s witnessed the beginnings of another new trend, the official recognition of fashion 'as a worthy form of cultural expression, making its entrée into distinguished museums, including the Metropolitan Museum of Art in New York [and] the Louvre in Paris'.[59] The Metropolitan Museum's Yves Saint Laurent 25-year retrospective exhibition in 1983–84 was groundbreaking in this respect. Before then, exhibitions at museums were conventionally limited to artworks or historic costume rather than current fashions. In an interview in 1996, Richard Martin discussed the interesting issue of the appropriation of art by the *couturier*, and his views pinpointed why the Saint Laurent exhibition was so pioneering, and why Saint Laurent was such an exceptional designer. For him, Saint Laurent's fashions had the same perceptions as art. The Mondrian dress, for example, 'made people think of the dress in terms of planar clothing by utilizing Mondrian as a kind of paradigm for the flatness that prevailed in that era'.[60] In announcing in 1985 the new Musée des Arts de la Mode in the Louvre's Pavillon de Marsan, Jack Lang, the Minister of Culture, underlined the role of the fashion museum as a component of the cultural and aesthetic domain:

'"There would no doubt be something slightly paradoxical in opening a fashion museum if fashion were just a seasonal trend ... a fashion museum is the history of practices and looks", Lang welcomed the ready-to-wear designer shows in the courtyard of the Louvre.'[61]

It was re-named the Musée de la Mode et du Textile and re-opened in 1997 in the Rohan wing of the Louvre as part of the 'Grand Louvre' project (the extension of gallery space into all the areas of the palace previously used as civil service offices).

Fashion continued to assume the status of an artistic event and to adopt the vocabulary of art when Issey Miyake held his first fashion 'installation', a term denoting an environment or space in a gallery specifically for a special exhibition. His *Issey Miyake Spectacle: Bodyworks* exhibitions held in Tokyo, Los Angeles and San Francisco in 1983 related his fashion designs to architecture. This was followed in 1988 by *Issey Miyake: A-Un Exhibition* in Paris which featured an astonishing array of his fabrics and fashion designed over several years, and in 1998 by the *Issey Miyake: Making Things* exhibition, also held in Paris, where his light, airy garments seemed almost to dance around the exhibition space, thus fulfilling his own uncompromising demand for total freedom and movement of the body.

An exploration of the connection between art and fashion reached its apogee in the 1996 Biennale of *Il Tempo e la Moda* held in Florence.

> 'In the cradle of the Renaissance, Valentino's scarlet gowns cosied up to Michelangelo in the Uffizi; Helmut Lang and Jenny Holzer expressed fashion and beauty through electronic language; Miuccia Prada and Damien Hirst offered a menagerie of live goats, rabbits and chickens; Jil Sander and Mario Merz created a wind tunnel blowing with autumn leaves.'[62]

The catalogue, entitled *Looking at Fashion*, stated that the aim of the exhibition was 'to explore a number of central issues of contemporary experience'. *Il Tempo et la Moda* was composed of seven large exhibitions: Art/Fashion; New Persona/New Universe; Visitors; Habitus, Abito, Abitare; Elton John Metamorphosis; Emilio Pucci; and Secret Love. The Art/Fashion exhibition was staged at the Guggenheim Museum SoHo in New York in 1997. It looked at the costume ideas propounded by the Futurists, the clothes and textiles of Sonia Delaunay, the art/fashion collaboration of Salvador Dalí and Elsa Schiaparelli, and the fashion work of Man Ray. Looking back at the Biennale, Ingrid Sischy, the co-curator, has remarked:

> 'That Biennale was an extension of something I did when I put Issey Miyake on the cover of *Artforum* in 1982 – and in the artworld, I can't tell you what a shocker that was. I am not trying to say that fashion and art are the same thing. I believe that the worlds were looking at each other and their strategies. With a Miuccia or a Helmut or

Issey Miyake, White, Brown and Black Silk Cotton and Linen Double Weave and Black Nylon Plain Weave Shirt Dress *(1985), (Cincinnati Art Museum, Gift of Arlene C Cooper). Miyake often used the vocabulary of art to describe his designs and exhibitions, one of which he described as an 'installation'.*

Gianni Versace, Metal Appliqué Halter-Neck Cocktail Top *(c. 1990), (Sotheby's, London). Versace made a close study of Byzantine art at the Metropolitan Museum of Art in New York.*

a Rei, it is not about wanting to be an artist, but about looking at each other and at their strategies.'[63]

Since the Biennale, many museums and art galleries have embraced fashion. Two fashion designers who were recognized for their special relationships with the art world were Gianni Versace and Giorgio Armani. With their intuitive flair for presentation and understanding of the power of imagery, both were in tune with the sensibilities of their time and helped define them. Versace exhibitions were held at the Metropolitan Museum of Art, New York, in 1997–98 and at the Victoria and Albert Museum, London in 2002–03. Versace had long associations with both museums, making endless visits in his careful research of art sources. He was preoccupied with the past, like so many fashion designers including Vivienne Westwood, herself the subject of an exhibition at the Victoria and Albert Museum in 2004. At the Metropolitan he especially studied the collections of Byzantine art, while at the Victoria and Albert, he was 'constantly in and out, quietly like any student. He was a most scholarly man'.[64] The exhibitions had sections on art inspirations, from Versace's interest in the heavy incrustations of metal found in Byzantine art, to the delicate floating designs of the early-20th century to the Warhol prints of Marilyn Monroe and James Dean. Versace was a savvy art collector with an impressive library and collection of paintings. Besides Warhol, he collected Picasso and Lichtenstein, who also made a significant impact on his dazzling designs. Versace had a distinctive style; he was a brilliant colourist who could mix patterns, textures and fabrics. He created an instantly recognizable image, which was one of his major contributions to late-20th-century fashion.

Giorgio Armani, the other great colossus of Italian fashion, was fêted at the Guggenheim Museum in New York and Bilbao in 2000–01 and at the Royal Academy of Arts in London in 2003–04. Through an innovative combination of light, sound and architectural elements devised by the artist and designer Robert Wilson, the London venue was a ravishing art installation in which to experience Armani's thematically grouped creations. Art and fashion interacted at many levels. The magnificent customized mannequins, with their sense of movement, were almost Beuys-like. The display of Armani's handbags had a Surrealist influence. They were pulled out from a wall with shadows behind them, reminiscent of the installations of Marcel Duchamp and Salvador Dalí. The Minimalism section of the exhibition revealed the extraordinary hues Armani derived from the same colour, evoking, for example, the paintings of Ad Reinhardt and Mark Rothko. Similarly, using the same colour with a vast array of

Giorgio Armani Fashions *(1986),*
(Fashion Research Centre, Bath)

different textures gave his designs the visual complexity of paintings. The pared-down effect of his style, with its pure, clean lines so immaculately draped and folded, created beautiful sculptural silhouettes. The exhibition gave a sense of an artistic personality working out his ideas in dress.

Norman Rosenthal, the exhibitions secretary of the Royal Academy of Arts, defended fashion's place in the art museum:

> 'The RA is hardly the first fine art museum to conceive of couture as living sculpture. The Metropolitan Museum of Art in New York has staged a number of exhibitions devoted to contemporary clothing and fashion, notably its 1984 retrospective of couturier extraordinaire Yves Saint Laurent. That show also caused the kind of furore

that has surrounded the Armani exhibition during its appearances in New York and London – the supposed ideological battle of high art versus popular culture. But while many say that fashion is too commercial to be treated as art – and of course, it is a huge industry – there has always been crossover between the two worlds. Think of Schiaparelli and the Surrealists or the Op art of Bridget Riley and fashion of the psychedelic '60s, to name just a couple of examples ... It's invigorating and, to my mind, essential, for museums to expose visitors to fresh visual experiences and ideas. A wider remit affords the public what Joseph Beuys called an expanded concept of art. And I'm certain that Beuys, whom I knew well and who was very fashion-conscious in his own way, would not have disapproved of Saint Laurent at the Met or Armani at the Royal Academy. I only wish that artists and curators alike would occasionally make more use of such mind-stretching concepts.'[65]

Many contemporary artists are incorporating fashion in their work. The photographer Cindy Sherman, in her 'Fashion' series, has photographed herself wearing clothes designed by Jean-Paul Gaultier, Issey Miyake and Jean-Charles de Castelbajac. Since 1983 she has produced more than three hundred of these self-portraits or self-transformations. Looking tense and dishevelled, with the garments hanging rather uncomfortably, the antithesis of models in fashion photographs, Cindy Sherman has used fashion to explore ideas and images of female identity that 'bear witness to a paradigm shift in the relationship between art and fashion'.[66]

The Courtauld Institute Gallery, London, held an exhibition during 2002–03 entitled *Excavated Mutilations: New Work by Conrad Atkinson*. Conrad Atkinson produced a series of works made in response to paintings and sculpture in the Courtauld Institute's collections. His pieces were displayed alongside their sources of inspiration in order to create a dialogue between the past and the present. In a number of his works he deployed clothing and embroidery. *A Collaboration on Scars between Fra Angelico, Conrad Atkinson and Vincent Van Gogh*, 2002, featured a Polo University Club Wool Jacket by Ralph Lauren with digitally produced embroidery. Responding to recurrent images of violence in the Courtauld Gallery's *Imago* Pietatis by Fra Angelico and Vincent Van Gogh's *Self-Portrait with Bandaged Ear*, the notion of comparing 'war wounds' was undermined by the flaccidity of the Ralph Lauren jacket.[67] In his review of the exhibition, Richard Cork wrote:

'Fascinated by the images of disfigurement, torture and crucifixion, especially in the late medieval and Renaissance paintings bequeathed by Lord Lee and Count Seilern, Atkinson decided to produce a sequence of works exploring the paradoxical notion of 'beautiful mutilations'. The paintings of blood and anguish he found at the Courtauld linked up, across the centuries, with his own interest in the imagery of the Aids virus and modern war ... Shocked by a Fra Angelico predella panel of the dead Christ standing in his tomb flanked by the lance and sponge used in the Crucifixion, he places

Conrad Atkinson, A Collaboration on Scars between Fra Angelico, Conrad Atkinson and Vincent Van Gogh *(2002), Polo University Club Wool Jacket by Ralph Lauren with digitally produced embroidery (Conrad Atkinson; courtesy Ronald Feldman Fine Arts, New York)*

the fatal wound on a jacket, where it stands out like a blood-smear at the scene of a crime. He also embroiders an equally unsettling mutilated ear on the sleeve. It is as if Atkinson has torn away the dressing from Van Gogh's *Self-Portrait with Bandaged Ear*, the most anguished image Courtauld ever purchased ... His searing yet disciplined intervention at the Courtauld often proves painful, prompting us to see the most familiar images in a raw and disconcerting light. He reminds us that Western art has often been centrally concerned with the tragedy of human suffering. In this respect, Atkinson's own work has much in common with the collections he interrogates here.'[68]

Whether commenting on themes such as identity, social issues or stereotypes, contemporary artists are utilizing fashion to explore new ideas and issues. As the boundaries continue to be pushed, more ways of engaging the viewer to see new possibilities in the interaction of art and fashion will be developed.

Fashion Mannequins, New York (2003), photograph:
William Mackrell (Private Collection)

✱ Notes

Introduction

1. F Boucher, *A History of Costume in the West*, new ed., London: Thames and Hudson, 1988, p. 191.
2. For Pisanello see Cabinet des Estampes, Musée du Louvre, Paris; Musée Bonnat, Bayonne; and Ashmolean Museum, Oxford; and for Jacopo Bellini see Cabinet des Estampes, Musée du Louvre, Paris.
3. For an example of a surviving Italian rowel-spur, dated c.1460, see Royal Armouries Museum, Leeds, Inv. VI. 322a.
4. V Steiker, 'Goddesses, Heroines and Wives', *ARTNews* (September 2001): p. 143.
5. *Ibid.*, p. 142.
6. I Chilvers, ed., *The Concise Oxford Dictionary of Art and Artists,* Oxford: Oxford University Press, 1991, pp. 381–82.
7. R B Simon, 'The Renaissance of the Sixteenth Century', *Arts of the Renaissance,* Sotheby's, New York, 25 January 2001, p.135.
8. G Vasari, *The Lives of the Artists,* Harmondsworth: Penguin, 1987, vol. 2, p. 304.
9. C Hope et al., *Titian*, London: National Gallery, 2003, p. 46 (exhibition catalogue).
10. *Ibid.*, pp. 40–41.
11. Steiker, *op. cit.*, p. 142.
12. Y Hackenbroch, 'Jewellery', 2. 1500–1630, *The Dictionary of Art,* London, 1996, vol. 17, p. 520.
13. *Ibid.*, p. 522.
14. For a discussion of 16th-century costume books see A Mackrell, *An Illustrated History of Fashion: 500 Years of Fashion Illustration,* London: Batsford, 1997, pp. 14–17.
15. J L Nevinson, 'The Origin of the Fashion Plate', *Actes du Ier Congrès international d'histoire du costume,* Venice, 1955, p. 2.
16. See K Hearn, *Marcus Gheeraerts II, Elizabethan Artist,* London: Tate Britain, 2002, pp. 41–51 (exhibition catalogue) for a discussion of pregnancy portraits.
17. 'The darlings of the moment who run about have no other thought than to be in fashion'. R Gaudriault, *Répertoire de la gravure de mode français des origines à 1815,* Paris: Cercle de la Librairie, 1988, pp. 8 and 29.
18. *Ibid.*, p. 27.
19. E Gordenker, *Anthony Van Dyck (1599–1641) and the Representation of Dress in Seventeenth-Century Portraiture,* Turnhout: Brepols, 2001, p. 3.
20. Mackrell, *op. cit.*, pp.32–33.
21. Gordenker, *op. cit.*, pp. 35–36.
22. '*Mode*...means in particular the manner of dress as received at Court.' A Furetière, *Essai d'un Dictionnaire Universel, contenant généneralement tous les mots François tant vieux que modernes...*, Amsterdam, 1685; Gaudriault, *op. cit.*, p. 8.
23. H Alexander, *The Fan Museum,* London: Third Millennium, 2001, p. 19
24. The Fan Museum, Greenwich, London, *A Fanfare for the Sun King,* 2003, (exhibition catalogue), p.1.
25. E and J de Goncourt, *Madame de Pompadour,* Paris: Charpentier, 1899. The Goncourt brothers coined this phrase.
26. E Goodman, *The Portraits of Madame de Pompadour: Celebrating the Femme Savante,* Berkeley: University of California Press, 2000, p.50.

Chapter 1

1. R John, 'Rococo', *The Dictionary of Art, op. cit.,* vol. 26, p. 491.
2. E and J de Goncourt, *French Eighteenth-Century Painters,* second edition, translated by R. Ironside, Oxford: Phaidon, 1981, p. 55; for Fiske Kimball see Philadelphia Museum of Art, *The Creation of the Rococo,* 1943, (exhibition catalogue) pp. 4–5.
3. See Goodman, *op. cit.*, Chapter 3 for Madame de Pompadour and the concept of the *femme savante.*
4. E and J de Goncourt, *La Femme au XVIIIe. siècle,* Paris: Charpentier, 1862; reprinted, Paris: Flammarion, 1982, p. 29.
5. M Delpierre, *Dress in France in the Eighteenth*

Century, New Haven and London: Yale University Press, 1997, p.1.

6. R John, 'Rococo', *The Dictionary of Art, op. cit.*, vol. 26, p. 499.

7. *Ibid.*, p. 500.

8. M Rosenthal and M Myrone, eds, *Gainsborough*, London: Tate Britain, 2002, p. 147 (exhibition catalogue).

9. L-S Mercier, *Le Tableau de Paris*, Amsterdam, 12 volumes, 1782–89, vol. 2, p. 215.

10. Rosenthal and Myrone, *op. cit.*, p. 162.

11. A Mackrell, 'Fashion Plate and Costume Book', *The Dictionary of Art, op. cit.*, vol. 10, pp. 822–24; Mackrell, *An Illustrated History of Fashion, op. cit.*, p. 73.

12. Rosenthal and Myrone, *op. cit.*, p. 178.

13. J Elkins, 'Style', *The Dictionary of Art, op. cit.*, vol. 29, p. 879.

14. Baron M Grimm, *Correspondance littéraire, philosophique et critique par Grimm...etc.*, ed. M. Tourneux, 16 vols, Paris, 1877–82, vol. 3, 1878, p. 432–33.

15. R John, 'Goût Grec', *The Dictionary of Art, op. cit.*, vol. 13, p. 233.

16. Royal Academy of Arts and the Victoria and Albert Museum, *The Age of Neo-classicism*, London: Royal Academy of Arts, 1972, p. lxvii (exhibition catalogue).

17. *Ibid.*, p. xxii.

18. L Petit de Bachaumont, *Mémoires secrets pour servir à l'histoire de la république des lettres en France depuis 1762 jusqu'à nos jours*, 36 vols, London, 1777–89, vol. 17, p. 226; J Baillio, *Elisabeth Louise Vigée Le Brun*, Fort Worth: Kimbell Art Museum, 1982, p. 47.

19. E L Vigée Le Brun, *The Memoirs of Elisabeth Vigée Le Brun*, translated by S Evans, London: Camden, and Bloomington: University of Indiana Press, 1989, p. 241.

20. Vigée Le Brun, *op. cit.*, pp. 27–28 and pp. 43–44.

21. Baillio, *op. cit.*, p. 47.

22. R. Martin, *The Ceaseless Century: 300 Years of Eighteenth-Century Costume*, New York: Metropolitan Museum of Art, 1998, p. 40 (exhibition catalogue).

23. F Métra, ed., *Correspondance secrète, politique et littéraire*, 18 vols, London, 1787–90, vol. 1, p. 179.

24. For a discussion of *La Gallerie des modes* and *Le Cabinet des modes* see Mackrell, *An Illustrated History of Fashion, op. cit.*, pp. 76–82.

25. Vigée Le Brun, *op. cit.*, pp.43–44.

26. Royal Academy of Arts, London, *The Age of Neo-classicism, op. cit.*, p. 62.

27. A Mackrell, *The Dress of the Parisian Élégantes with Special Reference to Le Journal des dames et des modes from June 1797 until December 1799*, M A thesis, London: Courtauld Institute, 1977, p. 45.

28. Duchesse d'Abrantès, *Mémoires*, 18 vols, Paris, 1831–35, vol. 4, p. 51.

29. J Carr, *The Stranger in France*, London: J. Johnson, 1803, p. 81, pp.88–89.

30. Mackrell, *The Dress of the Parisian Élégantes, op. cit.*, for a full discussion of the *Le Journal des dames et des modes*.

31. Sir J Reynolds, *Discourses on Art*, Introduction by R R Wark, London: Collier-Macmillan, and New York: Collier, 1966, pp.124–25.

32. Mackrell, *The Dress of the Parisian Élégantes, op. cit.*, p. 21.

Chapter 2

1. D Blayney Brown, *Romanticism*, London: Phaidon, 2001, p. 11.

2. A Mackrell, *Dress in le style troubadour, 1774–1814*, 2 vols, Ph D thesis, London: Courtauld Institute, 1987, vol. 1, Chapter 1, Part 3: Cult of le *bon vieux temps*.

3. Brown, *op. cit.*, p. 15.

4. C Baudelaire, *Baudelaire: Selected Writings on Art and Literature*, translated by P E Charvet, London: Penguin, 1992, p. 53.

5. A Hollander, *Fabric of Vision: Dress and Drapery in Painting*, London: National Gallery, 2002, pp. 119, 120.

6. F Chenoune, *A History of Men's Fashion*, translated by D Duisinberre, Paris: Flammarion, 1993, p. 9.

7. Hollander, *op. cit.*, pp. 120–21.

8. H Alexander, 'Even His Garden Secateurs were Fashioned by Hermès', *The Daily Telegraph* (6 March 2003), p. 13.

9. P Noon, *Constable to Delacroix: British Art and the French Romantics*, London: Tate Gallery, 2003, no. 52, p. 116 (exhibition catalogue).

10. Hollander, pp. 125, 127.

11. Boucher, *op. cit.*, p. 344.

12. Brown, *op. cit.*, pp84–85.

13. A Brookner, *Jacques-Louis David*, London: Chatto and Windus, 1980, p. 155.

14. Mackrell, *Dress in le style troubadour, op. cit.*, vol. 1, Chapter 6 for a discussion of costume books.

15. E-J Delécluze, *Louis David, son école et son temps*, Paris, 1855; reprinted, Paris: Macula, 1983, p. 313; S. Owenson [Lady Morgan], *La France*, 2 vols, London, 1817, vol. 2, p. 10.

16. Y Deslandres, 'Josephine and La Mode', *Apollo* (July 1977), p. 47.

17. Mme de Rémusat, *Mémoires de Mme de Rémusat (1802–1808)*, 3 vols, Paris, n.d., vol. 2, p. 54.

18. T Wilson-Smith, *Napoleon and his Artists*, London: Constable, 1996, p. 137.

19. Mlle Avrillion, *Mémoires de Mademoiselle Avrillion, première femme de chambre de l'Impérée sur la vie privée de Joséphine, sa famille et sa Cour*, Paris: Mercure de France, 1969, p. 68; on the Académie Celtique see M-C Chaudonneret, 'Musée des Origines: De Montfaucon au Musée de Versailles', *Romantisme* 84 (1994): pp. 23–24.

20. Delécluze, *op. cit.*, pp. 67–85.

21. Mackrell, *Dress in le style troubadour, op. cit.*, vol. 1, Chapter 1, Part 4: Lenoir's Medieval Shrine.

22. *Ibid.*, p. 68.

23. N Tscherny et al., *Romance and Chivalry*, London: Matthiesen Gallery, 1996, p. 72 (exhibition catalogue).

24. Delécluze, *op. cit.*, pp. 242, 244.

25. Mackrell, *Dress in le style troubadour, op. cit.*, vol. 1, Chapter 1 for the origins of *le style troubadour*.

26. *Le Journal des dames et des modes*, Paris, 1797–1839, no.1, 5 vendémaire an 13 (27 September 1804), pp. 2–3.

27. Mackrell, *Dress in le style troubadour, op. cit.*, vol. 1, Chapter 4 for the crucial role of Queen Marie-Antoinette in the development of *le style troubadour*.

28. *Mercure de France, littéraire et politique*, Paris, 1799–1820, 29 March 1806, p. 617; S Grandjean, *Inventaire d'après décès de l'Impératrice Joséphine*, Paris: [n.p.], 1964, p. 55, nos 49–62, nos 82–83; p. 57, nos 85–88, 92; p. 58, nos 110, 112–14, 121.

29. S Lee, 'Robert Lèfevre', *The Dictionary of Art, op. cit.*, vol. 19, p. 67.

30. D Scarisbrick, *Jewellery*, London: Batsford, 1984, p. 59; *Le Journal des dames et des modes, op. cit.*, no. 1, 5 vendemaire an 13 (27 September 1804), pp. 2–3.

31. *Ibid.*, no. 19, 5 nivôse an 13 (26 December 1804), p. 154. For the portraits of Madame la maréchale Ney and the comtesse de Périgord, including illustrations, see Mackrell, *Dress in le style troubadour, op. cit.*, vol. 1, Chapter 6, Part 2, pp. 237–39, and vol. 2, plates 136–37.

32. *Mercure de France, op. cit.*, 1 February 1806, p. 233.

33. Tscherny et al., *op. cit.*, p. 61; for illustrations of these paintings see Mackrell, *Dress in le style troubadour, op. cit.*, vol 2.

34. Grandjean, *op. cit.*, p. 51, no. 16; p. 52, no. 17; p. 66, no. 208; p. 68, nos 222–23; *Le Journal des dames et des modes, op. cit.*, 1807, plate 857; 1811, plates 1119 and 1127; 1812, plate 1201; 1814, plate 1365.

35. Grandjean, *op. cit.*, see for example, p. 52, no. 20; *Mercure de France, op. cit.*, 8 February 1806, p. 284.

36. F Benoît, *L'Art français sous la Révolution et l'Empire*, Paris: L-H May, 1897, p. 122.

37. L Courajod, *Alexandre Lenoir, son journal et le Musée des Monuments français*, 3 vols, Paris: H Champion, 1878–87, vol. 2, p. 8.; Delécluze, *op. cit.*, p. 244; M-C Chaudonneret, *La Peinture troubadour: Deux artistes lyonnais, Pierre Révoil (1776–1842), Fleury Richard (1777–1852)*, Paris: Arthena, 1980, pp. 15, 20–22, 117–18; *French Painting 1774–1830: The Age of Revolution*, Detroit: Wayne University Press, 1975, p. 586 (exhibition catalogue for Metropolitan Museum of Art, New York).

38. Noon, *op. cit.*, p. 127.

39. *Le Journal des dames et des modes, op. cit.*, no. 32, 28 February 1806, p. 256.

40. G Tinterow and P Conisbee (eds), *Portraits by Ingres: Image of an Epoch*, New York: Metropolitan Museum of Art, 1999, no. 35, pp. 150–51, p. 364 (exhibition catalogue); W R Johnston, *Nineteenth-Century Art: From Romanticism to Art Nouveau: The Walters Art Gallery, Baltimore*, London: Scala, 2000, pp. 14–16.

41. See Mackrell, *Dress in le style troubadour, op. cit.*, vol. 1, Chapter 2, Part 5, pp. 118–22 for costume books compiled during the First Empire.

42. F Masson, *Joséphine: l'Impératrice et la Reine*, Paris: Ollendorff, 1899, p. 367.

43. Mackrell, *Dress in le style troubadour, op. cit.*, vol. 1, p. 19.

44. Noon, *op. cit.*, pp. 127, 145.

45. Mackrell, *Dress in le style troubadour, op. cit.*, vol. 1, p. 228.

46. Noon, *op. cit.*, p. 115.

47. *Ibid.*, pp. 18, 124.

48. Boucher, *op. cit.*, p. 362.

49. Mackrell, *Dress in le style troubadour*, vol. 1, Chapter 6, Part 2, pp. 235–36 for the Empress Joséphine and the Scottish theme in *le style troubadour*.

50. *Ibid.*, p. 26; Grandjean, *op. cit.*, p. 50, no. 10; *Le Journal des dames et des modes, op. cit.*, no. 53, 15 June 1806, plate 730; no. 59, 15 July 1806, plate 737; no. 23, 25 April 1807, p. 184; no. 21, 15 April 1808, p. 168; no. 22, 20 April 1808, p. 176.

51. Mackrell, *Dress in le style troubadour, op. cit.*, vol. 1, pp. 259–61; *Petit courrier des dames*, 10 March 1829; vicomte T de Reiset, *Marie-Caroline, duchesse de Berry (1816–1830)*, Paris, 1906, pp. 367–71. (For the fashions of the Duchesse de Berry see Mackrell, *Dress in le style troubadour, op. cit.*, vol. 2; for the Empress Marie-Louise see Madame la duchesse d'Abrantès, *Mémoires*, 18 vols., Paris, 1831–1835, vol. XIV, p.285.)

52. P Chu and G P Weisberg, eds, *The Popularization of Images: Visual Culture under the July Monarchy*, Princeton: Princeton University Press, 1994, p. 8.

53. Boucher, *op. cit.*, p. 362.

54. P Chu, 'Pop Culture in the Making: The Romantic Craze for History', in *The Popularization of Images, op. cit.*, p. 178.

55. F Pupil, 'A Survey of National Historical and Literary Themes in French Painting', in *Romance and Chivalry, op. cit.*, p. 177; M-C Chaudonneret, 'Historicism and Heritage in the Louvre, 1820–1840: From the Musée Charles X to the Galerie d'Apollon', *Art History 4* (December 1991), p. 488.

56. Chu and Weisberg, *op. cit.*, p. 4. For fashion magazines during the July Monarchy and the artists who drew the fashion plates for them see Mackrell, *An Illustrated History of Fashion, op. cit.*, pp. 127–33.

57. D Scarisbrick, *Chaumet: Master Jewellers since 1780*, Paris: Alain de Gourcuff, 1995, pp. 74–75.

58. Scarisbrick, *Jewellery, op. cit.*, p. 50.

59. R John, 'Rococo Revival', *The Dictionary of Art, op. cit.*, vol. 26, p. 500.

60. S G Galassi *et al.*, *Whistler, Women and Fashion*, New Haven and London: Yale University Press, 2003, p. 104.

61. Tinterow and Conisbee, *op. cit.*, p. 15.

62. E and J de Goncourt, Journal: *Mémoires de la vie littéraire*, 4 vols, Paris: [n. p.] 1956, vol. 1, p. 1219.

63. D de Marly, *Worth: Father of Haute Couture*, second edition, New York: Holmes and Meier, 1990, p. 110.

Chapter 3

1. H Morgan, 'Art for Art's Sake', *The Dictionary of Art, op. cit.*, vol. 2, p. 530; B Farwell, 'Édouard Manet', *The Dictionary of Art, op. cit.*, vol. 20, p. 256.

2. Quoted in S May, 'Whistler: The Singing Butterfly', *ARTnews* (February 2003), pp. 116, 118.

3. S G Galassi, 'Whistler and Aesthetic Dress: Mrs. Frances Leyland', in *Whistler, Women and Fashion, op. cit.*, p. 95.

4. Anon., 'Aesthetic Movement', *The Dictionary of Art, op. cit.*, vol. 1, p. 170.

5. Morgan, *op. cit.*

6. L Lambourne, *The Aesthetic Movement*, London: Phaidon, 1996, p. 115.

7. E R and J Pennell, *The Whistler Journal*, Philadelphia: Lippincott, 1921, p. 301.

8. Lambourne, *op. cit.*, p. 32.

9. M F MacDonald, 'East and West: Sources and Influences', in *Whistler, Women and Fashion, op. cit.*, p. 58.

10. G Squire et al., *Simply Stunning: The Pre-Raphaelite Art of Dressing*, Cheltenham: Cheltenham Art Gallery and Museum, 1996, p. 42 (exhibition catalogue); for Pre-Raphaelite dress see also R Smith, 'Bonnard's *Costume Historique* – a Pre-Raphaelite Source Book', Costume 7 (1973), pp. 28 ff; L Ormond, 'Dress in the Painting of Dante Gabriel Rossetti', *Costume 8* (1974), pp. 26–29; and S M Newton, *Health, Art and Reason: Dress Reformers of the 19th Century*, London: John Murray, 1974, chapter 2.

11. E Aslin, *The Aesthetic Movement: Prelude to Art Nouveau*, London: Elek, 1969, pp. 81–82.

12. A Adburgham, *Liberty's: A Biography of a Shop*, London: Allen and Unwin, 1975. p. 14.

13. *Ibid.*, pp. 28, 51–52.

14. Galassi, 'Whistler and Aesthetic Dress', in *Whistler, Women and Fashion, op. cit.*, p. 104. For a colour illustration of the Liberty tea gown see p. 103.

15. Adburgham, *op. cit.*, p. 64.

16. de Marly, *op. cit.*, p. 116; S Blum, *Victorian Fashions & Costume from Harper's Bazar: 1867–1898*, New York: Dover, 1974, p. 233, caption to accompany the fashion plate, Charles Frederick Worth, *Tea Gown*.

17. G de Osma, *Fortuny: The Life and Work of Mariano Fortuny*, London: Aurum, 1994, pp. 16, 84, 88, 90.

18. J B Jiminez, *Picturing French Style: Three*

Hundred Years of Art and Fashion, Mobile, Alabama: Mobile Museum of Art, 2002, p. 133 (exhibition catalogue); Christie's, New York, *19th Century European Art*, sale catalogue, 23 April 2003, p. 16.

19. R Ash, *James Tissot*, London: Pavilion, 1992, plate 2.

20. K Lochman, ed., *Seductive Surfaces: The Art of Tissot*, New Haven and London: Yale University Press, 1999, p.12.

21. J Laver, *Vulgar Society: The Romantic Career of James Tissot* 1836–1902, London: Constable, 1936, p. 54.

22. Sotheby's, New York, *19th Century European Art*, sale catalogue, 29 October 2002, p. 79.

23. K Adler, '*Objets du luxe* or propaganda? Camille Pissarro's fans', *Apollo* (November 1992), p. 301; Lambourne, *op. cit.*, p. 44.

24. H Alexander, *Fans*, London: Batsford, 1984, p. 69.

25. Christie's, London, *Impressionist and Modern Evening Sale*, sale catalogue, 25 June 2002, p. 8.

26. Adler, *op. cit.*, p. 302.

27. The Fan Museum, Greenwich, London, *Masterpieces: An Exhibition celebrating the 10th anniversary of The Fan Museum*, 2001, no. 1 (exhibition catalogue).

28. Aslin, *op. cit.*, p. 79; M La Vallée, 'Art Nouveau', *The Dictionary of Art, op. cit.*, vol. 2, p. 562.

29. J H Rubin, *Realism and Social Vision in Courbet & Prudhon*, Princeton: Princeton University Press, 1980, p. 48.

30. J H Rubin, 'Realism', *The Dictionary of Art, op. cit.*, vol. 26, pp. 52–53.

31. Rubin, *Realism and Social Vision, op. cit.*, p. 49; Rubin, 'Realism', *The Dictionary of Art, op. cit.*, vol. 26, p. 53.

32. N Savy, 'Baudelaire', *The Dictionary of Art, op. cit.*, vol. 3, p. 392.

33. H Düchting, *Édouard Manet: Images of Parisian Life*, translated from the German by M Robertson, Munich: Prestel, 1995, p. 24.

34. *Ibid.*, p. 25.

35. *Ibid.*, pp.23–24; Farwell, *op. cit.*, p. 255.

36. Mackrell, *An Illustrated History of Fashion, op. cit.*, p. 141.

37. G L Mauner, *Manet: The Still-Life Paintings*, New York: Abrams, 2000, p. 130 (exhibition catalogue).

38. G Tinterow and G Lacambre, *Manet/Velázquez: the French Taste for Spanish Painting*, New Haven and London: Yale University Press, 2003, p. 51 (exhibition catalogue).

39. Mackrell, *An Illustrated History of Fashion, op. cit.*, pp. 132–33.

40. Mauner, *op. cit.*, pp. 130–37.

41. Baudelaire, *Selected Writings, op. cit.*, p. 391.

42. *Ibid.*, p. 424.

43. Farwell, *op. cit.*, p. 261.

44. R L Herbert, *Impressionism: Art, Leisure and Parisian society*, New Haven and London: Yale University Press, 1988, p. 178; see also M Roskill, 'Early Impressionism and the Fashion Print', *Burlington Magazine* (June 1970).

45. Christie's, London, *Impressionist and Modern Art Evening Sale*, sale catalogue, 3 February 2003, p. 20; J Selz, *Eugène Boudin*, translated by Shirley Jennings, New York: Crown, 1982, p. 57.

46. V Hamilton, *Boudin at Trouville*, London: John Murray, 1992, p. 19. For a colour illustration of *The Beach at Trouville – the Empress Eugénie* see frontispiece.

47. *Ibid.*, p. 46.

48. Herbert, *op. cit.*, p. 294.

49. B Denvir, *The Chronicle of Impressionism: An Intimate Diary of the Lives and World of the Great Artists*, London and New York: Thames and Hudson, 2000, p. 177.

50. K Sagner-Düchting, *Renoir, Paris and the Belle Époque*, translated by F Elliott, Munich and New York: Prestel, 1996, p. 63.

51. P Smith, *Seurat and the Avant-Garde*, New Haven and London: Yale University Press, 1997, p. 66.

52. See Mackrell, *An Illustrated History of Fashion, op. cit.*, pp. 136, 143 for *L'Art et la mode*.

53. Lochman, *op. cit.*, p. 9.

54. *Ibid.*, p. 8; Baudelaire, *op. cit.*, pp. 291–98 for 'The Modern Public and Photography'.

55. M Behaut, 'Gustave Caillebotte', *The Dictionary of Art, op. cit.*, vol. 5, p. 390.

56. M Simon, *Fashion in Art: The Second Empire and Impressionism*, London: Zwemmer, 1995, p. 134.

Chapter 4

1. M La Vallée, 'Art Nouveau', *op. cit.*

2. *Ibid.*

3. P Greenhalgh, *Art Nouveau 1890–1914*, London: Victoria and Albert Museum, 2000 (exhibition catalogue for V & A and the National Gallery of Art, Washington).

4. The Fan Museum, Greenwich, London, *Art Nouveau Fans*, 2000, unpaginated (exhibition

catalogue). See also W G Fischer, *Gustav Klimt and Emilie Flöge: An Artist and His Muse,* London: Lund Humphries, 1992; Sotheby's, London, *Gustav Klimt and Emilie Flöge: Artist and Muse,* sale catalogue, 6 October 1999; and M Dabrowski and R Leopold, *Egon Schiele: The Leopold Collection, Vienna,* Cologne: DuMont, 1997 (exhibition catalogue for the Museum of Modern Art, New York).

5. F Müller, *Art and Fashion,* London: Thames and Hudson, 2000, p. 4.

6. Olivier Coutau-Bégarie, Paris, *Collections Hamot,* sale catalogue, 29–30 April 2003, p 20; F Bercé, 'Eugène-Emmanuel Viollet-le-Duc', T*he Dictionary of Art, op. cit.,* vol. 32, p. 594. Musée Carnavalet, Paris, *L'Art de la soie, Prelle 1752–2002,* 2002, p.133 (exhibition catalogue).

7. Vallée, *op. cit.,* p. 564.

8. *Ibid.,* p. 564.

9. Mackrell, *An Illustrated History of Fashion, op. cit.,* p. 152.

10. A Mackrell, *Paul Poiret,* London: Batsford, 1990, p. 21.

11. J Robinson, *The Golden Age of Style,* London: Orbis, 1976, p. 38; Palais Galliera, Musée de la Mode et du Costume, *Paul Poiret et Nicole Groult: Maîtres de la mode Art Déco,* Paris, 1986 (exhibition catalogue).

12. S Tise, 'Art Deco', *The Dictionary of Art, op. cit.,* vol. 2, p. 519; Musée des Arts Décoratifs, *Les Années '25': Art Déco/Bauhaus/Stijl/Esprit Nouveau,* 2 vols, Paris, 1966, Vol 1: *Art Déco* (exhibition catalogue); Mackrell, *Paul Poiret, op. cit.,* p. 14.

13. S Tise, 'Art Deco', *The Dictionary of Art, op. cit.,* vol. 2, p. 520.

14. Mackrell, *Paul Poiret, op. cit.,* p. 20; T Benton, C Benton, and G Wood, *Art Deco 1910-1939,* London: Victoria and Albert Museum, 2003 (exhibition catalogue).

15. Mackrell, *Paul Poiret, op. cit.,* p. 20.

16. *Ibid.,* p. 9.

17. *Ibid.,* p.20; For a study of *Directoire* fashion plates from *Le Journal des dames et des modes* based on the collection in the Bibliothèque Doucet, University of Paris see Mackrell, *The Dress of the Parisian Élégantes, op. cit.*

18. Mackrell, *Paul Poiret, op. cit.,* p. 20.

19. N J Troy, *Couture Culture: A Study in Modern Art and Fashion,* Cambridge, MA: M I T Press, 2003, pp. 67–68.

20. P F Kery, *Art Deco Graphics,* London: Thames and Hudson, 1986, p. 231.

21. *Ibid.,* p. 232.

22.K Wayne, *Modigliani & the Artists of Montparnasse,* New York: Abrams, 2002, unpaginated (exhibition catalogue for Albright-Knox Art Gallery, Buffalo, New York); M Gee, 'Jacques Doucet', *The Dictionary of Art, op. cit.,* vol. 9, p. 196.

23. Troy, *op. cit.,* p. 77.

24. *Ibid.,* p. 77.

25. For the history of these fashion magazines see Mackrell, *An Illustrated History of Fashion, op. cit.,* chapter 5.

26. Fischer, *op. cit.,* p. 78.

27. P Cone (ed.), *The Imperial Style: Fashions of the Hapsburg Era,* New York: Metropolitan Museum of Art, 1980, p. 159 (exhibition catalogue).

28. *Ibid.,* p. 159. For a survey of cultural developments see K Varnedoe, *Vienna 1900: Art, Architecture and Design,* New York: Museum of Modern Art, 1986 (exhibition catalogue).

29. Mackrell, *Paul Poiret, op. cit.,* p. 49.

30. J Kallir, *Viennese Design and the Wiener Werkstätte,* London: Thames and Hudson, 1986, p. 97, see also pp.89–102; and A Völker, *Textiles of the Wiener Werkstätte 1910–1932,* New York: Rizzoli, 1994.

31. A-R Hardy, *Art Deco Textiles: The French Designers,* London: Thames and Hudson, 2003.

32. Fischer, *op. cit.,* p. 81.

33. *Ibid.,* p. 81.

34. Cone, *op. cit.,* p. 156.

35. Mackrell, *Paul Poiret, op. cit.,* p. 49.

36. *Ibid.,* p. 50.

37. *Ibid.,* pp. 53–54.

38. Kery, *op. cit.,* p. 269; Hayward Gallery, London, *Raoul Dufy 1877–1953,* London: Arts Council of Great Britain, 1983 (exhibition catalogue); Christie's, London, *Two Centuries of Design: The Bianchini Férier Collection,* sale catalogue, 27 July 2001, and Christie's South Kensington, London, *The Bianchini Férier Archive,* sale catalogue, 15 January 2003.

39. Mackrell, *Paul Poiret, op. cit.,* p. 17.

40. E Morano, *Sonia Delaunay: Art into Fashion,* New York: Braziller, 1986, p. 21; S Baron, *Sonia Delaunay: The Life of an Artist,* London: Thames and Hudson, 1995, p. 83; G Rayner, R Chamberlain, and A Stapleton, *Artists' Textiles in Britain 1945-1970,* Woodbridge, Suffolk: Antique Collector's Club, 2003, p. 14 (exhibition catalogue for the Fine Art Society, London).

41. Hardy, *op. cit.,* p. 126.

42. J Damase, *Sonia Delaunay: Fashion and Fabric,* London: Thames and Hudson, 1991, p. 61.
43. *Ibid.,* p. 59.
44. For an example of their work see Müller, *op. cit.,* p. 76.
45. Damase, *op. cit.,* p. 115.
46. R Martin, *Cubism and Fashion,* New York: Metropolitan Museum of Art, 1998 (exhibition catalogue).
47. Kery, *op. cit.,* p. 18.
48. *Ibid.,* p. 271.
49. A Mackrell, *Coco Chanel,* London: Batsford, 1992, pp. 18–19.
50. S Fillin-Yeh, *Dandies: Fashion and Finesse in Art and Culture,* New York: New York University Press, 2001, p. 44.
51. Mackrell, *Coco Chanel, op. cit.,* p. 31.
52. Kery, *op. cit.,* p. 272.

Chapter 5

1. C Beaton, *The Glass of Fashion,* facsimile edition, London: Cassell, 1989, p. 161.
2. Mackrell, *Coco Chanel, op. cit.,* p. 28; Jiminez, *op. cit.,* p. 137.
3. P White, *Elsa Schiaparelli: Empress of Paris Fashion,* London: Aurum, 1986, p. 49.
4. Mackrell, *Paul Poiret, op. cit.,* p. 77.
5. D Ades, 'Surrealism', *The Dictionary of Art, op. cit.,* vol. 30, p. 18.
6. J Mundy, *Surrealism: Desire Unbound,* London: Tate Publishing, 2001, unpaginated (exhibition catalogue for Tate Modern, London).
7. *Ibid.*
8. R Martin, *Fashion and Surrealism,* New York: Rizzoli, 1987.
9. J Tregidden, Review of *Fashion and Surrealism* by R Martin, in *Costume* 23 (1989), p. 145.
10. Mackrell, *Coco Chanel, op. cit.,* p. 55.
11. Martin, *Fashion and Surrealism, op. cit.,* p. 140.
12. *Ibid.,* p. 49. For an illustration of Coco Chanel's dress with a fish-scale pattern see Mackrell, *Coco Chanel,* op. cit., p. 46.
13. *Ibid.,* p. 49.
14. Hayward Gallery, London, *Addressing the Century: 100 Years of Art and Fashion,* 1998, p. 90 (exhibition catalogue).
15. *Ibid.,* p. 89.
16. R Martin, A Mackrell et al., *The Fashion Book,* London: Phaidon, 1998, p. 198.
17. Martin, *Fashion and Surrealism, op. cit.,* p. 50.
18. Mackrell, *Coco Chanel, op. cit.,* p. 50.
19. D Blum, *Shocking! The Art and Fashion of Elsa Schiaparelli,* Philadelphia: Philadelphia Museum of Art, 2003, p. 125 (exhibition catalogue).
20. F Baudot, *Fashion and Surrealism,* Paris: Assouline, 2002, pp. 14, 16; D De Marly, *The History of Haute Couture 1850-1950,* London: Batsford, 1986, p. 153.
21. *Woman's Journal* (January 1938), p. 43.
22. E Schiaparelli, *Shocking Life,* London: Dent, 1954, p. 51.
23. S Menkes, 'Fashion as Art...', *ArtReview* (September 2003), p. 44.
24. Christie's, New York, *Impressionist and Modern Works on Paper,* sale catalogue, 9 November 2000, p. 57.
25. Baudot, *op. cit.,* p. 76.
26. Blum, *op. cit.,* p. 136.
27. S Menkes, 'Schiaparelli's Revolutionary Legacy', *International Herald Tribune* (19 September 2003), p. 18.
28. Blum, *op. cit.,* p. 139.
29. White, *op. cit.,* p. 134.
30. Martin, *Fashion and Surrealism, op. cit.,* p. 136.
31. Ades, *op. cit.,* p. 23.
32. Baudot, *op. cit.,* p. 17; Menkes, 'Fashion as Art...', *op. cit.,* p. 48.
33. Müller, *op. cit.,* p. 11.
34. *Ibid.,* p. 11.
35. Baudot, *op. cit.,* p. 17.
36. Blum, *op. cit.,* pp. 254–55.
37. J Sherwood, 'Disgracefully Yours, the Queen Mother of Fashion', *The Independent on Sunday* (2 June 2002), p. 23.
38. F Baudot, *A Century of Fashion,* London: Thames and Hudson, 1999, pp. 154, 194.
39. White, *op. cit.,* p. 217.
40. 'Sayings of the Week', *The Observer* (1 November 1992): p. 22.
41. Y Saint Laurent, D Vreeland et al., *Yves Saint Laurent,* New York: Metropolitan Museum of Art, 1983, p. 27 (exhibition catalogue).
42. Müller, *op. cit.,* p. 11.
43. G Buxbaum, *Icons of Fashion: The 20th Century,* Munich, London, and New York: Prestel, 1999, p. 90.
44. Saint Laurent and Vreeland, *op. cit.,* p. 37; S Menkes, 'Saint Laurent reborn. Art as inspiration: 40 Years of YSL Fashion History', International *Herald Tribune* (5 March 2004), pp. 11, 13.
45. M Livingstone, *Pop Art: A Continuing History,* London: Thames and Hudson, 1990.

46. M Livingstone, 'Pop Art', *The Dictionary of Art, op. cit.,* vol. 25, p. 231.

47. M Livingstone, 'Andy Warhol', *The Dictionary of Art, op. cit.,* vol. 32, p. 862.

48. M Francis and M King (eds), *The Warhol Look: Glamour/Style/Fashion,* London and Boston: Little, Brown, 1997, p. 20 (exhibition catalogue for the Whitney Museum, New York, and the Barbican Art Gallery, London).

49. Baudot, *A Century of Fashion, op. cit.,* p. 259.

50. Francis and King, *op. cit.,* dust jacket.

51. L Goldstein, 'Hat Trick', *Time* Magazine (11 November 2002), p. 24.

52. Beaton, *op. cit.,* p. 259.

53. Martin and Mackrell, *op. cit.,* p. 27.

54. Buxbaum, *op. cit.,* p. 51.

55. B Quinn, *The Fashion of Architecture,* Oxford: Berg, 2003, p. 220.

56. Rayner *et al., op. cit.,* p. 82.

57. Baudot, *A Century of Fashion, op. cit.,* p. 244.

58. *Ibid.,* p. 306.

59. Müller, *op. cit.,* p. 14.

60. S B Kim, 'Is Fashion Art?', *Fashion Theory: The Journal of Dress, Body & Culture* 2/1 (March 1998), pp. 57–58.

61. Müller, *op. cit.,* p. 14.

62. Menkes, 'Fashion as Art...', *op. cit.,* p. 48.

63. *Ibid.,* p. 48.

64. N Foulkes, 'Making an Exhibition of Herself', *Night and Day* Magazine, *The Mail on Sunday* (4 August 2002), p. 25.

65. N Rosenthal, 'Fashion Statement: Defending Couture's Place in the Art Museum', *Art+Auction* (January 2004), p. 103.

66. Kim, *op. cit.,* p. 56.

67. A. Hudek, 'Excavating the Body Politic: An Interview with Conrad Atkinson'. *Art Journal,* (Summer 2003), p.11; www.courtauld.ac.uk/nof/demo/atk04.html.

68. R Cork, 'Courtauld and New', *The Times,* T2 section (5 November 2002), p. 19.

Bibliography

Abrantès, duchesse d', *Mémoires,* 18 vols, Paris, 1831–35

Adburgham, A, *Liberty's: A Biography of a Shop,* London: Allen and Unwin, 1975

Ades, D, 'Surrealism', *The Dictionary of Art,* vol. 30

Adler, K, '*Objets du luxe* or propaganda? Camille Pissarro's fans', *Apollo* (November 1992)

Alexander, H, *Fans,* London: Batsford, 1984

Alexander, H, *The Fan Museum,* London: Third Millennium, 2001

Alexander, H, 'Even His Garden Secateurs were Fashioned by Hermès', *The Daily Telegraph* (6 March 2003)

Anon., 'Aesthetic Movement', *The Dictionary of Art,* vol. 1

Antichità di Ercolano esposte, Le, 10 vols, Naples: Regia Stamperia, 1755–92; reprinted, Naples: Banco di Napoli, 1988.

Ash, R, *James Tissot,* London: Pavilion, 1992

Aslin, E, *The Aesthetic Movement: Prelude to Art Nouveau,* London: Elek, 1969

Avrillion, M-J-P d', *Mémoires de Mademoiselle Avrillion, première femme de chambre de l'Impératrice sur la vie privée de Joséphine, sa famille et sa Cour,* Paris: Mercure de France, 1969

Bachaumont, L Petit de, *Mémoires secrets pour servir à l'histoire de la république des lettres en France depuis 1762 jusqu'à nos jours,* 36 vols, London, 1777–89

Baillio, J, *Elisabeth Louise Vigée Le Brun,* Fort Worth: Kimbell Art Museum, 1982

Barnes, R, et al., *The 20th Century Art Book,* London: Phaidon, 1996

Baron, S, *Sonia Delaunay: The Life of an Artist,* London: Thames and Hudson, 1995

Baudelaire, C, *Baudelaire: Selected Writings on Art and Literature,* translated by P E Charvet, London: Penguin, 1992

Baudot, F, *A Century of Fashion,* London: Thames and Hudson, 1999

Baudot, F, *Empire Style,* London: Thames and Hudson, 1999

Baudot, F, *Fashion and Surrealism,* Paris: Assouline, 2002

Beaton, C, *The Glass of Fashion,* facsimile edition, London: Cassell, 1989

Beaton, C, *Self-Portrait with Friends,* London: Weidenfeld and Nicholson, c. 1979

Behaut, M, 'Caillebotte, Gustave', *The Dictionary of Art*, vol. 5

Benoît, F, *L'Art français sous la Révolution et l'Empire*, Paris: L-H May, 1897

Benton, B, C Benton, and G Wood, *Art Deco 1910-1939*, London: Victoria and Albert Museum, 2003 (exhibition catalogue)

Bercé, F, 'Viollet-le-Duc, Eugène-Emmanuel', *The Dictionary of Art*, vol. 32

Blayney Brown, D, *Romanticism*, London: Phaidon, 2001

Blum, D, *Shocking! The Art and Fashion of Elsa Schiaparelli*, Philadelphia: Philadelphia Museum of Art, 2003 (exhibition catalogue)

Blum, S, *Victorian Fashions & Costume from Harper's Bazar: 1867-1898*, New York: Dover, 1974

Boucher, F, *A History of Costume in the West*, new ed., London: Thames and Hudson, 1988

Brändstatter, C, *Klimt & Fashion*, New York: Assouline, 2003.

Brändstatter, C, *Wonderful Wiener Werkstätte: Design in Vienna 1903-1932*, London: Thames and Hudson, 2003.

Brookner, A, *Jacques-Louis David*, London: Chatto and Windus, 1980

Brown, D A (ed.), *Virtue and Beauty: Leonardo's Ginevra de'Benci and Renaissance Portraits of Women*, Princeton: Princeton University Press, 2002 (exhibition catalogue).

Browne, C, *Silk Designs of the 18th Century. From the Victoria and Albert Museum*, London: Thames and Hudson, 1996

Buxbaum, G, *Icons of Fashion: The 20th Century*, Munich, London, and New York: Prestel, 1999

Carette, Madame, *My Mistress, the Empress Eugénie; or, Court Life at the Tuileries*, London: Dean, 1889

Carr, J, *The Stranger in France*, London: J. Johnson, 1803

Chaudonneret, M-C, 'Historicism and Heritage in the Louvre, 1820-1840: From the Musée Charles X to the Galerie d'Apollon', *Art History 4* (December 1991)

Chaudonneret, M-C, 'Musée des Origines: De Montfaucon au Musée de Versailles', *Romantisme* 84 (1994)

Chaudonneret, M-C, *La Peinture troubadour: Deux artistes lyonnais, Pierre Révoil(1776-1842), Fleury Richard (1777-1852)*, Paris: Arthena, 1980

Chenoune, F, *A History of Men's Fashion*, translated by D Duisinberre, Paris: Flammarion, 1993

Chilvers, I (ed), *Concise Oxford Dictionary of Art and Artists*, Oxford: Oxford University Press, 1991

Chu, P, and G P Weisberg (eds), *The Popularization of Images: Visual Culture under the July Monarchy*, Princeton: Princeton University Press, 1994

Cone, P (ed.), *The Imperial Style: Fashions of the Hapsburg Era*, New York: Metropolitan Museum of Art, 1980 (exhibition catalogue)

Cork, R, 'Courtauld and New', *The Times*, T2 section (5 November 2002)

Cornu, P, *Préface à la réimpression de La Gallerie des modes et costumes français*, Paris, 1911-14

Courajod, L, *Alexandre Lenoir, son journal et le Musée des Monuments français*, 3 vols, Paris: H Champion, 1878-87

Dabrowski, M, and R Leopold, *Egon Schiele: The Leopold Collection, Vienna*, Cologne: DuMont, 1997 (exhibition catalogue for the Museum of Modern Art, New York)

Damase, J, *Sonia Delaunay: Fashion and Fabric*, London: Thames and Hudson,1991

De Marly, D, *The History of Haute Couture 1850-1950*, London: Batsford, 1986.

De Marly, D, *Worth: Father of Haute Couture*, second edition, New York: Holmes and Meier, 1990

Delécluze, E-J, *Louis David, son école et son temps*, Paris, 1855; reprinted, Paris: Macula, 1983

Delpierre, M, *Dress in France in the Eighteenth Century*, New Haven and London: Yale University Press, 1997

Denvir, B, *The Chronicle of Impressionism: An Intimate Diary of the Lives and World of the Great Artists*, London and New York: Thames and Hudson, 2000

Deslandres, Y, 'Josephine and La Mode', *Apollo* (July 1977)

Dictionary of Art, The, 34 vols, London: Macmillan, 1996.

Düchting, H, *Édouard Manet: Images of Parisian Life*, translated by M Robertson, Munich: Prestel, 1995

Elkins, J, 'Style', *The Dictionary of Art*, vol. 29

Ewing, E, *History of 20th Century Fashion*, fourth edition, revised by A Mackrell, London: Batsford, 2001

Fan Museum, *Art Nouveau Fans*, London, 2000 (exhibition catalogue)

Fan Museum, *Fanfare for the Sun King*, London, 2003 (exhibition catalogue)

Fan Museum, *Masterpieces: An Exhibition celebrating the 10th anniversary of the Fan Museum*, London, 2001 (exhibition catalogue)

Bibliography □

Farwell, B, 'Manet, Édouard', *The Dictionary of Art*, vol. 20

Fashion Institute of Technology, New York, *The Historical Mode*, 1989.

Fillin-Yeh, S, *Dandies: Fashion and Finesse in Art and Culture*, New York: New York University Press, 2001

Fischer, W G, *Gustav Klimt and Emilie Flöge: An Artist and His Muse*, London: Lund Humphries, 1992

Foulkes, N, 'Making an Exhibition of Herself', *Night and Day* Magazine, *The Mail on Sunday* (4 August 2002)

Francis, M, and M King (eds), *The Warhol Look: Glamour/Style/Fashion*, London and Boston: Little, Brown, 1997 (exhibition catalogue for the Whitney Museum, New York, and the Barbican Art Gallery, London)

Galassi, S G and M F MacDonald, *Whistler, Women and Fashion*, New Haven and London: Yale University Press, 2003

Gaudriault, R, *Répertoire de la gravure de mode française des origines à 1815*, Paris: Cercle de la Librairie, 1988

Gautier, T, *De la mode*, Paris, 1858

Gautier, T, *Émaux et camées*, édition définitive (1872), Paris: Garnier, 1943

Gautier, T, *Histoire de l'art dramatique depuis vingt-cinq ans*, 6 vols., Paris, 1858.

Gautier, T, *Histoire du romantisme*, Paris, 1874

Gautier, T, *Mademoiselle de Maupin*, translated by J Richardson, Harmondsworth: Penguin, 1981

Gee, M, 'Doucet, Jacques', *The Dictionary of Art*, vol. 9

Goldstein, L, 'Hat Trick', *Time* Magazine (11 November 2002)

Goncourt, E and J de, *L'Art du XVIIIe. siècle*, 12 vols, Paris: Charpentier, 1859–75

Goncourt, E and J de, *La Femme au XVIIIe. siècle*, Paris: Charpentier, 1862; reprinted Paris: Flammarion, 1982

Goncourt, E and J de, *French Eighteenth-Century Painters*, second edition, translated by R. Ironside, Oxford: Phaidon, 1981

Goncourt, E and J de, *Journal: Mémoires de la vie littéraire*, 4 vols, Paris, 1956

Goncourt, E and J de, *Madame de Pompadour*, Paris: Charpentier, 1899

Goodman, E, *The Portraits of Madame de Pompadour: Celebrating the Femme Savante*, Berkeley: University of California Press, 2000

Gordenker, E, *Anthony Van Dyck (1599–1641) and the Representation of Dress in Seventeenth-Century Portraiture*, Turnhout: Brepols, 2001

Grandjean, S, *Inventaire d'après décès de l'Impératrice Joséphine*, Paris: [n.p.], 1964

Greenhalgh, P, *Art Nouveau 1890–1914*, London: Victoria and Albert Museum, 2000 (exhibition catalogue)

Grimm, Baron M, *Correspondance littéraire, philosophique et critique par Grimm...etc.*, ed. M Tourneux, 16 vols, Paris, 1877–82

Hamilton, V, *Boudin at Trouville*, London: John Murray, 1992

Hardy, A-R, *Art Deco Textiles: The French Designers*, London: Thames and Hudson, 2003

Hayward Gallery, *Addressing the Century: 100 Years of Art and Fashion*, London: 1998 (exhibition catalogue)

Hayward Gallery, *Followers of Fashion. Graphic Satires from the Georgian period*, London, 2002 (exhibition catalogue)

Hayward Gallery, *Raoul Dufy 1877–1953*, London: Arts Council of Great Britain, 1983 (exhibition catalogue)

Hazlitt, Gooden and Fox, *The Age of Jazz*, London, 2002 (exhibition catalogue)

Hearn, K, *Marcus Gheeraerts II, Elizabethan Artist*, London: Tate Publishing, 2002 (exhibition catalogue)

Herbert, R L, *Impressionism: Art, Leisure and Parisian society*, New Haven and London: Yale University Press, 1988

Hollander, A, *Fabric of Vision: Dress and Drapery in Painting*, London: National Gallery, 2002

Hope, C, J Fletcher, M Falomir, J Dunkerton, N Penny, and C Campbell, *Titian*, London: National Gallery, 2003 (exhibition catalogue)

Hudek, A, 'Excavating the Body Politic: An Interview with Conrad Atkinson', *Art Journal* (Summer 2003)

Jiminez, J B, *Picturing French Style: Three Hundred Years of Art and Fashion*, Mobile, Alabama: Mobile Museum of Art, 2002 (exhibition catalogue)

John, R, 'Goût Grec', *The Dictionary of Art*, vol. 13

John, R, 'Rococo', *The Dictionary of Art*, vol. 26

John, R, 'Rococo Revival', *The Dictionary of Art*, vol. 26

Johnston, W R, *Nineteenth-Century Art: From Romanticism to Art Nouveau: The Walters Art Gallery, Baltimore*, London: Scala, 2000

Jones, C, *Madame de Pompadour. Images of a Mistress*, London: National Gallery, 2002

Kallir, J, *Viennese Design and the Wiener Werkstätte*, London: Thames and Hudson, 1986

Kery, P F, *Art Deco Graphics,* London: Thames and Hudson, 1986

Kim, S B, 'Is Fashion Art?', *Fashion Theory: The Journal of Dress, Body & Culture* 2/1 (March 1998)

Krell, G, *Vivienne Westwood,* London: Thames and Hudson, 1997

Lambourne, L, *The Aesthetic Movement,* London: Phaidon, 1996

Laver, J, *Vulgar Society: The Romantic Career of James Tissot 1836–1902,* London: Constable, 1936

Lee, S, 'Lèfevre, Robert', *The Dictionary of Art,* vol.19

Lehmann, U, *Tigersprung: Fashion in Modernity,* Cambridge, MA: MIT Press, 2000

Livingstone, M, *Pop Art: A Continuing History,* London: Thames and Hudson, 1990

Livingstone, M, 'Pop Art', *The Dictionary of Art,* vol. 25

Livingstone, M, 'Warhol, Andy', *The Dictionary of Art,* vol. 32

Lochman, K, ed., *Seductive Surfaces: The Art of Tissot,* New Haven and London: Yale University Press, 1999

Mackrell, A, *Coco Chanel,* London: Batsford, 1992

Mackrell, A, *Dress in le style troubadour, 1774–1814,* 2 vols, London: Courtauld Institute of Art, 1987

Mackrell, A, *The Dress of the Parisian Élégantes with Special Reference to* Le Journal des dames et des modes *from June 1797 until December 1799,* M A thesis, London: Courtauld Institute of Art, 1977

Mackrell, A, 'Fashion Plate and Costume Book', *The Dictionary of Art,* vol. 10

Mackrell, A, *An Illustrated History of Fashion: 500 Years of Fashion Illustration,* London: Batsford, 1997

Mackrell, A, *Paul Poiret,* London: Batsford, 1990

Mackrell, A, *Shawls, Stoles and Scarves,* London: Batsford, 1986

Martin, R, *The Ceaseless Century: 300 Years of Eighteenth-Century Costume,* New York: Metropolitan Museum of Art, 1998 (exhibition catalogue)

Martin, R, *Christian Dior,* New York: Metropolitan Museum of Art, 1996 (exhibition catalogue)

Martin, R, *Cubism and Fashion,* New York: Metropolitan Museum of Art, 1998 (exhibition catalogue)

Martin, R, *Fashion and Surrealism,* New York: Rizzoli, 1987

Martin, R, *Haute Couture,* New York: Metropolitan Museum of Art, 1995 (exhibition catalogue)

Martin, R, *Versace,* New York: Metropolitan Museum of Art, 1997 (exhibition catalogue)

Martin, R, A Mackrell, et al., *The Fashion Book,* London: Phaidon, 1998

Masson, F, *Joséphine: l'Impératrice et la Reine,* Paris: Ollendorff, 1899

Masson, F, *Le Sacre de la Couronnement de Napoléon,* Paris: Librairie Jules Tallandier, 1978

Mauner, G L, *Manet: The Still-Life Paintings,* New York: Abrams, 2000 (exhibition catalogue)

May, S, 'Whistler: The Singing Butterfly', *ARTnews* (February 2003)

Melot, M, 'Gavarni, Paul', *The Dictionary of Art,* vol 12

Menkes, S, 'Fashion as Art ...', *ArtReview* (September 2003)

Menkes, S, 'Saint Laurent reborn. Art as inspiration: 40 Years of YSL Fashion History', *International Herald Tribune* (5 March 2004)

Menkes, S, 'Schiaparelli's Revolutionary Legacy', *International Herald Tribune* (19 September 2003)

Mercier, L-S, *Le Nouveau Paris,* 6 vols, Paris, 1798

Mercier, L-S, *Le Tableau de Paris,* 12 vols, Paris, 1782–89

Métra, F (ed.), *Correspondance secrète, politique et littéraire,* 18 vols, London [n.p.], 1787–90

Metropolitan Museum of Art, *French Painting 1774–1830: The Age of Revolution,* Detroit: Wayne University Press, 1975 (exhibition catalogue)

Morano, E, *Sonia Delaunay: Art into Fashion,* New York: Braziller, 1986

Morel, B, *The French Crown Jewels,* Antwerp: Fonds Mercator, 1988

Morgan, H, 'Art for Art's Sake', *The Dictionary of Art,* vol. 2

Müller, F, *Art and Fashion,* London: Thames and Hudson, 2000

Mundy, J, *Surrealism: Desire Unbound,* London: Tate Publishing, 2001 (exhibition catalogue)

Murger, H, *Scenes de la vie de bohème,* Paris: Calmann-Levy, 1861

Musée Carnavalet, *L'Art de la Soie, Prelle 1752–2002,* Paris, 2002 (exhibition catalogue).

Musée des Arts Décoratifs, *Les Années "25": Art Déco/Bauhaus/Stijl/Esprit Nouveau,* 2 vols, Paris, 1966 (exhibition catalogues)

Musée Galliera, Musée de la Mode de la Ville de Paris, *Europe 1910–1939, quant l'art habillait le vêtement,* Paris, 1997 (exhibition catalogue)

Musée Galliera, Musée de la Mode de la Ville de

Bibliography

Paris, *Souvenirs muscovites 1860–1930*, Paris, 2000 (exhibition catalogue)

Neufville, É de, *Physiologie de la femme*, Paris, 1842

Nevinson, J L, 'The Origin of the Fashion Plate', in *Actes du Ier Congrès international d'histoire du costume, Venise, 31 aôut–7 septembre 1952*, Venice: Centro internazionale delle arti e del costume, 1955

Newton, S M, *Health, Art and Reason: Dress Reformers of the 19th Century*, London: John Murray, 1974

Newton, S M, *Renaissance Theatre Costume and the Sense of the Historic Past*, London: Rapp and Whiting, 1975

Noon, P, *Constable to Delacroix: British Art and the French Romantics*, London: Tate Gallery, 2003 (exhibition catalogue)

Ormond, L, 'Dress in the Painting of Dante Gabriel Rossetti', *Costume 8* (1974)

Osma, G de *Fortuny: The Life and Work of Mariano Fortuny*, London: Aurum, 1994

Owenson, S [Lady Morgan], *La France*, 2 vols, London 1817

Palais Galliera, Musée de la Mode et du Costume, *Paul Poiret et Nicole Groult: Maîtres de la mode Art Déco*, Paris, 1986 (exhibition catalogue)

Partsch, S, *Gustav Klimt: Painter of Women*, translated by M Robertson, Munich and New York: Prestel, 1994

Pennell, E R and J, *The Whistler Journal*, Philadelphia: Lippincott, 1921

Perrot, P, *Fashioning the Bourgeoisie: A History of Clothing in the 19th Century*, translated by R Bienvenu, Princeton: Princeton University Press, 1994

Philadelphia Museum of Art, *The Creation of the Rococo*, 1943 (exhibition catalogue)

Philadelphia Museum of Art, The Detroit Institute of Arts, and the Grand Palais, *The Second Empire. Art in France under Napoleon III*, Paris, Imprimerie Blanchard Le Plessis-Robinson, 1978 (exhibition catalogue)

Poiret, P, *Art et phynance*, Paris: Lutétia, 1934

Poiret, P, *My First Fifty Years*, translated by S Haden Guest, London: Gollancz, 1931

Quinn, B, *The Fashion of Architecture*, Oxford: Berg, 2003

Rayner, G, R Chamberlain, and A Stapleton, *Artists' Textiles in Britain 1945–1970*, Woodbridge, Suffolk: Antique Collector's Club, 2003 (exhibition catalogue for the Fine Art Society, London)

Reiset, vicomte T de, *Marie-Caroline, duchesse de Berry (1816–1830)*, Paris, 1906

Reynolds, Sir J, *Discourses on Art*, Introduction by R R Wark, London: Collier-Macmillan, and New York: Collier, 1966

Robinson, J, *The Golden Age of Style*, London: Orbis, 1976

Rosenblum, R, *Ingres*, New York: Harry N Abrams, 1985

Rosenthal, M, and M Myrone, eds, *Gainsborough*, London: Tate Britain, 2002 (exhibition catalogue)

Rosenthal, N, 'Fashion Statement: Defending Couture's Place in the Art Museum', *Art+Auction* (January 2004)

Roskill, M, 'Early Impressionism and the Fashion Print', *Burlington Magazine* (June 1970)

Royal Academy of Arts, *Giorgio Armani: A Retrospective*, London, 2003 (exhibition catalogue)

Royal Academy of Arts, *Reynolds*, London, 1986 (exhibition catalogue)

Royal Academy of Arts, *Tamara de Lempicka: Art Deco Icon*, London, 2004 (exhibition catalogue)

Royal Academy of Arts and the Victoria and Albert Museum, *The Age of Neo-classicism*, London, 1972 (exhibition catalogue)

Rubin, J H, *Realism and Social Vision in Courbet & Prudhon*, Princeton: Princeton University Press, 1980

Rubin, J H, 'Realism', *The Dictionary of Art*, vol. 26

Sagner-Düchting, K, *Renoir, Paris and the Belle Époque*, translated by F Elliott, Munich and New York: Prestel, 1996

Saint Laurent, Y, D Vreeland et al., *Yves Saint Laurent*, New York: Metropolitan Museum of Art, 1983 (exhibition catalogue)

Savy, N, 'Baudelaire, Charles', *The Dictionary of Art*, vol. 3

Scarisbrick, D, *Chaumet: Master Jewellers since 1780*, Paris: Alain de Gourcuff, 1995

Scarisbrick, D, *Jewellery*, London: Batsford, 1984

Schiaparelli, E, *Shocking Life*, London: Dent, 1954

Selz, J, *Eugène Boudin*, translated by Shirley Jennings, New York: Crown, 1982

Seznec, J, *Salons/Diderot*, 4 vols, Oxford: Clarendon Press, 1957–67

Sherwood, J, 'Disgracefully Yours, the Queen Mother of Fashion', *The Independent on Sunday* (2 June 2002)

Siegfried, S L, *The Art of Louis-Léopold Boilly. Modern Life in Napoleonic France*, New Haven and London: Yale University Press, 1995

Silverman, D, *Art Nouveau. Fin-de-siècle France,* Berkeley: University of California Press, 1989

Simon, M, *Fashion in Art: The Second Empire and Impressionism,* London: Zwemmer, 1995

Simon, R B , 'The Renaissance of the Sixteenth Century', *Arts of the Renaissance,* New York: Sotheby's, 25 January 2001 (sales catalogue)

Smith, P, *Seurat and the Avant-Garde,* New Haven and London: Yale University Press, 1997

Smith, R, 'Bonnard's *Costume Historique* – a Pre Raphaelite Source Book', Costume 7 (1973)

Squire, G, C Wilson, and S Wilson, *Simply Stunning: The Pre-Raphaelite Art of Dressing,* Cheltenham: Cheltenham Art Gallery and Museum, 1996 (exhibition catalogue)

Steiker, V, 'Goddesses, Heroines and Wives', *ARTNews,* (September 2001)

Stern, R, *Against Fashion: Clothing as Art, 1850–1930,* Cambridge, MA: MIT Press, 2003

Syson, L, et al., *Pisanello: Painter to the Renaissance Court,* London: National Gallery, 2001 (exhibition catalogue)

Tinterow, G, and P Conisbee (eds), *Portraits by Ingres: Image of an Epoch,* New York: Metropolitan Museum of Art, 1999 (exhibition catalogue)

Tinterow G, and G Lacambre, *Manet/Velázquez: the French Taste for Spanish Painting,* New Haven and London: Yale University Press, 2003 (exhibition catalogue)

Tise, S, 'Art Deco', *The Dictionary of Art,* vol. 2

Tregidden, J, Review of *Fashion and Surrealism* by R Martin, in *Costume 23* (1989)

Troy, N J, *Couture Culture: A Study in Modern Art and Fashion,* Cambridge, MA: M I T Press, 2003

Tscherny, N, G S Sainty, and M-C Chaudonneret, *Romance and Chivalry,* London: Matthiesen Gallery, 1996 (exhibition catalogue).

Vallée, M La, 'Art Nouveau', *The Dictionary of Art,* vol. 2

Varnedoe, K, *Vienna 1900: Art, Architecture and Design,* New York: Museum of Modern Art, 1986 (exhibition catalogue)

Vasari, G, *The Lives of the Painters, Sculptors and Architects (Le Vite dei più eccllenti pittori, scultori ed architettori Italiani),* first published in 1550; a second, enlarged edition appeared in 1568); reprinted, 2 vols, Harmondsworth: Penguin, 1987.

Vecellio, C, *De gli habiti antichi et moderni di diverse parti del mondo,* Venice, 1590; facsimile reprint, Bologna: Inchiostroblu, 1982.

Vecellio, C, *Habiti antichi et moderni di tutto il Mondo,* Venice, 1598; facsimile reprint (illustrations only), New York: Dover, 1977.

Vertès, M, *Art and Fashion,* translated by G Davis, New York and London: Studio Publications, 1944

Victoria and Albert Museum, *Fashion 1900–1939,* London, 1975 (exhibition catalogue)

Vigée Le Brun, E L, *The Memoirs of Elisabeth Vigée Le Brun,* translated by S Evans, London, Camden and Bloomington: University of Indiana Press, 1989

Viollet-de-Duc, E-E, *Dictionnaire raisonné du mobilier français de l'époque carlovingienne à la Renaissance,* 6 vols, Paris, 1858

Völker, A, *Textiles of the Wiener Werkstätte 1910–1932,* New York: Rizzoli, 1994

Wallace Collection, *Catalogue of Miniatures,* London: The Trustees of the Wallace Collection, 1980

Wallace Collection, *Catalogue of Pictures,* 4 vols, London: The Trustees of the Wallace Collection, 1985–92

Wayne, K, *Modigliani & the Artists of Montparnasse,* New York: Abrams, 200 (exhibition catalogue for Albright-Knox Art Gallery, Buffalo)

White, P, *Elsa Schiaparelli: Empress of Paris Fashion,* London: Aurum, 1986

White, P, *Poiret,* London: Studio Vista, 1974

Wilcox, C (ed.), *The Art and Craft of Gianni Versace,* London: V&A Publications, 2002

Wilcox, C, *Vivienne Westwood,* London: V&A Publications, 2004

Wilson-Smith, T, *Napoleon and his Artists,* London: Constable, 1996

Wilton, A, *The Swagger Portrait: Grand Manner Portraiture in Britain from Van Dyck to Augustus John, 1630–1930,* London: Tate Gallery Publications, 1992 (exhibition catalogue)

Index of artists, art movements and fashion designers

Numbers in italics refer to pages on which illustrations appear.

Index □